The **Foxfire** Book of Appalachian Cookery

The **Foxfire** Book of Appalachian Cookery

Edited by T. J. Smith

REVISED EDITION

With a new foreword by **Sean Brock**

THE UNIVERSITY OF NORTH CAROLINA PRESS

Chapel Hill

This book was published with the assistance of the
Fred W. Morrison Fund of the University of North Carolina Press.

© 2019 The Foxfire Fund, Inc.

Chapter opening illustrations by Mckaylin Hensley

Manufactured in the United States of America

Designed by Richard Hendel

Set in Chaparral Pro and Fresco Sans by Rebecca Evans

The University of North Carolina Press has been a member
of the Green Press Initiative since 2003.

Cover illustration by Jessie Doyle. Used by permission of
Southern Exposure Seed Exchange.

Library of Congress Cataloging-in-Publication Data

Names: Smith, T. J., 1977– editor. | Brock, Sean, writer of preface.

Title: The Foxfire book of Appalachian cookery / edited by
    T. J. Smith ; with a new foreword by Sean Brock.

Description: Revised edition. | Chapel Hill : The University of
    North Carolina Press, [2019] | Includes index.

Identifiers: LCCN 2019008135 | ISBN 978-1-4696-5461-4
    (cloth : alk. paper) | ISBN 978-1-4696-4754-8 (pbk : alk. paper) |
    ISBN 978-1-4696-5410-2 (ebook)

Subjects: LCSH: Cooking—Appalachian Region, Southern. |
    Appalachian Region, Southern—Social life and customs. |
    LCGFT: Cookbooks.

Classification: LCC TX715 .F826 2019 | DDC 641.5975—dc23
    LC record available at https://lccn.loc.gov/2019008135

Contents

Foreword

SEAN BROCK

First and foremost, sitting here in front of a blank page about to write the foreword for *The Foxfire Book of Appalachian Cookery* is about as surreal as it gets for me. I am beyond thankful to have been bestowed this important privilege. I have to admit, I never saw this coming when I discovered this book in my late teens. I had moved to Charleston, South Carolina, to attend cooking school and came across it in the library. I was struck by the honest black-and-white images, the familiar dialect, and the food of my family within its pages.

I'll never forget the emotions and memories from my childhood that flooded my mind and soul that day. I became obsessed with this book and began to collect the other *Foxfire* volumes as they popped up at yard sales or on eBay. It was my visual aid to show all the cooks I worked with where I came from and how old-fashioned the food was there. Most people flinched at the images of chickens getting their necks rung before supper or cute little animals being skinned. All I could think about was squirrel gravy on top of a cathead biscuit. These reactions were a surefire sign that most people in cooking school hadn't grown up the way I did. I would no longer take those sorghum potlucks or strings of leather breeches hanging on the porch for granted. I began to dig in to my family's traditions and badger my Grandma Audrey about her kitchen and garden wisdom. That's the sign of a good book, one that inspires gratitude and incites childlike curiosity.

I was born in Wise County, Virginia, butted right up against the Kentucky state line. We lived in Scott Roberson Holler, up a steep, winding, and barely paved road on "Brock Hill." I grew up around rough and tough coal miners and even stronger Appalachian women who all shared a deep love for good food, family, and hospitality. We always ate together and pretty much never went to restaurants. I was raised the Appalachian way: running barefoot around the garden and in the kitchen by my momma's side. Cooking for the family was a rite of passage.

Every time I pick up this book I learn something new. I swear my copy smells like a skillet of corn bread after all these years. Just today I was reading about bleaching apples, and now I can't wait for the first basket to arrive so that I can try this hillbilly alchemy out at home. I also recently ran across the tradition of drying pumpkin slices over the hearth again. I decided to serve them at a guest chef dinner, painting them with reduced pumpkin juice in hopes that they would resemble Japanese *hoshigaki* (dried persimmons). It worked!

These aforementioned inspirations are why this book is important and will continue to be important long after we are gone. Most of this material lives on through generations only by word of mouth. None of this has been captured in big glossy cookbooks or overproduced food TV shows. This thought is interesting and also worries me sick. I can't sit back and watch the complexity of this culture dwindle away like the stripped mountaintops from years of irresponsible coal mining and natural resources management. Those practices have placed a black cloud over the economy and landscape of those gorgeous and magical mountains.

Appalachian cooks take pride in not writing recipes down or measuring ingredients. They take pride in working a wood stove by feel and not by glaring at a thermometer or asking Alexa to set a timer. They love teaching the art of a hog killing and preserving food for tougher times. Foxfire became privy to this back in the 1960s and started doing the work that has helped guide my career. The spirit of those high school kids who took to the woods in 1966 will always shine a light on the right path to celebrating this food.

The recipes are written as oral histories, and I wish all cookbooks were laid out this way. For some reason most cookbook publishers just don't have the courage. A special connection to the food forms when I am able to picture the time and place of these amazing people through the high art of Appalachian storytelling. I hope this book will give you a glimpse into the family reunions, holiday feasts, and church suppers that hold these communities together. At the very least, it may inspire you to pass some of this wisdom on, so the generations after us will pickle by the signs and bury heads of cabbage in their backyards for years to come.

Acknowledgments for the Revised Edition

We would like to acknowledge the work of Kami Ahrens, Amelia Golcheski, and Audrey Thomas, without whom this revised edition would not have been possible.

We thank our Foxfire student, freshman Mckaylin Hensley, for her beautiful illustrations throughout the book.

We also thank Sean Brock for his sincere love and appreciation for this cookbook and for his counsel in its re-editing.

Last, we dedicate this edition, in part, to Anthony Bourdain and his work in introducing new audiences to the value and importance of cultural foodways to the world at large and who reminded us, "Food is everything we are. It's an extension of nationalist feeling, ethnic feeling, your personal history, your province, your region, your tribe, your grandma. It's inseparable from those from the get-go."

T. J. Smith

Acknowledgments for the Original Edition

This book is the result of a project that was started in 1980 by Margie Bennett (a *Foxfire Magazine* advisor) and three students: Rosanne Chastain, Kim Hamilton, and Dana Holcomb. What started out as a summer project evolved into a much larger task, yet a more challenging one for both the students and the organization.

The material collected by these students was compiled as a special issue of the *Foxfire Magazine* for our magazine subscribers. Realizing the amount of unpublished information about Appalachian cooking still in our files, in addition to the quantity of available unrecorded information in this area, we continued the research for a larger publication—the second Foxfire Press book—about the foods and the people who prepare the food in our part of the country. Each day we were amazed and excited about the vast amount of information we continued to find but, because we already had enough material for two cookbooks, we had to stop the search and start putting together a manuscript. Maybe someday the material left out of this book will appear in another volume.

So many people tend to get involved with this sort of project, and there are always those who should receive some special recognition.

As always, Foxfire is indebted to the numerous students who were involved with the interviews and the taking of photographs, but I want to especially acknowledge Chet Welch, Allan Ramey (who also took the cover photographs), and Tammy Ledford for their enthusiastic and dedicated energy during the final production of this book. Without them this book would never have been finished on time.

To all our friends who welcomed us into their homes with such warmth and enthusiasm to share with us again their knowledge of something we knew so little about; and to those very special folks like Nora Garland, Ruby Frady, Mary Pitts, Rittie Webb, and Albert and Ethel Greenwood, among many others, who refused to let us leave without eating a meal with them or at least sampling their foods, I express my gratitude. Without all these people this book would not exist.

Special thanks to Ruth Cabe and Judy McCracken for their advice and dedicated time testing recipes despite one of the hottest summers ever to hit this part of the country. I also recognize all the students, parents, friends, faculty, and staff who assisted in finding and testing recipes. And for Susan Davis, who always answered the plea for help at the eleventh hour, I give thanks.

Appreciation is extended to the Atlanta Historical Society for its encouragement and support in initiating this project.

Some of the interviews and photographs in this book were conducted in collaboration with the Georgia Education Television Network.

Funding for the first year's operation of the Foxfire Press was provided by the Georgia Council for the Arts. This book was under development during that year.

Linda Garland Page

The **Foxfire** Book of Appalachian Cookery

Introduction

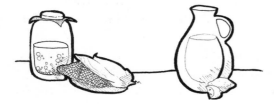

In this renaissance of food and food culture, an age of entire television networks dedicated solely to food and cooking, when seemingly every restaurant in every town has a collection of Yelp reviews, and practically everyone (yes, *everyone*) has an opinion about something so regionally attuned as barbecue, it's hard to imagine a time when culturally focused cookbooks, especially those from the American South, weren't flying off the shelves, but 1984 was one such time. As it would happen, that was the year E. P. Dutton released *The Foxfire Book of Appalachian Cookery*.

The mid-1980s were not a great time for food culture. It was a time of fast and convenient food. The microwave was the most popular appliance in the kitchen. The public demand was for meals that were quick and affordable. For those of us who were children in the eighties, our earliest food memories are as likely to be of Mom or Dad coming home with a bucket of the Colonel's secret recipe as of a home-cooked meal. So when the first edition of this cookbook, a book about hardscrabble living and crafting meals from scratch, was released in 1984, you may guess that it wasn't on everyone's wish list.

By the time UNC Press released a paperback edition, in 1992, things were not much different in terms of food's place in the broad popular culture. Emeril Lagasse, considered by many to be a pioneer of our now food-savvy society, was still a year from his first television appearance. Folks remained drawn to the convenience of eating out, but instead of fast food, the buzz was mostly about chain restaurants (anyone else remember what a big deal Applebee's was?). Grilling was gaining ground as a popular weekend foodie pastime, but nothing like today's age of mushikamados on practically every suburban back deck. America's love affair with curated menus and farm-to-table freshness was still but a glint—and mainly on the East and West Coasts—in our collective eye. So, when UNC Press's *Foxfire Book of Appalachian Cookery* appeared, most of the public still wasn't ready to start frying ramps or kneading out biscuits.

This is all to say that maybe the time wasn't right then, but now . . . now, we are in a very different time. Now is a time when the public has embraced food as something more than just fuel for our bodies. Now is a time when so much of the population is aware of how food can change our perspective on everything from health to global politics. Specifically related to Foxfire, now is a time when southern foodways stock is cruising ever upward.

For well over a decade, much of the foodie world's attention has been on food traditions from the South. Blue-chip traditions such as barbecue (and all its regional nuances) and New Orleans creole cuisine have enjoyed the larger share of the spotlight, along with more focused foodways such as those found in the low country or in southern urban centers. Recently (and most exciting for all of us here), the food-ways of Southern Appalachia have started to get attention. Through the work of such organizations as the Appalachian Food Summit and the Southern Foodways Alliance, the foodie world is being exposed to Southern Appalachian fare like cornmeal gravy and smoked apples. Thanks to Facebook groups and urban supper clubs, folks are sharing recipes and trying their hands at Southern Appalachian recipes. It's a remarkable thing to behold, especially for someone who was raised in these mountains.

This moment in American food culture feels like the right time to take a closer look at our little cookbook, dust it off, rethink it for today, and put it back out into the world. In order to do so, I'd like to walk you through how we came to this book in the first place.

In 1972, *The Foxfire Book* was published by a group of high school students in Rabun County, Georgia. It was an incredible endeavor undertaken by the students, who were empowered by their teachers to take ownership of how their community was interpreted and presented to a broad audience. It was a product born out of *The Foxfire Magazine*, which began just five years earlier. Students in the Foxfire program approached the magazine and, later, the book with maturity and tremendous vision. For that first book, they knew that they needed content with impact—words and images that effectively communicated the cultural traditions of their communities while holding the attention of their readers. None of them really knew just how far their words would reach, but they knew that, no matter if the book was read by one person or one million, they wanted to make a good impression.

To that end, the students intuitively chose to include several articles about food-related subjects in that first book, such as cooking over an open hearth and churning butter. Food is common ground. For many of us, our introduction to different cultures comes in the form of food. We all need it, and if we're paying attention to just how big food culture has become, most of us love it with true zeal. Many of us love exploring new tastes and sensations. Food is, in this folklorist's opinion, the folk culture gateway drug. Foodways are the passport with which we visit culture without having to hop on a plane or even get into our cars. This book uses food traditions as an introduction to a rich culture and derives its success from the authenticity and intimacy of each interview. Here were young Appalachians collecting, documenting, and interpreting their culture. The people the students interviewed weren't "others": they were family, friends, and neighbors.

It was only natural that, in those intimate spaces, conversations about food and foodways were abundant. Who doesn't like talking about food? Although the content of Foxfire books is often organized around specific topics, the actual interviews are more organic, moving from subject to subject as both interviewer and contact perform a dialogic dance. The process for a Foxfire interview isn't necessarily to go into an initial sit-down with something specific in mind—more often than not, the prepared questions are general, geared toward putting the interviewee at ease and learning about his or her life experiences. It is from that process (and the resulting transcription) that new questions form and follow-up interviews are scheduled to dig deeper on specific topics. In *The Foxfire Book*, the chapters on preserving fruit and vegetables, churning butter, and mountain recipes grew out of interviews that weren't focused on those subjects. It was through this process that *The Foxfire Book of Appalachian Cookery* began to take shape. *Foxfire Magazine* advisor Margie Bennett and three of her students, Rosanne Chastain, Kim Hamilton, and Dana Holcomb, followed this process, first, to a special edition of *The Foxfire Magazine* and, ultimately, to the first edition of this book.

I'm going to be straight with you: I'm not a chef. There is little in the way of formal training or expertise that makes me a good candidate to edit a cookbook beyond the fact that I happen to be the sitting executive director at Foxfire. However, I am a folklorist and I love food and I love cooking and cookbooks. I find it impossible to resist a Junior League or garden club cookbook from a used book sale. I am also blessed with a staff that includes a number of folks who love food and cooking and cookbooks even more than I do, and I've enlisted their help in rethinking this publication, namely our assistant curator, Kami Ahrens, and two graduate interns, Amelia Golcheski and Audrey Thomas. I've also reached out to some chef friends (including the author of this edition's foreword) for input and perspective. With our collective heads working together, we sat down with *The Foxfire Book of Appalachian Cookery* and thought about how we could make it better. This is what we came up with.

First, we tackled organization. We felt that there were too many chapters in the original publication. It was clearly laid out in the tradition of cookbooks from that period, which meant that it didn't *feel* like a Foxfire book. And what's the point of having "Foxfire" on the cover if it doesn't feel like a Foxfire book? The organization of the material was antiquated, inconsistent, and a bit illogical. So, to address those issues, we've taken the book down from seventeen chapters to ten, reorganizing them in a way that is more organic. As you might guess, that means we had to reorganize the content as well. It's been an interesting exercise, to say the least. There was a wealth of material—from stories and memories to the recipes themselves—and we were given the difficult task of keeping the book to the same or fewer pages. We wanted to add new material, but to do so, we had to cut out some of the old. I tasked several of our more food-savvy staff with identifying those recipes that may be less accessible to readers and replacing them with recipes that were easier to accomplish. In some instances, we removed recipes that were redundant, in which there were two or more listings of essentially the same dish. All in all, we feel that we have streamlined and improved the recipe offerings. There were then countless discussions on where to put things in the context of the new chapter headings. Oftentimes, a recipe could be as equally at home in one section as another, so a lot of our organizational decisions came down to the subjective opinions of one or more of the folks working on this book.

During the reorganization, we identified one topic, touched on briefly in the first edition, that is enjoying something of a revival: curing meat. Although this process might be inaccessible for most folks, we recognize that there is an audience of chefs, charcuterie makers, and homesteaders who are interested in learning how meat was cured with salt and sugar and, in some instances, wood smoke. When we started shuffling things around in the new organizational scheme, we felt the need to add a chapter on smokehouses and curing processes. Our archives as well as early issues of *The Foxfire Magazine* contain a wealth of information on these subjects. We used these resources to put together a detailed chapter on curing meat that we hope you enjoy.

Before I let you go, I want to raise a topic of importance to us at Foxfire, which revolves around issues that have arisen from our popular culture's new interest in traditional foodways. As a representative of an organization charged with the curation and interpretation of Southern Appalachian culture, I would be remiss if I did not point out that Southern Appalachia, while currently romanticized in a variety of popular contexts, is a region facing significant challenges. Changing demographics, rural gentrification, the exploitation of natural resources, the loss of unskilled labor jobs, the rise in drug and alcohol addiction, and growing childhood obesity are just a few. I mention this to you, our readers, to illuminate your understanding of these trials and in the hope that your appreciation for this region (as demonstrated in your purchase of this book) grows into an awareness of its obstacles and that you may be inspired to help in our navigating those obstacles.

On that note, while the spotlight on cultural foodways has its benefits, it also has some dark consequences. As food has moved into the sphere of popular culture and mass media, it has fallen prey to the supply-and-demand dynamics of cultural trends. This presents a challenge to many regional foodways that originally emerged out of necessity and limitations on resources and accessibility. Poor people know how to survive, and when it comes to food, that survival often depends on their ability to use anything edible— from the lights, or lungs, of a pig to the tail of an ox. This approach to food manifests itself in now-familiar dishes like Jamaican oxtail or Cajun boudin. As with boudin, these recipes often make use of something foodies call offal, which is most often defined as the internal organs and entrails of a butchered animal. Likewise, historically cast-off cuts of meat, such as oxtail and skirt steak, are finding their way into suburban homes around the country. And, as is the way with supply and demand, the popularity of these foods has driven up prices—in some instances, pricing out the very people from whom these food traditions derive.

In Appalachia, we are seeing this very phenomenon. Recently a friend and I were discussing the growing popularity of ramps. Naively, I commented that at least folks were having to travel into Appalachia to buy ramps from smaller produce stands and were, as a result, supporting a small farmer. My friend deadpanned, "You can buy ramps in Whole Foods." I was at a loss for words. Such is the way of popular culture, but I ask our readers to be mindful of this. I'm not suggesting that you not enjoy ramps (good on ya, if you do) or souse meat or any of the other wonderful foods in this book, but I am asking that you consider making that drive into Appalachia to buy your ramps and perhaps explore how you can contribute to helping this region navigate today's challenges.

So, there it is—rather, *here* it is. We hope that those of you just discovering this book find our collection entertaining and informative, and we invite you to explore our other books. For those of you who have loved and cherished the early editions of *The Foxfire Book of Appalachian Cookery*, we hope you enjoy reading the book through a new lens *and* discovering the new material we've included.

Our wish for this volume is to add something valuable to the growing conversation about southern foodways, specifically Southern Appalachian foodways. We encourage all of you, our readers, to reach out and share your thoughts on what we've put together here, and perhaps share a recipe or two of your own with us that may find its way into a future volume from Foxfire. We invite you to join us at our table and relish in the stories and flavors collected and preserved through this wonderful organization we call Foxfire.

Prologue

The most appropriate way to set these recipes, instructions, and stories in their proper context is to begin with part of an interview we conducted with Ada Kelly, who died at the age of ninety-five, two weeks before the manuscript for this book was delivered to the publisher.

A former schoolteacher, Ada lived on a large farm in Rabun County, Georgia. By the time Foxfire was started in 1966, she was a grandmother many times over, and students visited her frequently to get her to teach them how to make items like bonnets made of cornshucks (see *Foxfire Book 3* [1975], pp. 461–64) that she remembered from her largely self-sufficient childhood. Well into her later years, she pursued the creative outlets that gave her so much pleasure—drawnwork, knitting, crocheting, making rugs and quilts, and creating beautiful compositions of wildflowers and leaves pressed between velvet and glass in wooden frames. She remembered her youth with much clarity, and she had such perspective on life in the mountains in general that she was consulted more than once by the scriptwriters for the Broadway play *Foxfire* to ensure its accuracy and authenticity. She was one of our favorite people.

The year before I was born, my father built a four-room log cabin with two rooms downstairs and two up. We moved into the building just before I was born, and I lived there until I was eighteen. We had a very comfortable house and a large fireplace with a hearth that came way out [into the room]. There was eight children in our family, and we all pitched in and helped with the work on the farm and was really a close-knit family. We had good parents. They were strict with us and expected us to do what was right, and that has always stuck with us. We kept a lot of

Ada Kelly.

cattle and some horses and some hogs and raised practically everything we used. We had sheep, and my mother and father would shear the wool. We washed, carded, and spun the wool, and my mother wove it into material. She made practically all our clothing by hand. It was customary for the children to work with the parents in most everything they did, and it was a matter of survival for everybody to do their part.

In the summertime we'd get up about daylight, and my father was usually in the fields with his crop just after daylight. We all had our job to do, and we all went on and did it and didn't ever think about not doing it. It was just a part of life. I wonder sometimes when I hear children say these days, "I don't want to." We never did say that. Just whatever there was to do, we all pitched in.

It was our job as children to shell corn and feed and look after the sheep and help do the milking as we got large enough. I remember shelling corn at night by hand to take to the mill the next day. We'd sit by the fire and shell a bushel of corn by hand. They didn't have much wheat bread then—most of it was corn bread. And we raised rye, so we had a lot of rye bread then.

I look back on my childhood, and I think I was as happy as any child that ever grew up. My father and mother were very hard workers. My father was a general farmer, and he always had a lot of animals and grew our pork, beef, and vegetables. He hauled produce in a wagon—apples and chestnuts. He'd go from here in a wagon down as far as Washington, Georgia, and Royston and all down in there to sell it. He'd probably be gone two weeks, and he'd always bring us something special, things I looked forward to. We'd always be glad for him to come home.

He also did a good bit of carpentry work, and he tanned leather. He'd bring it in, and that's one thing he did at night. He'd just work with that leather, rub it and scrape it and get it pliable so he could make it into shoes, harness, and all those kinds of things.

Mother did the cooking and helped with the milking and gardening and looking after the family in general. She visited the sick a lot and did a lot of knitting. She made all our clothes by hand till I was about ten years old. She cooked on the fireplace, too. They had a wire hung down in the chimney, and it had a hook on it. They'd hang their put on that hook, and food would cook a long time there. They also had a big iron pot that they put vegetables in, and they'd stack one pan on top of another in that pot. You could cook vegetables and meat and anything that you had to boil in there. Or they had two or three great big iron [Dutch] ovens with lids, and they'd bake a chicken pie in one, potatoes in one, and bread in the other one. With a big family it took lots to eat.

And that's the best food you've ever eat—cakes, egg custards, chicken pies, and boiled vegetables. When they'd have quiltings, they'd cook all kinds of things for a day or two on the fireplace. The women'd gather and bring their little children. The children would play outside, and everybody's have the best time in the world. We always had a good dinner on Sundays, too. We had lots of wild strawberries, and we'd have strawberry pies, and we'd have cabbage and turnips and pork and homemade sausage and rye bread.

I wouldn't want to go back to cooking on the fireplace, though. Sometimes I bake potatoes on my fireplace in the wintertime out of curiosity, I guess, mostly. But they are good. Well, some things are better cooked on the fireplace—corn bread and *big old fat biscuits cooked on the fireplace was just out of this world! I don't think any stove has cooked them as good; I really don't. I remember very well when we got our first cookstove. I was about eleven years old, and my father had built a new dining room and kitchen onto the house. I remember how proud I was we had a stove. It had a great big oven. We'd cook pones of corn bread in there and baked sweet potatoes and Irish potatoes. And we'd fry meat in a frying pan.*

My father wasn't a hunter, but everybody had hogs and cows and grew their own pork and beef. We'd kill and dress a beef occasionally and quarter it up and sell three quarters to some of the neighbors—a quarter apiece. One [family] would sell to the others, and another time another one would kill a beef and do the same thing. And he'd hang the hind quarter we kept up in the smokehouse where the air circulated and dried the best beef you've ever eat. It was just as tender. We've done that since I've lived here, but that was a good many years ago. And he'd salt-cure the pork, pack it down in a wooden box that he'd made, and, after it got cool, he'd put a layer of salt and spread it all out till it'd cure. Then when we'd need meat we'd go and cut off what we needed. We never was out of ham and fatback and bacon, and most of the people, unless they was just extremely poor, would've had their own meat. You just spread it out and salted it down about the next day after you killed it. They let it cool, and then they just covered it with salt. That was the best meat you've ever eat— some of the best hams and ham gravy.

We used to have plenty of vegetables and fruits all winter, and they were delicious. We got lots of wild berries—huckleberries, blueberries, blackberries— and we always did a lot of canning. We filled all our jars and sealed them with beeswax and cloth rags.

Take a clean rag cloth, dip it in hot beeswax and put three or four layers of that over a stone jar. And believe it or not, it kept just as good as anything keeps now. We dried blackberries and huckleberries, too.

Now, on roasting ears being dried—they just cut the kernels off and spread them out on cloth until they dried, and then they stored them in a jar or container of some kind. Then you could cook them when you got ready. And pumpkins, they cut them in round strips and hung them on strings up in their kitchen. They'd dry. You'd just cook them like you would a fresh pumpkin.

They also did what they called bleaching apples. They'd cut up a tub full of apples and put a little sulfur in a saucer and strike a match to it and set it in there and cover the tub and it'd burn. Nearly everybody made a tub of that, and we had those bleached apples for the winter.

Everybody grew cabbage in that country [Scaly, North Carolina], too. If you ever go up there now, the whole country's in cabbage. They've always grown some, and they'd cut the cabbage up by the tubs full and make big barrels of kraut. They'd just put layers of chopped cabbage and layers of salt, weight them down with a smooth plank with a cloth under it and over it, and just let it set there till it got sour. It'd keep all winter long. You'd just go to that tub and dip out the kraut and fry it a little. That was it except to eat it.

And they stored a lot of food whole. They'd bury cabbage and potatoes and turnips and apples in the ground. They'd dig a rather deep hole and put their hay or straw in the bottom of the pit so the food wouldn't come in contact with the dirt and fill that hole full of whatever vegetables or fruit they wanted to save there. Then they'd put some more straw on top of it and cover it with a deep layer of soil, and when they wanted some of it to use, they'd dig a hole into that, get them out some, and cover it back up. And that food'd keep just as perfect there, or more so, than it would in any cellar you'd ever see.

So we didn't suffer for something to eat. Very few people did unless they was somebody that was sick, and then the neighbors would take care of them. So it was a good life after all.

1 The Hearth

As far as the good part of it,
I don't know if cooking today is any better.
—*Unknown participant*

Of all the remembrances Foxfire students have shared about Aunt Arie Carpenter, one that is talked of most concerns her popping corn in her fireplace whenever the students would visit. It's a tradition that we have carried forward at the Foxfire Museum and Heritage Center in our Savannah House—an 1820s-era log cabin from the Savannah Community in western North Carolina—where we often pop corn in the fireplace for visiting elementary schoolchildren to sample. The kids and their teachers are always fascinated by the process and often remark that ours is the best popcorn they've ever had. There's just something special about food cooked over a wood fire.

Open-hearth cooking is presently enjoying something of a resurgence. Restaurants from Savannah to Seattle are incorporating wood-fire or open-hearth cooking in recipes for their menus. Classes and workshops focused on cooking over an open wood flame are growing in popularity. Festivals centered around traditional wood-fired fare such as barbecue and smoked meats are held in practically every state in the nation. Even here, at Foxfire, classes in open-hearth cooking and wood-stove cooking are a part of our heritage skills class offerings.

A number of factors could be attributed to this renewed interest in wood-fire cooking, but our very simple point of view on the subject is that folks are drawn in by the intimacy of the process. Cooking in this way is intentional and attentive. One cannot place a pot over the flame and walk away. Cooking over a fire requires care and patience. It asks us to stop, be present, and focus. Wood-fire cooking is all at once meditative and actively engaging. As we struggle with the fast pace of modernity, there is something special about those opportunities we can find to slow down, unplug, and take a moment (or, if we're lucky, several moments) to dedicate our attention to a singular task. And whether that singular task is baking biscuits in a wood stove or preparing a dish on your backyard grill, cooking over a wood fire is altogether a splendid, rewarding experience. What's more, with just a few basic tools, it is extremely accessible. Our hope for this chapter is simply that you find inspiration here to meet this approach to cooking wherever you can and have that experience.

Fireplace Cooking

Cooking in the fireplace is simple, but it requires a great deal more time and effort than using a stove. As Nora Garland told us, "Cooking over a fireplace was hotter than cooking over a wood stove. After all, you were right down over the fire. And there was a lot of extra bending and stretching, but people didn't think nothing about it then. They was used to it."

For cooking, there must be a hot bed of coals—a process that takes several hours for a new fire to produce. Hickory and other hardwoods were especially popular for sustained heat. Aunt Nora stressed the importance of keeping the wood in a shed. She said, "We didn't want no wet wood, and when it turned in to rain, we'd all go running to bring in wood and stack it on the porch."

Many fireplaces had a fixed, horizontal iron bar running from side to side about three feet above the fireplace floor. Others had a bar, or crane, that was hinged to the side wall of the fireplace so that it could be swung in and out.

Aunt Arie Carpenter pops corn for Foxfire students.

On these bars, pots and kettles with a handle, or bale, would be hung from S-shaped hooks.

People used these pots, suspended over the fire, for warming soups and stews, heating large quantities of water, and boiling meat and vegetables. On a horizontal bar there was room for pots of stewed meat, leather breeches (see pages 37–38), and boiled cabbage hung side by side for a complete meal. If the fire got too hot, or if something needed only to be kept warm, the pot could be slid along the bar to the side or swung partly out of the fireplace.

The Dutch oven—a heavy, round iron pot with a handle and an iron lid that has a half-inch lip all the way around the edge—was one of the most common cooking utensils. Dutch ovens were usually used for baking bread and biscuits, but they could also be used for baking cakes and potatoes, roasting meats, and heating soups and stews. Some of the older Dutch ovens and skillets had rounded bottoms and three little legs. One variation looks like a large frying pan with four small legs and is often called an old-timey oven or an old bread oven. Today, a trivet can be used to rest a skillet or Dutch oven over hot coals. You can find trivets of all sizes online or at specialty cookware stores, or if you are especially industrious, you can fabricate one in your home blacksmith forge.

While the Dutch oven was sometimes used out of doors, like most cast-iron cookware it was usually used inside by the fireplace, placed on hot coals raked directly onto the hearth. Both lid and oven were preheated before using, the oven being preheated on the coals themselves and the lid directly on the fire. When the oven and lid were hot enough, the bread dough—or whatever was to be baked—was poured into the oven and the

Aunt Arie tends potatoes cooked in a Dutch oven. Necessary fireplace implements—shovel and poker—stand beyond the oven.

lid set on top with pothooks. Coals would then be piled on top of the lid for additional heat, the lip around the edge keeping them from rolling off. You had to be careful that the coals under the oven were not too hot, or the food would burn. The lid could be much hotter than the bottom, as it was not directly touching what was being baked.

Here's how to bake corn bread in a Dutch oven:

Carefully grease the whole inside of the oven with a piece of pork rind. Then preheat the oven and the lid on the coals. Mix up the batter by combining 2 cups of cornmeal, 1 cup of flour, 1 cup of buttermilk, and a spoonful each of salt and soda. Sprinkle a handful of cornmeal on the sides and bottom inside the oven so the bread won't stick, and then pour the batter in, making sure the oven is level so the bread will be the same thickness all around. Using some tongs, place the lid on the oven and cover it with hot coals. The bread will be ready in 15 to 20 minutes, depending on how hot the coals are. It can be cut right in the oven and taken out with a fork or large spoon.

Marinda Brown found out for herself how deceptively easy this method of cooking corn bread can be:

We used to cook in iron pots. We had iron tea kettles and Dutch ovens with the little legs and the lid you put your coals on. A little while back I thought I had found a recipe to make corn pone like my mother used to make in a Dutch oven, and I went ahead and made up the batter and built a fire. I put on a lot of coals, and I was going to have some good corn pone. I got it too hot, though, and burned it up. I never have tried it anymore.

For frying, coals were raked out onto the hearth and the frying pan was set directly on them. When boiling a small amount of water or making coffee, people would set the kettle on a few coals right up against the fire. An even quicker method was to place the kettle right on top of the burning wood. Again, a trivet can be a useful tool for cooking in this way.

Meat was broiled simply by holding it over a bed of hot coals on the end of a long, sturdy fork with a wooden handle. Popcorn was popped ("parched") by putting the shelled kernels in a covered metal box that had small holes punched in it. The box was attached to a long wooden handle and shaken directly over the fire. Aunt Arie used a device like this to pop corn for the Foxfire students visiting her, and it's what we use here at the museum.

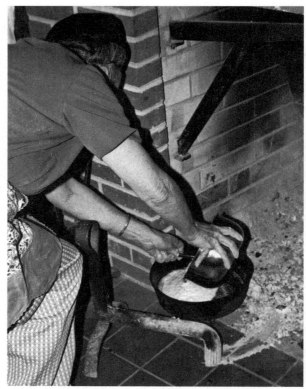

Fay Long stoops to pour corn bread batter into her preheated Dutch oven.

Foods such as potatoes, corn, onions, and nuts—still in their protective coverings of skins, shucks, and shells—could be roasted by burying them in hot ashes for insulation and then placing live coals on top of the ashes. Ash cakes were baked by wrapping the dough in cloth, placing them in a cleaned-out corner of the fireplace, and covering them with ashes and coals. They were supposed to have a delicious flavor when baked this way, but it was difficult to control the heat and keep the bread clean. Sometimes small cakes were cooked directly on the fireplace shovel, which was handheld or propped over the firedogs while the cakes cooked.

Aunt Fay checks the progress of her bread by carefully wielding a poker. Note the pothooks at her feet and the pot of bear meat suspended from a crane in the fireplace.

mantel. And Aunt Nora supplied us with another down-to-earth way to take advantage of fireplace heat: "We used to sit chairs around the fireplace and hang clothes over them to dry. We had to. We don't have winters now like we used to. Back then, snow would lay on the ground six inches deep for weeks, so we *had* to dry our clothes by the fire."

During the winter, fires were kept going all day. At night, ashes were heaped over the coals to keep them hot until morning. A fire would start up again "just like you poured kerosene oil on it" when fresh wood was added. In the warmer months, the fire would be started up only when it was time to cook, and ashes would be raked over the coals to save them when no fire was needed. Homes were once constructed with dogtrots (covered breezeways) separating kitchen from living quarters mainly because the extra heat generated by fires continually maintained there made the room uncomfortable in warm weather.

Arie Meaders's account of her mother's cooking on a fireplace is one of the most vivid we collected:

The more common use for the shovel, however, was in the habitual task of cleaning out the fireplace. As Nora Garland said, "Mother always put the ashes on the beans she was growing in the garden. We'd put out the fire, move the firedogs, shovel out the ashes, and scour the fireplace out, too. We only did that about once a month because that was a *job*. You'd have to get down on your hands and knees with a rag and scrub."

Fruits, vegetables, and meats were often dried by the fire for several days to preserve them. The food would be placed on the hearth away from the direct heat or strung and suspended from the

My mother had a large [Dutch] oven, and I've got it here if none of them's not carried it off. It's got three legs, but it don't have any handle. She used pot hooks to go in the eyes that was in the oven. She'd set the oven on the fire and get it hot, and then she'd pull some coals out and set the oven on that. She'd put the lid in the fireplace and get it good and hot, and then she'd put coals on it [on top of the oven]. She'd make her bread up this way [making rolling and patting motion with two hands] into three pones that went around in that big oven. She'd put her bread in, put the lid on, and get that oven hot enough to cook that bread.

When she went to make a pie, it was the same way. If she was gonna make a tart pie, she had little tart pie pans that she used to make pies from fresh apples in. She'd make her pies and set them in that big oven. She'd have it ready to cook them pies done by the time she'd get another batch of pies made up. And when that one was done, she'd take it out and put another one in. She cooked a lot that way, but I wouldn't get but just one or two cooked!

She had a big pot to cook beans or green beans or turnips in, or boil backbones and spareribs in, or anything you was gonna have like that. I've seen pots that hang over the fire. They're cranes—our uncle had one—but we didn't have anything like that. Everything went out on the hearth. The beans would sit right in front of the fire and just cook on one side. She'd put coals around it to keep it cooking all around, and she'd turn it around every once in a while and let the other side cook.

Then we had a great big old frypan with a big long handle, and that's what she fried her meat in. She'd pull coals out on the hearth and set that pan right on them, and the meat would just cook. It was good. She'd pull the coals out and put her coffeepot on there, too. She'd always have a kettle that she "het" her water in—or she "heated" her water in. People laugh at me for say "het" [laughing]! She'd have her water hot, and she'd pour it in there on her ground coffee. It wasn't but a few minutes till the coffee would boil, being as the water was already hot and the coals was under it.

Right before dinner you'd have three or four different things going at the same time in the coals. You had to stay right there with it [laughs]! My mother liked fireplace cooking better than her wood stove. She was raised to it, and she'd manage it pretty good! Of course, when she went to make her cobbler pies, she'd use her stove because she couldn't get her cobbler pan in the oven and she could get it in the stove.

Law, I remember them blackberry pies she used to make! When she'd make one they'd be so many flies they'd nearly eat you up! It took two to mind the flies off the pie so the rest could eat. We had no screens nor nothing like that, but, oh, we had flies then—my, my. It was terrible. We'd use a brush from the shade tree a lot of times to keep them from the table. And we had a cane about that long [indicating three feet] we got off the creek bank, and we'd roll so many layers of paper on part of it and then split the paper with scissors. That made a pretty good fly brush. Somebody had to stand over the table while everybody else was eating. It had to be done, or they'd eat a fly! Us biggest children was always the ones that done it. Sometimes we'd sit at the table with our hand propped on the table scaring flies. I don't see how in the world people lived. It wasn't no wonder they had lots of typhoid fever back then.

Exie Dills is another contact who, as she says, "cooked on a fireplace right smart."

I'd always do baked bread or potatoes in an oven in front of the fire. You've got to have a whole lot of live coals, and you put you out some on the hearth and put your oven down on them. If you wanted to you could lay strips of meat on top of your potatoes to bake them, and if you didn't you could just rub grease on the potatoes. Bake them with the jacket on, put your lid on, and cover that lid with coals. It wouldn't take sweet or Irish potatoes either one but about forty-five minutes to bake. And I have baked bread in that oven time and again, even sweet bread. We called it gingerbread back then. We'd make it with syrup, a cup and a half to two cups of homemade cane syrup and one egg and pour in there. Lay the ginger to it heavy [laughing]. Work your dough pretty *stiff—don't leave it soft—and pat it in that greased oven. Make two cakes, leave the open space in the middle, and just put one cake on each side of your oven. That would make it cook in the middle better, you see. It would run together a little, but not like if it was put in whole. Just cover your lid with coals and bake it.*

We found that many women had a soft spot for the old ways of fireplace cooking, and on occasion, a few still practice it:

LOLA CANNON: *In winter it was very nice to put a skillet on the hearth in front of a good fire and rake the coals from the fire under the skillet and bake corn bread and potatoes. The oldsters still think that the food had a better flavor then than it does now, but that may just be our idea.*

LETTIE CHASTAIN: *My grandma used to make the best corn bread I ever had in her Dutch oven. She'd bake cakes and everything. And she'd hang a little black pot over the fire and cook peas. You know dried peas will stay through the winter, and we had to have the fire in the fireplace anyways, so that's how she cooked them.*

ICIE RICKMAN: *We have a fireplace in yonder and a fireplace upstairs. My husband's mother cooked in yonder on that big one. She had a skillet with legs and a lid on it. She cooked bread and the best cakes in it. It sure is good that way. His mama and daddy had a wood stove, but they just loved to cook on those old fireplaces. You ought to eat some of their good beans they cooked. The old folks did things the hard way, didn't they?*

BESSIE BOLT: *I still cook here on the fireplace with a black pot. It's about the best cooking there is, I think. I prefer it. I could own all these modern kind, but I don't care for them. I use my old wood fireplace and wood heater—just myself here and the Lord.*

Having turned her pothooks into a handle, or "bale," Aunt Fay lifts the finished bread from the ashes. The S-shaped hook from which pots are hung can be seen on the right.

Wood Stove Cooking

For most of our first contacts interviewed by Foxfire students in the late 1960s, cooking on a fireplace was a memory from childhood. Their firsthand experiences in wood-fire cooking were almost exclusively with wood cookstoves. As Addie Norton reminisced:

I can remember the first stove that we ever had. Daddy took off some stuff to market. You know, we used to take things off of the farm and journey into Georgia and swap it for things we needed at home. I think now, honey, I believe that he paid for it with potatoes or turnips or some or something or other he had raised on the farm.

Now, that's been many years, but I can remember it just like it was yesterday. He found a little number seven stove. It's a little bitty thing. And we put that thing up and some of them said, "You'll set the house afire when you put a fire in that thing." I said, "It won't do no such thing." Daddy said it wouldn't either, but everybody that came in was afraid of that stove [laughter]. We put a fire in it and we cooked on it for a long time. I thought it was the most wonderful thing to have a stove to cook on and not have to cook on a fireplace. Finally we got a number eight, I think. It was bigger than a number seven. But I remember that little number seven stove, honey. I can just see it sitting over there in the corner. It set on legs, up, oh, about that far from the floor to keep it from catching a-fire down below. But I can just see that sitting over there on one side of that chimney. I just imagine now the first meal cooked on it was for breakfast, and I just guess it was bacon and eggs and maybe corn bread. I don't know, maybe biscuits. Whatever we had, that's what we had for breakfast. And syrup, butter, milk and things like that. 'Course we always had plenty of that.

Back when I bought my wood cookstove, my son said, "Mother, why didn't you put on a few more dollars and get an electric stove?" At that time the elective stove wouldn't have cost much more than that one did—around toward a hundred dollars then. I told him, I said, "For the simple reason, son, I don't want one." I never had cooked with electricity or anything. I had always used wood or coal, and I'm

not afraid of it, honey, and I am afraid of gas and electricity at my age. You know, you've not got the mind to remember things that you had when you was young. And I was afraid at that time to have one—afraid I'd forget something and leave it turned up. But you see, if I put a fire in that wood stove and go out of the house, it's not gonna get hotter. It's gonna get cooler. That wood's gonna burn up and it's not gonna hurt nothing. If I go out and leave the electric stove on, I'm liable to catch the house on fire or something like that. I'm afraid to risk my own judgment about things like that. And I really and truly love the heat from a wood stove or a coal stove better that all your electric or anything else you can get. Yes, ma'am. I love my own heat and I absolutely freeze to death when I go to the boys'. Some of them's got electricity and some of them's got this and some of them's got the other, but I still love my old stove right there. I get awfully black and nasty with it, but I still love the heat. I reckon it's because I was raised on it and I don't know anything [else]. I don't like an electric stove. I'd burn up everything I tried to cook, or I'd do something to it that wasn't right.

Often a first cookstove was, for newlyweds, one of the bare essentials for setting up housekeeping. Billy and Annie Long recalled with some regret the fate of their first stove. Billy said, "The first stove we had was one of those big blue ranges with a warming closet over the top and a hot water heater on the side by the firebox. When the house burned up it went to pot, and we never did try to cook on it no more. The roof fell in and broke it.

Yeah, I'd went to [the town of] Clayton. Neal and a fellow was cleaning out the chicken house, for we was fixing to put in some more chickens. They all come in and eat dinner, and after they got through they went on back to work. Neal had been spraying the chicken house, and he'd just went out the back door and started up to the chicken house when he heard something. He looked around, and the house was afire where the flue come out. We had a little old hose pipe and a standpipe right there in the yard. He hooked all that up, but that thing was burning so big by then he couldn't do no good. So they run in here and begun to carry stuff out of the front rooms while the kitchen was burning.

Annie continued: "We picked the kettle up that went with the stove and run out with it. It's all we got out of the kitchen."

In *Foxfire Book 3* (pp. 470–71), Aunt Nora Garland related the story of her first acquaintance with the wood-burning cookstove:

The first [cook]stove I ever saw in my life was a Wilson Patent Stove. My mother had been to her Aunt Jane's, right here in town, and found out that she had a stove. Well, she wanted one; so she came back home and wanted Daddy to know about it. He told us to go back to Aunt Jane's [and find out where she ordered it]. It finally came, and they put it up and built a fire in it. We got the wood, thinking that it was the awfullest thing in this world—people still cooking on a fireplace. We hadn't had a stove and this one—with two little eyes at the top—was the first one that came out.

The neighbors came in to see it, and it began to smoke. Well, Mama watered the fire out of it and walked to Aunt Jane's to see what was the matter with it. Aunt Jane said, "Honey, the newness is burning off it. The polish will soon burn off, and it will be alright."

We were so happy with that stove. We baked a batch of bread on it. We had had to bake that in the

Arie Meaders proudly holds one of her son's famous face jugs.

fireplace, but we didn't have to after we got the stove. And people came in to see what was happening, and from then on nearly everybody tried to get three dollars to get them a stove. This must have been about 1906. I'm eighty-two now, but I must've been five or six. I remember that stove so well. We even made a poem about it:

So well do I remember
The Wilson Patent Stove
That Father bought and paid for
With cloth the girls had wove.
All the neighbors wondered
When we got the thing to go
They said it would burst and kill us all
Some twenty year ago.
But twenty year ago,
Just twenty year ago
They said it would burst and kill us all
Just twenty year ago.

It never did burst. It was a stove like any other
stove, but we hadn't never saw one before.

Whatever the risks, wood stoves were considered to be an improvement over fireplaces for cooking, but they obviously still required a lot of attention. Dry kindling and wood had to be cut to fit the firebox and kept on hand. When Annie Long said that she liked to cook on a wood stove, her husband retorted with a laugh, "Getting wood was the biggest thing she didn't like, I think." Blanche Harkins said, "I wouldn't want to have to cook on a wood stove now" because "that wood is messy."

Stove wood should be stacked in a woodshed or on the back porch where it will be protected from the weather. The drier the wood is, the faster a fire will become hot enough to cook on. Wet or green wood must dry first in the fire before it can burn and tends to smoke more than dry wood. Green wood also causes creosote buildup inside cookstoves.

We asked for some general instructions on where to install a wood-burning cookstove. If there is not a brick or rock wall for the stove to stand against, we were told that the back of the stove should be least thirty-six inches from the

The classic Home Comfort wood stove, owned by Mr. and Mrs. Andy Webb.

Sometimes cast-iron kettles were the only things salvaged from a house fire.

Split wood and logs were kept near the stove in any handy receptacle.

wall, allowing room for the stovepipe. The sides should be no closer than twenty-four inches from a wall, as most wood-burning stoves are not insulated.

Stoves are often installed with bricks under the legs to lift them higher off the floor. This helps prevent the floor from being overheated and the iron legs from making impressions or holes in the floor. The stovepipe should be installed according to the manufacturer's instructions. A general list of recommendations and precautions follows:

- Stove must be eighteen inches from *any* wall.
- Flue pipe should be put together with metal screws only.
- Chimney caps were not recommended in the first edition, but we have found that a screen and a cap on the stovepipe not running through a chimney is a good precautionary measure.
- Don't place flammable objects on or near the heater when you have a fire.
- Never use wet or green wood because of creosote buildup.
- Have your chimney checked every other year and cleaned to prevent chimney fires.
- Before hooking a stove or heater up to a used chimney, be sure to check for cracks in the flue and for buildup in pipes.
- Ashes should be emptied when the ash box is half full to keep the grate from warping.
- Before dumping, make sure ashes contain no live coals. A slight breeze is all it takes to fan them to life and start a fire where they are dumped.

Jake Waldroop splits wood.

(above) *An early cookstove with a variety of cookware; cloths have been placed under the front legs to level the stove.*

(left) *Stovepipe inserted into a chimney.*

In a wood cookstove, the fire is built in the firebox located on the left-hand side of the stove, right under the cooking surface. To save time, people used coals right from the fireplace to start a fire. However, to start a fire "from scratch" in your firebox, first shake the ashes from the previous fire down into the ash box and open the dampers (see diagram of stove parts). You may want to line the bottom of the firebox with a sheet of newspaper to prevent new coals and small kindling from falling down into the ash box.

Kindling is used to start the fire. Corncobs, chips from the woodpile, broomstraw, paper, and small pieces of pine wood—"pine knots" and "light" or "fat" wood—are excellent as kindling. While these pieces of pine light quickly, they "outsmoke anything" and may be preferred to start non-food-related fires only. In the past, people would pour a small amount of kerosene into a container and stand some corncobs up in it. These kerosene-soaked corncobs were used as kindling for starting a fast fire. However, we advise against using any such fuel for a wood cookstove in the house. As a compromise, we suggest using small starter sticks or similar products, which are generally made from compressed wood shavings and wax. Do not use large starter logs. A box of firewood and one of kindling should be kept in the kitchen, readily available near the stove.

Caution: Pouring any flammable liquid directly onto hot coals or into a fire is very dangerous and should never be done. As Gladys Nichols said, "I wouldn't advise nobody to do that. You're liable to explode yourself." We were also cautioned by our contacts to maintain the area around the stove or range, keeping it free of combustible materials—flammable liquids, dust, lint, paper.

You should never use or store gasoline or cleaning fluids in the area where the range is located. Additional cautions include the fact that frozen wood with ice or snow on it may smother fire or even crack the casting of the stove, and wood that has been saturated with salt water will cause corrosion of the metal and should not be used at all.

Lay a few pieces of crushed paper on the grate, cover them with kindling, and light the paper with a match. When the fire begins burning well, turn the damper on the stovepipe until it is almost closed. This holds the heat in the stove instead of letting it go up the chimney. However, if the fire begins to die out or smoke excessively, open the damper again for a few minutes, allowing more air into the stove, and it will blaze up again.

Add a few more small pieces of wood, then start adding large pieces of stove wood as a bed of coals is built up. As Addie Norton explained to us: "After you get your fire burning, you get wood that's cut down and split up. It takes about two sticks to a fire and keeps fire so much longer than little ones. You don't have to be putting wood in the stove so often. If it burns up quick, you got to keep it going. The biggest trouble with a wood stove is you have to keep feeding wood to it. If you want it about the same heat, you get it as hot as you want it, and then just put in a stick or two at a time—enough to keep it the same way—and you can keep it that way all day by putting in one or two sticks at a time."

Any kind of dry wood may be used for the fire in a wood cookstove. Oak, hickory, poplar, pine, and sassafras were mentioned most often by people we interviewed here in northeastern Georgia. Oak and hickory are hardwoods, making the hottest fire and burning longer. They were

Parts of the stove (top)
and diagram of the cooking
surface (bottom).

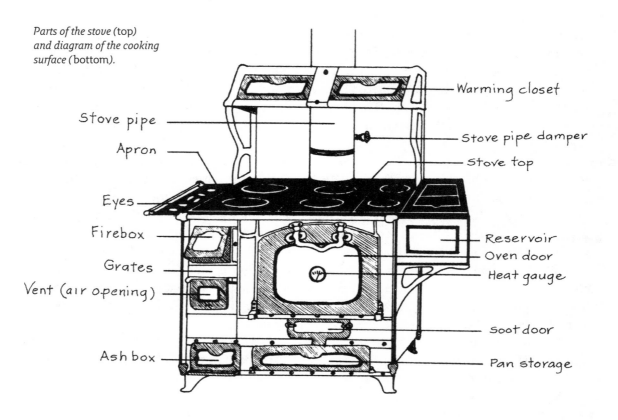

Warming closet

Stove pipe

Apron

Stove pipe damper

Stove top

Eyes

Firebox

Reservoir

Oven door

Grates

Heat gauge

Vent (air opening)

Soot door

Ash box

Pan storage

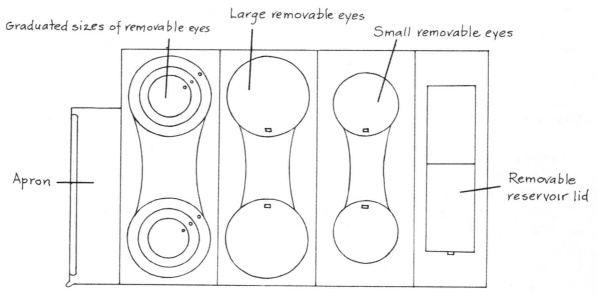

Graduated sizes of removable eyes

Large removable eyes

Small removable eyes

Apron

Removable reservoir lid

The wood may be added to the fire through the firebox door or through one of the eyes over the firebox. The better way, we were told, is through the eye, because when the firebox door is opened there is a risk of hot coals falling out on the floor. Food being cooked on this eye may be moved to the apron on the left while this process takes place.

The floor of the firebox is a metal grate. The ashes from the cookstove's fire fall through to the ash box, a drawer directly beneath the firebox. Some women told us that each evening, after they finish washing the dishes, they empty the ash box, putting the ashes on the garden, as they make a good fertilizer. There is a rod that can be attached to the grate and turned to empty the firebox of any ashes that haven't fallen through. The eye lifter is used to move this rod.

The cooking surface of a wood stove usually has six eyes. Sometimes they are all the same size, sometimes of varying sizes. The left side of the stove, directly over the firebox, is the hottest place on the top of the stove. The heat under the eyes cannot be regulated individually, so pots have to be moved from one to the other, according to how much heat is required. To get the most heat, the eye over the firebox can be lifted off and the pot or pan can sit directly over the fire. Daisy Justus said, "You could take the eye off, and the pot would fit down right over the fire. If you wanted to simmer anything, you could push it back over the cooler part of the stove." Cast-iron kettles and pots are the only ones recommended for placing immediately over the flames, because of their weight. The eyes on the left side of some stoves have graduated sizes so that, no matter what diameter, a pan will fit snugly over the flames. Most stoves have basically the same

Hands still floury from rolling out dumplings, Fay Long opens her firebox to add wood.

overwhelmingly favored for heaters, but we were cautioned that "oak'll burn up your firebox" in a cookstove. Pine, poplar, sourwood, and sassafras are softwoods and burn more quickly. They are good when starting a fire and may be followed by sticks of hardwood, if desired. Once the fire is established, the temperature in the stove can be maintained by adding one or two sticks of wood at twenty- to thirty-minute intervals. Fireboxes are usually large enough to take firewood sixteen to eighteen inches long and two to three inches in diameter.

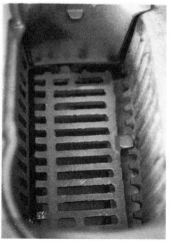

(above) *Most wood cookstoves have a large cooking surface and can accommodate numerous pots and pans.*

(left) *Grate.*

four- or six-eye surface, although one larger range that Foxfire documented had a flat griddle on top for frying things like pancakes, eggs, and bacon.

The oven is usually located on the right-hand side of the stove and is heated from the left and top by the circulation of heat from the firebox. The heat flows from the firebox through a four-inch-high air space directly under the cooking surface to the reservoir on the other side.

Leftovers or food ready to serve may be kept in the warming closet until mealtime. This is a metal compartment about six inches deep located above the cooking surface at about eye level, with

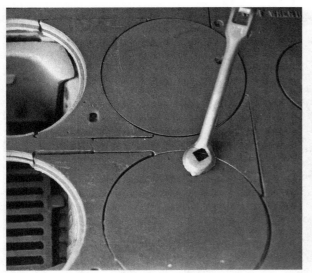  

The eye lifter is being used to turn the rod that operates the grates, dumping ash from the firebox to the ash box.

Firebox (top) *and ash box* (bottom) *doors stand open.*

Ash box.

either enamel or iron doors to protect the food. There is enough heat in the warming closet to keep food warm for several hours.

The reservoir is a copper, steel, or iron box. If iron, the reservoir has an enameled lining that is easily cleaned. The first reservoirs sat on top of the right-hand eyes and could be moved when the eyes were needed for cooking. The more modern reservoir is usually located on and attached to the right end of the stove. On many newer wood cookstoves the reservoir holds about six to eight gallons of water, the water taken out with a dipper or pot. Reservoirs will rust out eventually if the enamel gets chipped or cracked, but they are made to be easily replaced.

Most women we interviewed said that they kept the reservoir filled with water warming for dishwashing and baths. As bread crumbs or other food might fall into the water in the reservoir, a kettle of fresh water was always kept on the stove for coffee or tea or for adding to food that was cooking.

Daisy Justus told us: "We used the water in the reservoir to wash dishes. We washed anything we had—black kettles, too. If you wanted something to get to boiling real quick, like cooked beans, you added hot water from the reservoir."

The air vents, or dampers, are very important parts of the wood-burning stove because they control the fire and the amount of heat in the stove. On most of the cookstoves we were shown there were three dampers: one beside the firebox (the vents slide to permit air and can be closed completely or partially); a second on the stovepipe above the stove (a handle twists to open or close it); and a third inside the stove, usually located directly beneath the eyes on the extreme right side, and the cook can turn this "up," to open the damper and let air draw the heat up the stovepipe, or "down," to close the damper and

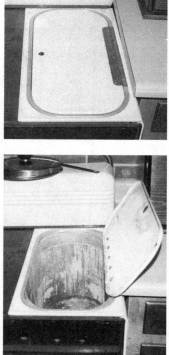

All the eyes on the stove can be removed with the lifter, a tool that comes with most wood cookstoves.

Two views of an enamel-lined reservoir.

A warming closet ready to be filled with food.

The firebox damper with its vents opened.

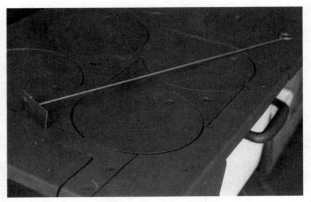

A soot rake on the cooktop.

hold the heat inside the stove and around the oven.

Once the fire is burning steadily, and you want to keep a maximum temperature in the stove for cooking on top and for using the oven, the dampers should all be completely open. To lower the temperature, close the air vent to the left of the firebox. More heat may be directed to the oven and the front of the stove by turning the damper on the stovepipe down.

Some people "hold" a fire in their stoves from one meal to the next by adding a large piece of wood at the end of their cooking and then closing the damper on the stovepipe. This way, very little air gets to the fire, and the wood burns slowly. When ready to begin preparing the food for the next meal, the damper is opened, more wood is added to the firebox, and the fire will usually begin to flame up as soon as the air reaches it. When the stove is not in use, the dampers are kept closed because air will sometimes circulate down through the chimney and blow ashes and soot into the house.

Maintenance of a wood cookstove includes disposing of ashes and soot routinely. Every two to three days, the soot should be raked off the oven top and from the rest of the inside of the stove using a soot rake. The ashes can be pushed through into the firebox or raked to the soot door, which is usually located under the oven or on the bottom right side of the stove beside the oven and under the reservoir. From here the soot can be raked into a pan or onto paper and thrown out. If soot is not cleaned out frequently but allowed to build up inside the stove, the fire will not heat the stovetop as well. Bread will not cook inside the oven as quickly if soot builds up on the oven's top. Soot can also accumulate inside the stovepipe. To clean it, tap along the pipe. Since, as one contact told us, "Gravity worked back then, too," the soot will fall through and under the oven, where it may be taken out the soot door.

Addie Norton described the cleaning process she goes through: "I used to clean the ashes out of my stove about every three or four days when the ash box would get full. But now, since I don't cook as much, about once a week and sometimes not that often. The ash box holds about a half bushel of ashes. I got a little old rake that I clean it out with. Stick that little rake down in there and rake

Mary Cabe tests the heat in her oven.

it all out of there. Then it heats better in the bottom, but I don't want it to heat too much in the bottom of it, so I don't clean it out underneath as much as I could."

While many people may dispose of their ashes in their gardens and flower beds, there are those who find other uses for them, as Addie does: "Oh, I throw mine, usually, out there in the road. It gets bad, and I take them coals out there and put them in the trenches in the road and it keeps my road filled up [laughter]. That's where I put mine this winter, most of them."

A large fire is not needed for cooking, as told by many of our sources. It is possible to begin cooking some foods on top of the stove within five or ten minutes after a fire has been started. However, it usually takes thirty minutes or more before the oven is hot enough to begin baking, especially in a larger stove. Aunt Lola Cannon told us that her mother would put a piece of white paper in the oven, and she could tell by the way the paper browned if the stove was ready to bake cakes and bread. It should turn a golden brown in five minutes. An indicator for some was to have a pot of coffee on top of the stove, and when the fire was hot enough to boil the coffee, the oven was hot enough to begin baking.

Learning to adjust the temperature in the oven of a wood stove takes some trial and error. There are thermometer gauges on the oven doors of

Examples of two styles of temperature gauges on a wood cookstove.

Most ovens had only one rack.

most later models, but these act as warning signals rather than as regulators. Besides, old-time stoves rarely had them, and many of the people we interviewed first learned to cook without the convenience of a thermometer. Gladys Nichols's statement, "If you cook regular like I did for all my years, you an' just guess at it and tell when it's what it ought to be," was repeated by several of the older women we interviewed.

A fairly constant temperature can be maintained in the oven by adding one or two sticks of dry wood as you notice the thermometer dropping a little below the desired heat. To cool down the oven while baking, the oven door may be opened a few minutes or the damper (on the stovepipe) adjusted by closing it down, to bring in less air, making the fire burn more slowly.

The temperature gauge on the oven door should read between 300 and 350 degrees Fahrenheit for baking cakes, and they are usually placed on the middle rack of the oven. The wood cookstoves owned by most of the women we interviewed had only one rack in their ovens, although some did mention adjustable racks with two or three positions. Some of them told us that they place a pan of water on the top rack and their cake on a rack below the water. Heat in the oven is concentrated at the top, where it enters from the firebox, there being no means of fan-forcing or otherwise circulating the heat around the oven. Thus, when the pan is placed *between* the cake and the hottest area of the oven, the water absorbs much of the heat and prevents the top of the cake from getting too brown before it is completely cooked inside.

We were warned to keep a closer watch on anything we were baking in the oven of a wood stove than we ordinarily do when using a modern gas or electric oven because of the fluctuations in temperature if wood is not added as needed. The fire might burn out and the temperature drop while a cake is baking. For something that takes an hour to bake, the fire may need to be tended three or four times to maintain the temperature. However, when baking bread or a cake for that long, vibrations from tending the fire—such as slamming the door—can jar the food and cause it to fall. In addition, if something tends to cook more on one side than the other, it has to be turned around at regular intervals.

Addie Norton explained what had to be done if you didn't have a thermometer:

You would just have to judge it by the way you was baking. You don't want to bake a cake too fast. You don't want to brown it on top before it begins to get done in the bottom. They's a lot of ways you can tell about your cookstove if you've had on as much as I have and cooked on one all your life, you know. You know exactly how to handle it. I can keep that one cool just the way I want it or I can get it too hot. You can tell very easy when your oven's too hot. The heat outside tells you. You just have to wait till it cools down. You just have to take your biscuits or whatever you got in there out and let it cool down. You can't take the wood out.

For some of the women we interviewed, this constant vigilance and the time required before the stove was ready for baking—both of which slowed down the cooking process—were the major drawbacks to wood-stove cooking. That, and the constant battle with wood. As Margie Ledford said,

I didn't like cooking on a wood stove. It was too much hard work. You've got to keep poking those coals and putting wood in it to keep it hot, especially if you're going to can. That's hard, because you've got to keep the pressure up and you've got to keep the same temperature. I don't have to do that anymore. Just like milking a cow—I don't have to do that anymore, either. People say that that was back in the good old days, but they weren't that good. Of course, used to you had time but you had to have time to cook and carry your wood in and keep your stove going. But now you don't have time. Besides, it was a lot harder work, and that's not my cup of tea. Electric stoves are easier, especially when you get to feeling like you don't want to wrestle a load of wood every little while.

In general, however, our contacts' preference for a wood stove was very widespread. Exie Dills liked a wood stove better for safety:

I always cooked on a wood stove up till we moved down here. About ten years ago I cooked my first meal on an electric stove. I never will get used to that thing. I have to watch whenever I start to turn a knob because sometimes instead of turning it off I turn it up. I get it hotter all the time in place of cooler. A wood stove won't cook maybe as quick, but on my old stove out yonder I'd cook bread or biscuits above electric on it any day.

I've burned my fingers a few times [on wood stoves], but nothing bad—not like the other day on an electric. I burned my hand the other morning on steam the worst I was ever burned in my life over a cookstove. I went to turn the blooming thing off, and the water for coffee was setting there on the electric stove boiling. I just reached up and turned it off, and I never noticed that steam coming right up under there. My land alive, how that did hurt! I never was burned that way by a kettle, coffeepot, or nothing else on a wood stove.

Cast-iron and aluminum pots and pans are equally at home on a wood stove.

Marinda Brown also dislikes, at times, the quick, constant heat of the electric or oil stove: "I don't believe that I've burned up as much food with a wood stove as I have with an electric stove. With an electric stove, I turn on my burners and turn around to do something else and forget. It gets hotter quicker, and so it takes more moisture to cook on the electric stove than on the wood stove. And we used to cook in ironware a lot. The water didn't evaporate as fast in that as it does in the newer methods of cooking."

And women like Stella Burrell simply preferred the taste of food cooked on a wood stove. As she stated,

I think maybe the slow process of cooking on a wood stove makes the flavor really good, especially in green beans and things like that. I had a skillet that had *the iron lid over it, and you could put about three chickens in it to fry. You would brown your chicken real quick, put it all back in the pan and put it on the back of the stove. Put just a little water in it, and let it sit there and steam. It would be soft. It wouldn't be crisp unless you left it a long time, but it would cook slow, and it would be cooked all the way to the bone. It just had a* delicious *taste.*

Even women who disliked cooking with wood retained an affection for their old stoves. Belle Ledford, for example, admitted, "I've heard a lot of people say that food tastes better cooked on a wood stove, but to me it doesn't and I didn't like cooking that way better, but I almost cried when we sold our wood stove. I certainly got attached to it, and if I had had the room, I would have kept it. I would not have gotten rid of it."

A Word on Cooking Utensils

Many people attribute the superior taste of wood-stove-cooked food to the pots in which it was cooked rather than to the stove itself. While most pots and pans used on electric and gas stoves work just as well on wood cookstoves, skillets, Dutch ovens, kettles, and pots made of cast iron were long the first—and perhaps only—choice of people in this area.

When we asked Addie Norton what kind of pots and pans she used to use, she answered, "Oh, iron ones, just like I do now. I used to have some old big pots, you know, iron pots. They've never been a mess of beans or anything cooked that's as good as they are in that old black pot, and what makes the difference I don't know. They make the best old beans you ever tasted [laughter]. I never have liked beans as good since I quit cooking in that old iron pot."

Gladys Nichols agreed, saying, "Today's way of cooking is better, but I believe I'd rather have beans with a piece of fatback meat in them cooked about three hours in the old iron pot. And if you fry your meat, a cast-iron frying pan is the best cooker there is. It's a little heavy and ugly looking, but it cooks better."

Cast-iron pots and skillets must be treated, or seasoned, to prevent foods from sticking and to keep them from rusting after being washed. To season, when they are new or have to be cleaned as described above, grease well with lard or vegetable shortening. Preheat the oven to a hot temperature, place the pan inside, and turn off the oven or let the fire gradually die down while the pan seasons for thirty minutes.

Soot, of course, will build up on cast-iron cookware when placed directly over the flames, and it needs to be cleaned off with sand or some

Cast-aluminum kettle.

Wash pots often held hominy, lard, or stew as well as served for the day's washing.

type of rough scouring pad. Dishrag (luffa) gourds used to be one choice, as many homemakers grew these in their yards for just such use.

If a cast-iron pot or kettle becomes rusty from disuse, scour it with ashes or white sand to remove the rust. After washing it out thoroughly, fill it with cold water and heat for fifteen or more minutes, after which the pot should

A "spider" or fritter pan (two views).

be thoroughly dried to prevent further rust. It should then be good as new and ready to heat water or cook in once more.

Many cooks even believe the iron cookware to be healthier. Daisy Justus, for example, disputes the sales pitch of the stainless-steel and copper-bottomed pot peddlers: "All these pots and pans that the salesman talks about and how nasty that old iron cooking was. I believe it was in a nurse's book or something said the iron gave you iron out of that cooking—I mean like it was *good* for you."

Today, we can say with some confidence that Daisy Justus and many of the other contacts were correct in their statements about health benefits of cooking with cast iron. In 1986, just two years after the publication of this book, an article in the *Journal of the American Dietetic Association* found that cooking with iron does, in fact, increase iron levels in food anywhere from 8 percent to as much as 2000 percent. The variations in increased iron levels are attributed to factors such as moisture, acidity, and cooking times of the foods prepared in iron cookware (H. C. Brittin and C. E. Nossaman, "Iron Content of Food Cooked in Iron Utensils" [1986]). Thanks to modern manufacturers, like Lodge, Finex, and Victoria, cast iron is maintaining its place among the must-haves of cookware.

2 The Garden

When I plant my garden, I wanta plant it on the right time of the moon.
—*Mrs. E. N. Nicholson*

Like many rural Americans in the early to mid-twentieth century, Appalachians relied heavily on the bounty of their gardens and fields. As Esco Pitts recalls in *Foxfire Book 4* (1972, p. 223), "Then you couldn't just go to the store and buy much stuff 'cause they wasn't much stuff to buy. And then people just made their living just got the practice of making their living at home." Most homes in Appalachia had a large vegetable garden where people would grow such supper staples as beans, summer squashes, tomatoes, okra, and the like. Some larger families would also plant field crops such as corn and cabbage as well as larger plots of white (or Irish) potatoes and sweet potatoes.

The questions of what to plant and when to plant varied from person to person, but there was a general consensus throughout Southern Appalachia on these topics. Mrs. E. N. Nicholson, like quite a few in the area, believed in planting by signs. In her interview for *The Foxfire Book* (1972), she declares, "I was brought up in that day, and I can't help from believin' in it. When I plant my garden, I wanta' plant it on the right time of the moon. But most of that's forgotten now." Whether by the signs or not, most folks would begin their planting following Easter Sunday, starting with heartier plants that could take a little cold snap now and again, and then adding warmer weather plants as the days grew longer and summer approached.

Today, home gardens are coming back in a big way in Southern Appalachia. Some sustainable growers are even finding ideal plots of bottomland to cultivate and begin smaller commercial operations. Produce stands and local farmers' markets featuring organic, non-GMO, and heirloom varieties of fruits, vegetables, and

Jerusalem artichokes, a popular tuber in the area for more than a hundred years, is making a modest comeback on some smaller, organic farms.

flowers are becoming more and more popular in the region. Even right here in Foxfire's backyard, growers are reintroducing long-forgotten varieties, such as the Jerusalem artichoke, an edible tuber abundant in the area throughout the nineteenth and early twentieth centuries.

Beans

Of all vegetables native to our region, beans were the most popular and prevalent. New varieties of hybrid beans have replaced the old. Several of our contacts remembered their favorites, no longer grown here.

FLORENCE BROOKS: *There's altogether a difference—people ain't got none of the old-fashioned bean seed they used to have. People's stuff used to be a whole lot better than what is now. The beans ain't near as good as they used to be. We had what we called greasy-back beans—I've not seen any of them in years. They were little white beans in a white pole bean. You can eat the greasy-back bean*

either green or dried. For a dried bean, after they get dry on the vine, you pick them, put them in a sack, and beat them out with a stick. The beans fall out of the pod. We planted green beans and cornfield beans. We always planted the cornfield full of them, so we'd have beans that'd dry up and we'd have our own soup beans.

HARRY BROWN: *We didn't have any half-runners back in those days, we had cornfield beans. We'd pick them after they got large enough. We'd take them and break them like we were going to cook them, and set down with a big needle and string them on a thread. [We called them] leather breeches. People didn't can so much like they do now.*

As Harry Brown noted, some years ago leather breeches were indeed a solution to preserving beans before the popularity of canning jars (for pickled beans, another favorite long-term way to keep beans, see page 59). His wife, Marinda, contributed her method of making leather breeches:

Leather breeches is something that people used way back in the past, and it's a simple food that has lots of nutrients. I guess a lot of people practically lived on it way back years ago. You gather the beans in an early stage when the pod begins to get sort of full. You string them just like you would string beans, with a needle and thread. Then tie that and hang them up on the wall and let them dry. They're a little tough and brittle when they dry, but they'll keep there all along until you use them up. When you get ready to cook them, soak them overnight. You can bread them, but most people just take them off the string and cook them just like you would green beans—the pod along with the beans—with a piece of bacon or fatback. They're pretty good. Of course, they don't taste anything like green beans. I keep mine, and my

At Andy Webb's, leather breeches hang to dry.

bean seed if I ever save any, either in the refrigerator or freezer because the weevils get in them.

Daisy Justus gave her recipe for making leather breeches:

String and break green beans as if you were going to cook them. Spread thinly and dry thoroughly or thread a big needle with no. 8 thread and string them up. Dry until they rattle and put them in a cloth bag, tied securely. Keep dry and on sunny days put them

in sun for a while. To cook these beans, wash well and put them in warm water to soak overnight, then cook as any dried beans. Cover beans with water, add salt and a piece of salt pork. Bring to a boil, then cook slowly for two or three hours. The longer they cook the better they are. If you use a pressure cooker, cook for about thirty minutes, then remove; cover and cook them dry.

Rittie Webb also discussed leather breeches: "We usually cook leather breeches all day. We boil them hard for a while and then run the water out of them to get the dried taste out. Then we add more water and cook them with a piece of meat all day. They are good. We'd have green beans, pinto beans, or leather breeches. We'd change around on beans."

There were almost as many "best ways" to cook green beans as there were women who talked with us:

GRANNY GIBSON: *Green beans are the best in an old black pot. I just put them in a pot with some water and some grease or a piece of pork and cook them three or four hours—not all day. I usually have them for dinner on Sundays.*

ADDIE NORTON: *Pick a mess of green beans from the garden. String and break them into one-and-a-half- to two-inch pieces. Wash them thoroughly afterwards. Put bacon or streaked pork meat for seasoning into a pot. Add the beans and add water to cover the beans. Cook until the beans are tender. You may want to add more water along to keep the beans from burning, but you want to have most of the water cooked out when they are done.*

ARIZONA DICKERSON: *My mother always cooked her beans in an iron pot on the fireplace. They're not good if you don't cook them down to the grease. A lot of people don't know how to cook beans.*

They leave water in them. I cook mine down to the grease, but not burned.

DAISY JUSTUS: *I peel Irish potatoes and put on top of my green beans—cook them together. I let the beans get practically done before putting the potatoes in. Some people put small pods of okra on top of the beans instead of potatoes.*

LOLA CANNON: *I barely cover the beans in water. I add salt to taste. Then I add a little sugar. If you'll add half as much sugar as you do salt, it improves the flavor of your green beans.*

OCTOBER BEANS
GRANNY GIBSON

"The mountain people used these beans as a substitute for soup beans, which don't grow here. They can be eaten fresh when young and tender, but people usually dried them, shelled them, and stored them for later use. To cook, parboil beans for five minutes, using about a quart of water to a cup of beans. Drain the water, rinse the beans off, and add another quart of water per cup of beans and [salt] pork about big as your fist (sliced). Cover and simmer until tender."

SOUP BEANS
RUTH HOLCOMB

"I cook soup beans. I pour two cups of ketchup into one quart of beans and add one teaspoonful of sugar. I put raw bacon and sliced onions on top of the beans and cover with water. I salt the beans to taste and cook them until they're done."

GOURD BEANS

A truly unusual "bean" was introduced to us by Connie Chappell. She grows something called the gourd bean. It looks like squash, but it is longer and green. Some people say it tastes like squash, but Mrs. Chappell says the gourd bean has a better taste. Mrs. Chappell was living in Scataway, just outside of Hiawassee, Georgia, when she found out about the vegetable:

I found out about the gourd bean about forty something years ago. We were working for a man hoeing corn, and [his wife] had some fixed for dinner. We ate them at that man's house that day for dinner, and he give us seed of them, and we planted them, and I've been growing them ever since. I don't know if you can freeze and can them. I haven't tried, but I don't like squash frozen; so I know I wouldn't like them. Some people call them guinea beans, but we know them as gourd beans.

You can cut a mess off of one when it's young and the place will just heal over and keep growing. I have grown them to be four and five feet long, but this year mine haven't got that long because of the dry summer. They're easy to care for. You just plant them and work them like anything else. You don't have to dust them or anything like that. The best time to plant them is early in the spring when you plant your garden. You can use almost any kind of soil [laughs], but you can't plant them in red soil. I use regular fertilizer, but you can use manure if you ain't got fertilizer for them. You have to have something for the gourd bean to run on. I usually have mine growing on the hog lot fence. Then they are ready to pick in a month or two. The best time to pick them is when they're eight to ten inches long, when they're young and tender.

[To cook them] you just take and peel the outside peeling off, and wash them in the sink in cold water. Let the water run over them, then get a towel and dry them off and slice them just like you do a squash, and fry them. When you cook them, put them in your grease and fry them like you do regular squash. I fry

Connie Chappell with her amazing gourd bean.

them in just a little Crisco or just any kind of grease I've got. They taste different from squash—they've got a better taste, and the taste is not strong.

To get the seed you just have to bust that hard shell with something. They're just like gourd seed; if you take them for seed, let the frost hit them. The vines usually run to be very long. They ain't, a bug bothered them this summer. The pigs have, though. The pigs tore the vines nearly all up [laughs].

Beets
Beets were often raised for pickling (see chapter 3), but they could be eaten in various other ways. Lucy York said, "Beets can be stored like cabbage. When ready to prepare them, scrub them and boil, adding a small amount of vinegar to the water. Cook until tender."

HARVARD BEETS
OLENE GARLAND

1 tablespoon cornstarch
½ teaspoon salt
½ cup mild vinegar or 6 tablespoons
   vinegar and ¼ cup cream
3 cups cooked sliced beets
½ cup sugar
2 tablespoons butter

Cook and stir the first 3 ingredients in the top of a double boiler. When clear, add the beets and place the pan, covered, over hot water for ½ hour. Just before serving, heat the beets again and add the butter. Yield: 6 servings.

SAUTÉED BEETS
Peel and slice raw beets. Place slices in butter in a frying pan. Cover and let simmer about 20 minutes. When tender, season with salt and pepper.

Cabbage
Cabbage is another standard fall vegetable in the mountain diet. It is locally grown in quantity for sale to grocers. Several women offered cooking tips:

RUTH HOLCOMB: *Wash cabbage thoroughly and cut into squares. Put into a pot and cover with water. Add salt to taste and season with meat or bacon grease. Boil until cabbage is tender—about two hours.*

ARIZONA DICKERSON: *Don't cover cabbage when cooking as this keeps odor in. Cook without the lid.*

LUCY YORK: *After the cabbage has been cooked tender, you can pour the water off and fry the cabbage in a pan with some bacon grease.*

FRIED CABBAGE
1 head cabbage, chopped
4 teaspoons lard or other shortening
Salt and pepper to taste

Put about an inch of water in a large frying pan and bring to a boil. Put all the cabbage and lard in, season it, and cover. Simmer for about 25 to 30 minutes.

See recipes for slaw in chapter 10.

Carrots
Granny Gibson says, "I have never cooked carrots too much, but I usually just cut them up and boil them. They're supposed to be good for your eyes." Carrots were first eaten raw or boiled, but they eventually found their way into modern casserole dishes. These are a recent introduction, however. As Dorothy Beck says, "They didn't even know what casseroles was when I was growing up."

CARROT CASSEROLE

ARIZONA DICKERSON

1 pound carrots, cooked and mashed

1 small onion, diced

1 small green pepper, diced

½ cup milk

⅓ cup sugar

1 cup cracker crumbs (half for topping;
*   half in mixture)*

½ cup soft butter (a little for topping;
*   remainder for mixture)*

Salt and pepper to taste

Mix together all ingredients, except for the topping. Pour into a casserole dish. Add crumbs and butter on top. Bake in a 350°F oven for 30 minutes until brown. Yield: *5 servings.*

CARROT-APPLE SALAD

1 cup grated raw carrots

1 cup chopped celery

½ cup chopped peanuts

Mayonnaise

Lettuce

1 large tart apple, cored and sliced

1 sweet red pepper, cut in strips

1 green pepper, cut in strips

Blend carrots, celery, and nuts with desired amount of mayonnaise. Serve on lettuce, garnished with slices of apples and strips of peppers. Yield: *8 servings.*

CARROT-PINEAPPLE SALAD

1 cup grated raw carrots

1 cup chopped celery

1 slice pineapple, diced

1 cup chopped pecans

Mayonnaise

Blend together the carrots, celery, pineapple, and pecans. Toss with a small amount of mayonnaise and serve. Yield: *8 servings.*

Corn

Corn was one of the most important crops, used as a staple for both people and their animals. Folks ate it fresh on or off the cob. They used it dried to make cornmeal (see chapter 8), parched corn, hominy, and grits, and sprouted it to make moonshine. They also raised and dried popcorn. The dried fodder, or leaves, was used to feed animals, and the shucks could be used to bottom chairs or could be made into mats, scrub mops, hats, horse collars, and various other things.

Florence Brooks recalled some of these diverse uses for corn: "Up there on Scaly Mountain, we didn't waste nothing. We used every blade of fodder and every top, every shuck. We'd always cut our tops and pull our fodder along about September. They let us kids out of school for two weeks to do that. Then after about three frosts we'd start gathering it. And we used corn for eating and grinding into meal."

Some folks ground corn by hand with a homemade grinder (similar to a manufactured grater, but coarser). Inez Taylor was one of these: "I make gritted corn for Daddy a lot now. I just take the corn where it's too hard for anything else, and I put it on a gritter and grit it. Then I just put salt and a little sugar in it, put it in the pan and cook it just like corn bread."

Diversions from the daily routine were few, and families took advantage of every opportunity to turn work into a social event. Corn harvesting time was no exception, as Bessie Underwood notes: "We used to have corn shuckings when I was a young girl. You had to cook then, but you just cooked up big pots full of chicken and dumplings, beans, potatoes, cobbler pies, baked sweet potatoes, and stuff like that."

Jake Waldroop adds: "We'd get our corn gathered up in the fall of the year, and then we'd have corn shuckings. We'd ask in ten or fifteen men. We'd get in women folks, too, and they would bunch in and get supper. They'd kill chickens and we'd have fresh meat. They'd make pies and custards and fix the awfullest dinner or supper ever you saw. We'd get the corn all shucked out, and they'd dance till daylight."

Most of the time corn was prepared simply. Granny Gibson told us: "Whenever I was growing up we'd go to the field and get just regular old field corn. Just cut it off and put it in the pan and fry it; or you could boil it, either way. I thought it was good. Sweet corn's took its place now. It's good, too."

SOME BASIC CORN RECIPES

BERTHA WALDROOP: *For boiled corn on the cob, shuck and silk your fresh corn. Put the ears of corn in boiling water. When the water returns to a hard boil, put the lid on the pot and continue to boil for ten to fifteen minutes more.*

LUCY YORK: *Cut fresh corn off the cob. Put it in a frying pan with a small amount of butter or grease. Add water, if needed, and cook a short time—just long enough to get it tender.*

INEZ TAYLOR: *I remember my mother's fried corn. She cut it off the cob real thin, and she'd put her some butter in one of those old iron skillets and put the corn in that hot butter and just stir it till it thickened. Lots of times she'd put it in the oven and it would brown on the top and the bottom. There's nobody could cook it like she did.*

BLANCHE HARKINS: *Parching corn— shell dried corn off the cob in the fall or wintertime. Toast it in the oven like parching peanuts.*

It was possible to create relatively complicated concoctions using only readily available ingredients and a little imagination: Skin the corn with homemade lye. Cook corn by boiling. Cook dried beans. Put corn and beans together in same pot, cook some more. Add pumpkin if you like, and cook until pumpkin is done. Add to this a mixture of cornmeal, beaten walnut and hickory nut meats, and enough molasses to sweeten. Cook this in an iron pot until the meal is done. Eat fresh or after it begins to sour. Some of this may be fried in hot grease. This mixture will not keep very long unless the weather is cold.

The arrival of the supermarket in the mid-twentieth century introduced Appalachian cooks to a variety of different spices, such as paprika, which generated new recipes like the one Arizona Dickerson shared with us.

CORN AU GRATIN
ARIZONA DICKERSON
2 egg yolks, well beaten
1 cup cooked corn
1 small onion, chopped
1 small green pepper, chopped
2 tablespoons shortening
1 cup cooked rice
½ cup grated cheese
Salt and pepper to taste
Dash of paprika
Strips of bacon

Mix together beaten egg yolks and corn. Sauté onions and green peppers in the shortening and add to egg and corn mixture. Lightly fold in cooked rice. Place half of mixture in a baking dish, add ¼ cup cheese, salt, and pepper, then remaining corn mixture. Cover with remaining grated cheese. Dust with paprika and lay strips of bacon across the top. Bake in a 400°F oven for 20 minutes, or until bacon is cooked. Yield: *6 servings*.

Garden Greens

While cultivated collards, turnip greens, and mustard varieties have been known to escape or naturalize and grow wild in old garden plots, it is common practice to plant them in early spring, at the start of the season, and again in late summer and early fall with other cool weather crops. People also planted late cabbage and turnips for storing through the winter, and the fall garden assured them of a good supply of fresh greens after the warm weather crops finished coming in.

Esco Pitts elaborates:

For a fall crop, we planted turnips and cabbage in September. Sometimes we'd put out late multiplying onions in the fall (around September) and have onions all winter. We buried the turnips along with the cabbage to keep them through the winter. Usually, my mother planted [collards] in the fall of the year. Around the latter part of July or the first of August, she'd sow a collard bed, and when they come up a good size to transplant, she'd have a row in the garden. Collards are not much good till the frost bites them—it makes them better to eat.

Turnip and mustard greens still appeal widely to the Appalachian palate. Ione Dickerson said,

"My son didn't like turnip greens, so I gave him a nickel a bite to eat them. He got rich fast like that [laughter]! It's a funny thing—he loves greens now. Dr. Neville told me one time, 'If they don't eat it when you put it on the table, put it on again until they *do* eat it!'"

RUTH HOLCOMB: *Wash the greens thoroughly. Put them in a pan and cover with water. Put top on the pan and bring greens to a boil. Scrape new potatoes and boil on top of the greens. Add salt to tastes. Cook until tender, one or two hours. Season with bacon grease or butter.*

GRANNY GIBSON: *I've tried raising spinach, and I never could do nothing with it. It just wouldn't grow for me. Mustard greens and turnip greens do good, though. You have to boil them with grease in them. I usually cook mine with peanut oil or some kind of oil made out of sunflower seeds, but people used to just cook it with fatback.*

MARGIE LEDFORD: *I don't like poke salad, but I love turnip and mustard greens. You put a piece of meat in the water when you cook your turnip greens and cook them good and tender. When you get them tender, drain the water out of them. A lot of times I take and cook mine in a pot of meat grease. Now that's what makes them good. Have you some grease in one of them big skillets and put them in there and slow fry them where they won't scorch or anything till they are real good and tender. Mix up some seasoning in there, and they will melt in your mouth if you're a hillbilly! Most hillbillies like turnip greens.*

RITTIE WEBB: *Let mustard greens cook about thirty minutes and season them. You don't have to fry it if you put the seasoning in while it's in the pot. Of course, a lot of people do fry it. Leonard used to eat his raw.*

Hominy

While the making of hominy is not exactly an easy undertaking, it was yet another way in which the taste of common corn could be altered to add variety to the Appalachian diet. Hominy is served as a starchy vegetable, like rice, and is made from the kernels of dried corn. The outer husks of the kernels are removed by boiling the shelled corn in the water. Hominy is usually prepared outdoors in a large cast-iron pot over an open fire.

Granny Gibson briefly explained this time-consuming process:

People used to tie ashes and corn in a sack and boil them a pretty long time in an old iron pot. The water going through the ashes makes lye. That's what makes the outer part of the corn kind of scale off, and what you have left is hominy. You just wash it and wash it to get the lye out, and then you put it back in the pot with just pure water and cook it until it gets tender. Keep adding water to it because it just keeps swelling. Then you take it out, put some grease in it and fry it. It takes all day to make it, but it was good.

A more detailed account of how to produce homemade hominy follows:

The first thing that must be done in the making of hominy is to prepare the lye. It is made by pouring water through oak or hickory ashes that have been saved from the fireplace. During a demonstration by Bessie Kelly, the ashes were placed in a large metal barrel, which had a spouted hole in the bottom. Several gallons of water were slowly poured over them. The water soaking through the ashes leached out the potash, or lye, and this dripped into a plastic container. (Plastic, iron, or porcelain can be used, but not aluminum, as the lye will corrode it.) This should take about two hours. (For more detailed information about ash hoppers, see *The Foxfire Book*, p. 156, and *Foxfire Book 4*, p. 478.)

Two gallons of shelled corn are put into a large iron wash pot and the two gallons of lye are added. Then two gallons of water are added. More water is poured in as needed to keep the corn covered and to prevent its sticking to the bottom of the pot. The lye-corn mixture must cook until the skins start coming off the corn. This usually takes four to six hours. Stir the mixture occasionally to prevent sticking. All the corn is then removed from the pot, the lye water poured off, and the pot washed out. Thoroughly rinse the lye off the corn. Place corn back into the clean pot and cover with clear water. Boil the corn again until the skins come completely off. The hominy comes to the top of the pot and can be scooped out, ready to eat plain or fried in butter. If you want to preserve the hominy, it can be frozen or canned.

HOMINY

1 cup hominy

4 cups boiling water plus 1 teaspoon salt

Drop the hominy into the salted boiling water in the top of a double boiler. Place over hot water and steam, covered, for 1 hour, or until tender. Serve with cream or melted butter.

Rittie Webb uses "bought lye" today for making hominy:

My mother used to make hominy out of homemade lye, and I have too. It makes it taste better than this lye we buy. It gives it a kind of sweet taste. Of course, now I use the bought lye. You take about a gallon of water and put it in an iron kettle and let the water start boiling. Then you put the lye in. I use about a teaspoonful of lye to a quart of water. When the water starts boiling, get the lye dissolved

A barrel used for dripping lye when making hominy.

Hominy was most frequently made in an old cast-iron wash pot.

The final, ready-to-eat product is brought up on the paddle used to stir the hominy.

good in there, and then put in the corn. I put in about a half a gallon of corn, and that way you make enough. Then you stir it with a wood-handled spoon. Make sure the skin is all off of it, and take it out of the kettle and wash it real good about three times in a [different] pan. Wash the kettle, too. Put the hominy back in the kettle, in some clean water and boil again. You have to stir the hominy pretty often, till it comes to the top and you can see it. [It will] make your water get thick. Then it swells up and it will make your kettle full directly. I start cooking my hominy early in the morning and it takes me all day to get it cooked enough. By night, it's all right to eat. It's a job to make hominy. I like to eat it right out of the kettle. Most of us put it in a pan with some bacon grease, salt it, and fry it just a little before we go to eat it, and that gives it a good taste.

Okra

Another popular vegetable was the prickly pod called okra, which was introduced to the Americas by West African slaves. Okra has been widely adopted throughout southern foodways and is a staple of summer gardens throughout the region.

FRIED OKRA

Slice the okra about ½-inch thick, roll in meal and salt, and fry in grease until light brown and crispy.

OKRA AND GREEN BEANS

BELLE LEDFORD

"I steam okra on the top of green beans. Just before your green beans get done, pick out the tender, young okra pods. Cut their stems off, but don't cut into the okra. Put them on top of the green beans and let them steam while they finish cooking. Don't stir the beans, or you'll stir the okra down in them."

Onions

Onions are most frequently fried.

FRIED GREEN ONIONS

BELLE LEDFORD

"My mother used to fry green onions [spring onions or scallions]. When they were young and tender, you could eat the tops, too. She'd cut them up and fry them all together, the tops and the onions."

SCALLOPED ONIONS

Wash onions and boil until tender. Drain well and layer onions in a baking dish. Sprinkle each layer with soft bread crumbs, grated cheese, salt, and paprika. Pour hot bacon drippings over the onions. Bake in moderate 375°F oven until top is brown.

BOILED ONIONS

Place whole, sliced, or skinned onions in a boiler, covering them with salted water. Boil onions until tender. Drain well. Serve with melted butter or drop into a boiling white sauce.

Potatoes

Both white, or what were more commonly called Irish, and sweet potatoes were commonly grown throughout Southern Appalachia. White baking potatoes are found on most American dinner tables now, and sweet potatoes have lost some of their former popularity in this region. However, sweet potatoes were often chosen over Irish potatoes for their flavor reminiscent of pumpkin and similar squash varieties, and they were often more available than winter squashes.

ESCO PITTS: *When he dug his sweet potatoes, my father always let them dry in the sunshine. Then he'd bring them in the kitchen and put them back of the stove. He'd sort out all the small, long, stringy potatoes that weren't big enough to try to eat.*

LUCY YORK: *You may boil your sweet potatoes until they are tender. Then peel them, mash them up, and add sugar and butter to taste. Or you may peel them raw, slice into quarter-inch pieces, and fry in hot grease until tender.*

RUTH HOLCOMB: *Wash sweet potatoes and rub them dry with a cloth. With the peels still on, lay them in a pan that is greased lightly. Wash and dry cabbage leaves and lay them on top of the potatoes. Put in a hot stove and bake until soft and tender. The cabbage leaves hold the steam in.*

BAKED SWEET POTATOES

Today people use this same recipe, but with the addition of orange or lemon juice and cinnamon.

6 to 8 sweet potatoes, cooked and peeled
4 tablespoons butter
¼ cup honey

Place potatoes in a baking dish. Combine butter and honey and pour over potatoes. Bake in a hot (400°F) oven for 15 to 20 minutes, basting frequently.

HONEY SWEET POTATOES

⅔ cup honey
½ cup butter
1 teaspoon salt
8 to 9 sweet potatoes

In a well-greased baking dish, spoon the combined honey, butter, and salt between layers of sliced sweet potatoes. Bake in a moderate (350°F) oven for 30 minutes, basting frequently.

SWEET POTATO SOUFFLÉ

ARIZONA DICKERSON

1 cup milk
1 tablespoon butter or margarine
2 tablespoons sugar
½ teaspoon salt
2 cups cooked sweet potatoes, mashed
2 eggs, separated
1 teaspoon nutmeg
¼ cup raisins
¼ cup nuts, chopped

Scald milk. Add butter, sugar, and salt. Stir until butter is melted. Add to sweet potatoes. Stir until smooth. Beat yolks and whites of eggs separately. Stir yolks into potato mixture, and then add nutmeg, raisins, and nuts. Fold in stiffly beaten whites and pour into buttered baking dish.

If desired and obtainable, arrange 5 marshmallows over the top. Bake in a moderate (350°F) oven for 20 to 25 minutes or until set. Use as main course or dessert. Yield: *6 servings.*

FRIED SWEET POTATOES

Inez Taylor remembers her mother's fried sweet potatoes. "She'd put just a little grease in the pan, and she'd slice them [sweet potatoes] just like you do Irish potatoes. She'd put them in the pan and put a cup of sugar on them. Then she'd dampen that sugar with water and put those in the oven till they browned."

IRISH POTATOES

As mentioned above, Irish, or white, potatoes remain staples in the Appalachian, and national, meat-and-potatoes diet. They are baked, fried, mashed, put into pies, and eaten with gravy and dumplings.

ADDIE NORTON: *Irish potatoes, everybody eats Irish potatoes in North Carolina. I don't know about everywhere else, but everybody here eats Irish potatoes about every meal. I told my daddy one time, I said, "I've eat potatoes till I don't think I'll ever want any more," and I never have wanted any more.*

And I could then fry some of the best Irish potatoes I believe I ever seen, and you know how I done? Done the hard way. I put them on and boiled them and took the skin off of them, and then I mashed them up while they was hot. I mashed them up with salt and pepper and worked that salt and pepper in them, you know, and then I made them up in patties and put them in a pan of grease and fried them. You can't find nothing no better than that if you love Irish potatoes. They would just get as brown as they could on both sides. They was good, even if I did cook them.

I bake Irish potatoes. I also peel them and boil them, then mash them, adding salt, pepper, butter, and milk to make them creamy. To fry them, I slice three or four potatoes very thin, like potato chips; put in a frying pan with hot grease, and season with salt and pepper. Cover, and cook until light brown, turning occasionally.

LOLA CANNON: A good-sized potato will bake in the wood stove in about two hours.

IONE DICKERSON: My grandmother used to make this recipe. Cook and mash potatoes and brown sausage. In a casserole dish place a layer of potatoes and then a layer of sausage until both are all used. Bake until bubbly or cooked through at 300 degrees for fifteen to twenty minutes or until done.

RUTH HOLCOMB: For gravy and potatoes, I peel small new potatoes and boil them until they are tender. I mix three tablespoons of flour in two cups of milk and put this into the potatoes and cook them two or three more minutes, until that gravy's thick. Take from stove and stir in one tablespoon butter and a dash of black pepper and salt to taste.

POTATO CROQUETTES WITH CORNMEAL

BELLE LEDFORD

In making potato croquettes, most people use flour, but I like the cornmeal. You take cooked potatoes. You can use leftover stewed or creamed potatoes, but if I was just going to begin from the first, I'd cook about four or five medium-sized potatoes. Put one egg in that, and if you wanted two eggs, you could put two in it. I dip out between a fourth and a half cup of cornmeal in my hand and add that with about a half a teaspoon baking powder. Then put in about a tablespoon or two of chopped onion. That cornmeal and the egg helps it to hold together.

Sometimes you have to put a little milk in it to moisten it up if it's too dry. Make it out into little cakes and fry them in grease.

IRISH POTATO DUMPLINGS

1 quart potatoes, peeled and quartered
1 1/2 to 2 quarts water
Salt and pepper to taste
1 tablespoon butter or margarine
1 cup milk
1 recipe for biscuit dough

Peel and quarter potatoes. Put them in a pot, cover with water, add salt and pepper and butter. Boil until the potatoes are tender. Add milk. Roll biscuit dough out 1/4-inch thick, cut in 2-inch squares, and drop into the rapidly boiling water in which the potatoes are cooking. Cook dumplings 1 minute, remove the pot from the heat, and serve hot.

NANNY'S POTATO PATTIES

JAN JARROD

1 (16-ounce) package frozen whole kernel corn
   or 1 can whole kernel corn
1 small onion, finely chopped
1/2 cup chopped green onion
1/2 teaspoon pepper
2 tablespoons oil
2 cups mashed potatoes
1/2 cup flour
2 eggs, lightly beaten
3/4 teaspoon salt

Mix all ingredients well. Drop by heaping teaspoons of mixture into a hot, well-greased skillet, and fry on both sides until browned.

CREAMED POTATO SOUP

2 cups sliced potatoes

2 cups water

Salt and pepper to taste

Butter to taste

½ cup milk

1 tablespoon flour

Peel and slice potatoes, cover with water in a saucepan, and add enough salt, pepper, and butter for taste. Boil until tender. Mix milk and flour in a jar and shake until well mixed, then add to potatoes. Let the mixture boil 2 to 3 more minutes, until broth is slightly thick. If the broth becomes too thick, add more water or milk. Yield: *4 to 5 servings.*

POTATO SOUP WITH CORNMEAL

BELLE LEDFORD

I make potato soup and I put cornmeal in it. My mother used to make it, and she didn't have any recipe. When [my daughter] Mary Ann was a little girl, every time she got sick, she'd say, "Grandmother, make me some potato soup." And [Mary Ann] still cooks it. When I'm at her house, I say, "Cook me some potato soup."

She puts about a quart of water and about a quart of sweet milk [regular milk] on the stove and gets it to cooking. Then she puts her potatoes in. I guess she uses about six good-sized potatoes and cuts them up fine. She puts one or two stalks off of the celery in, cut up fine, and you can put an onion in if you want it. She just puts cornmeal in until she gets it as thick as she wants it. The last time I fixed it, I think I used a half a cup for that much soup. Season it good with butter and cook it. She always makes a big pot full when she makes it, because we all eat it. She makes it much better than I do, too."

Pumpkins

Lucy York describes preparations for pumpkins and cushaws: "Peel and slice them up. Cook in a small amount of water until soft like applesauce. They can then be served as a vegetable. They have a sweet taste, but more sweetening could be added, if desired. Usually sorghum syrup is used." For more sweet pumpkin recipes, see chapter 9. For pumpkin bread, see chapter 10.

FLORENCE BROOKS: *We used to eat slices of pumpkin fried in grease.*

FRIED PUMPKIN OR SQUASHBLOSSOMS

MARGARET NORTON

1 egg

½ cup milk

½ cup flour

Pumpkin or squash blossoms

Grease for deep frying

Make a thin batter using egg, milk, and flour. Dip the blossoms in the batter and fry in deep hot grease. Serve as you would any vegetable.

PUMPKIN CAKE

MARGARET NORTON

1½ cups butter or corn oil

2 cups sugar

3½ cups flour

2 teaspoons baking powder

2 teaspoons soda

1 teaspoon salt

2 teaspoons pumpkin pie spice

2 cups cooked mashed pumpkin

4 eggs, well beaten

2 teaspoons vanilla

1 cup chopped nuts

1 cup raisins or other dried fruit

Cream together butter and sugar. Sift together dry ingredients, using 1 cup of the flour, and add to creamed mixture along with the pumpkin. Add eggs and vanilla, beating well. Fold in nuts and raisins, which have been mixed with remaining ½ cup flour. Bake in a greased and floured loaf pan in a 400°F to 450°F oven for 60 minutes.

Squash

Many varieties of squash were cultivated in the mountains. Some of these were served as vegetables, but others had a chameleon quality that varied according to the spices and flavorings added to them (for example, see Cushaw or Pumpkin Pie on pages 172–73).

HARRY BROWN: *Everybody planted their cucumbers and squash on the tenth day of May—they called it Vine Day. You can plant squash earlier, but old people always planted squash, kershaws, and Hubbard then. Cushaws are pulp filled and grow great long. They're white and have a neck to them kind of like crookneck squash, only great big. They were really good to fry like sweet potatoes or to slice up and put butter and sugar on them. Just put them in the stove and bake them.*

When local people say "squash," they generally refer to yellow crookneck summer squash. The following preparation ideas were contributed with this type in mind:

HATTIE WATKINS: *When you're frying squash, you can put in some green tomato slices or okra rolled in cornmeal, and cook it all at the same time.*

BELLE LEDFORD: *I dip my squash in cornmeal when I fry it. Don't many people fry squash just one layer at a time in a pan and brown it on each side. My children liked it better that way. After they got large*

enough to be cooking themselves, I'd say, 'I'll fix one pan full. If you want more, you can fix more. You can fix as many as you want to.' It takes a long time to stand over it and fix it that way.

ARIZONA DICKERSON: *If squash are small, slice crossways like you would tomatoes for sandwiches. If they are large, slice longways into quarters; then slice into quarter-inch pieces. Roll the pieces in cornmeal or flour and salt and pepper. Fry in a pan with a small amount of oil or grease. Turn over when browned. Remove and drain on brown paper when cooked on both sides.*

SQUASH SOUFFLÉ
ARIZONA DICKERSON
3 tablespoons butter or grease
1 cup hot milk
1 cup fine dry bread crumbs
2 cups cooked squash
½ teaspoon salt
⅛ teaspoon pepper
1 tablespoon grated onion
2 eggs, beaten
1 cup grated cheese (try different cheeses to
   vary the dish)

Melt the butter in the hot milk and pour over bread crumbs. Mix with the squash, salt, pepper, onions, and eggs; pour into a buttered baking dish and sprinkle the cheese over the top. Bake in a 350°F oven for 20 to 30 minutes. Yield: *6 to 8 servings.*

Granny Gibson describes a way of preparing winter squash: "There's different ways to cook squash. You can stew them or fry them or bake them. Edith out here bakes hers sometimes. You just cut them [lengthwise] through the middle, lay them in the pan, put some butter on them, and bake them in the stove. They're good."

Tomatoes

ESCO PITTS: "I never saw a tomato till I was ten or twelve years old. My daddy wouldn't hardly go to the table if there was tomato on there. He said they wasn't a hog would eat them and so he wasn't going to eat them. Tomatoes was something we never saw in our young days."

FRIED GREEN TOMATOES

LOLA CANNON: *Pick tomatoes before they start showing any sign of ripening. Wash and slice tomatoes; roll in a mixture of flour or meal and salt and pepper and fry in hot fat. Brown on both sides.*

BERTHA WALDROOP: *Use green tomatoes before they show any sign of ripening. Wash and slice just as you would for tomato sandwiches. Roll the slices in cornmeal and flour or a mixture of the two. Heat grease in a frying pan and put the slices in. Salt and pepper them. Then turn them over to brown on the other side. When browned, remove and drain on brown paper or paper towels and serve.*

STEWED TOMATOES

Remove skins and slice tomatoes into a pot. Place over the heat and let stew in their own juice 15 to 20 minutes. Add desired amounts of salt and pepper; add some butter. Stew for another 15 minutes.

TOMATO PIE

4 cups canned tomatoes
1 cup milk
½ cup sugar
Pie dough of choice

Pour tomatoes into a pan that can be placed in the oven. Add salt to taste. Stir in sugar and milk. Make up a dough just like for a cobbler pie and roll or press the dough out. Bring the tomato mixture to boiling on top of the stove. Lay dough on top of the tomatoes, letting the juice boil through. Boil until dough is done (cooked through). Then put in a 350°F oven to brown on top, about 5 to 10 minutes.

CHASE SOUP

GLADYS NICHOLS

This recipe is named for Gladys Nichols's son Chase, who liked it so much.

4 cups ripe tomatoes, quartered
1 small onion, chopped
2 tablespoons flour
2 cups milk
Salt and pepper to taste
Butter or lard

Cook together ripe tomatoes and chopped onions until onions are tender. Blend flour into milk and mix into tomatoes. Add enough salt and pepper to taste. Bring to a boil, then simmer about 5 minutes. Season with butter or lard. Yield: *6 servings.*

TOMATO SOUP

ANNIE LONG

1 pint peeled, canned tomatoes
2 cups water
1 carrot, cubed
1 small onion, chopped fine
1 bay leaf
2 cloves
1 teaspoon salt
Dash of pepper
4 cups soup stock

Place all ingredients in large saucepan. Cover and cook for 1 hour, or until carrots are tender. Remove cloves and bay leaf before serving. Serve as is or place in the blender and purée before serving. Yield: *4 servings*.

Turnips, Rutabagas, Parsnips

Turnips were a popular by-product of greens, and rutabagas and parsnips were prepared much the same way.

FLORENCE BROOKS: *We raised great big turnips—people don't raise turnips like they did then. Old people had great large turnips back then, and they had them all the winter. Lot of times they'd have to plow those old turnips up and push them aside to plant again in the spring. And my father went to the field with a big basket [to gather the cast-aside turnips] and we'd put on pots of them to eat.*

BELLE LEDFORD: *I stew or steam rutabagas until they're done, mash them, and put a little butter in them. I don't fix them often, but I have a son-in-law that likes them. When he visits if it's in season I cook them for him because he doesn't get them at home.*

MARGIE LEDFORD: *I don't like parsnips, but, now, I like rutabagas. I cook them just like turnips. Get a piece of meat and put it in there and get it to boiling; then put the rutabagas in. I put a little bit of sugar in them.*

RUTH HOLCOMB: *Wash and peel parsnips. Put in a pan with a piece of ham bone or other meat. Cover with water, add one teaspoon sugar and salt to taste. Boil until almost dry, about three hours. They are then ready to serve.*

EXIE DILLS: *You can fry them or you can boil them. Take them backbones you know, and put a bunch of them on top of the parsnips and cook them. They was pretty good, I thought.*

Other Vegetable Recipes

Other vegetables made appearances on the table, often in medleys or soups.

SPLIT PEA SOUP
BELLE LEDFORD
2 cups dried split peas
3 quarts water
Ham bone or 2-inch cube of salt pork
½ cup chopped onion
1 cup chopped celery
½ cup chopped carrot
2 cups soup stock or 2 cups milk
1 bouillon cube
2 tablespoons butter
2 tablespoons flour
Salt to taste

Soak peas for 12 hours in water to cover by 2 inches water. Drain the peas and put in a large kettle. Add water and ham bone or salt pork and simmer, covered, for 3 hours. Add chopped onions, celery, and carrots; simmer, covered, 1 hour longer. Put soup through a food mill or blend in a blender. Chill and skim off all fat. Add soup stock or milk, if thinner soup is desired. If using milk instead of soup stock, add the bouillon cube, butter, and flour paste to soup stock before adding the milk. Add salt to taste. Cook until thickened and well done. Yield: *16 to 20 servings*.

CREAM OF BROCCOLI SOUP

BELLE LEDFORD

2 tablespoons butter

1 onion, chopped fine

2 tablespoons flour

5 cups chicken broth

1 pound fresh broccoli, cooked

½ teaspoon salt

¼ teaspoon pepper

½ cup whipping cream

Grated lemon rind from 1 to 2 lemons

Sauté onions in heated butter in a saucepan for 3 minutes, until softened. Add the flour and stir in the chicken broth. Cover and simmer 20 minutes. Mix together the cooked broccoli and 1 cup of the liquid. Bear or process in a blender until smooth. If necessary, strain to remove strings and lumps. Return purée to the soup mixture in saucepan. Add salt, pepper, and whipping cream, and heat to boiling. Serve in warm bowls and garnish with desired amount of lemon rind. Yield: *6 servings.*

3 The Springhouse

I've got a good, bold spring.

—Unknown participant

A large factor in deciding where to start a new farm was access to a dependable source of clean cold water. As noted in *Foxfire Book 2* (1973), this supply would be necessary not only for drinking water, as well as water for livestock and irrigation, but also for the construction of a springhouse where certain foodstuffs could be preserved. Before the convenience of electricity and such appliances as refrigerators and freezers (and even after those were available), many folks depended on a springhouse to keep foods fresh. These small structures were built over or near springs, and the cold flowing water cooled milk, cheese, butter, and meat, as well as pickled and canned goods. Although electric refrigeration was widely available when the first Foxfire interviews were conducted, some folks still kept a springhouse to keep their food fresh.

Many in these parts have fond memories of springhouses and their drier counterpart, the root cellar, filled with jars of canned and pickled fruits and vegetables, as well as bushels of heartier produce, including apples, potatoes, onions, and cabbage, which could be stored over many months without preservation. In this chapter, we celebrate preserved foods that often called a springhouse or root cellar home over the long winter.

A Word on Root Cellars

A group of Foxfire students happened upon a root cellar on one of their drives around the area. Chet Welch explained, "This root cellar was found accidentally by Tammy Ledford, who spotted it from a car window. The outside cellar is now rare. Today most people store their food in a basement. Since we didn't know who owned this root cellar, Tammy, Allan Ramey, and I decided

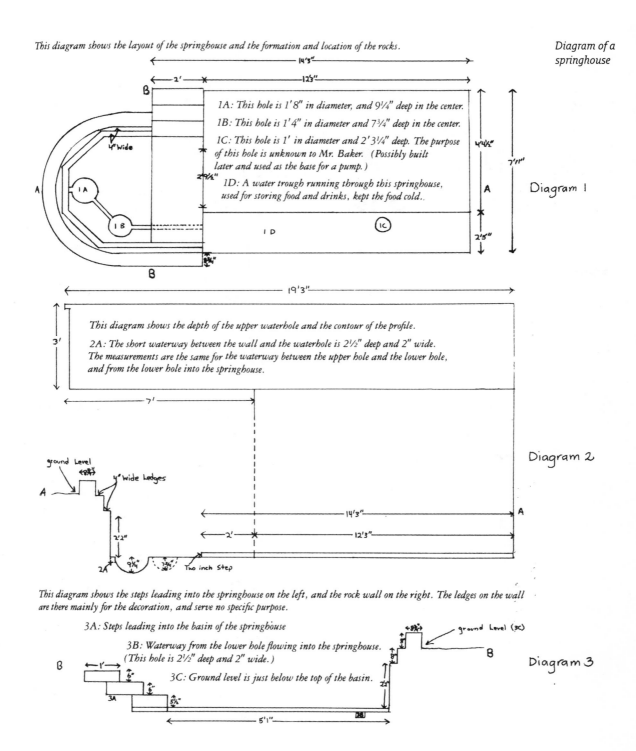

This diagram shows the layout of the springhouse and the formation and location of the rocks.

Diagram of a springhouse

1A: This hole is 1' 8" in diameter, and 9¼" deep in the center.

1B: This hole is 1' 4" in diameter and 7¾" deep in the center.

1C: This hole is 1' in diameter and 2' 3¼" deep. The purpose of this hole is unknown to Mr. Baker. (Possibly built later and used as the base for a pump.)

1D: A water trough running through this springhouse, used for storing food and drinks, kept the food cold.

Diagram 1

This diagram shows the depth of the upper waterhole and the contour of the profile.

2A: The short waterway between the wall and the waterhole is 2½" deep and 2" wide. The measurements are the same for the waterway between the upper hole and the lower hole, and from the lower hole into the springhouse.

Diagram 2

This diagram shows the steps leading into the springhouse on the left, and the rock wall on the right. The ledges on the wall are there mainly for the decoration, and serve no specific purpose.

3A: Steps leading into the basin of the springhouse

3B: Waterway from the lower hole flowing into the springhouse. (This hole is 2½" deep and 2" wide.)

3C: Ground level is just below the top of the basin.

Diagram 3

While not commonplace today, it wasn't too long ago that local springs were used for keeping foods cold.

The front view of a springhouse, showing how racks were carved and laid into the ground.

The racks in the springhouse were carved out by Babe LeCount. This photo shows the precision of his work.

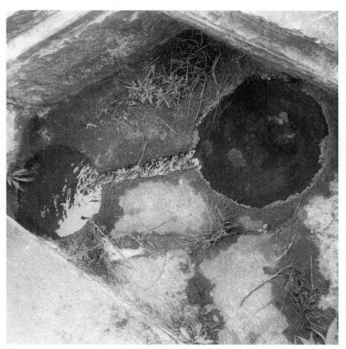

The water comes into the large hole (note the ripples) and runs through the trough into the smaller hole. From there it goes into the building.

one day that we should just drive up and ask about it. We were greeted by Albert and Ethel Greenwood, who kindly invited us to the cool of their porch. They talked about their root cellar, and Ethel shared with us her favorite recipe for preserving fruits, and then Albert told us about the root cellar."

ALBERT GREENWOOD: *We built our root cellar about two years after we moved here in 1961. I measured it off up the bank. I wanted it built seven feet into the bank and when I got it dug, I only had six. I lost a foot. The slope of the ground made the difference, but I didn't know that till after it was done. I just dug down and back—kept digging it out. The wood in the ceiling and doors is chestnut out of an old-timey house in Dillard, and the rest is oak. When I first built it, I went down to Franklin [North Carolina] to the sawmill and got some sawdust. I put that on the overhead ceiling to insulate it. The tar paper that was on it went bad and went to leaking. I just put a sheet of this black plastic over it and that stopped the leak. I just keep putting off fixing it.*

When you have a real cold winter a root cellar's about the only way you can keep anything from freezing. It was so cold last winter, so I had an oil lamp that I lit in the night. I've checked the temperature a few times in there, and I don't think it ever got below 38 degrees [Fahrenheit]. I didn't think anything would freeze, but I just wanted to be sure. I had potatoes in there, and they're a mighty easy thing to freeze.

The ground is what gives it more protection than anything. You can take potatoes out of the cellar, pour them out on the ground, cover them with hay and then cover them up with dirt. They won't freeze. Ethel keeps all the canned goods and all the flowers

she can get in the root cellar during the winter. We've got so many flowers right now it looks like we might not get them all in there. I put that window in there to let in light on the account she had a whole lot of flowers. When you put them in the dark, why, they'll die. They's no ventilation nowhere in that root cellar. I've seen them fixed with a pipe about four inches wide out the top. The pipe had a little top to it to keep rain from going down through it.

I'll tell you, if I had a place of my own and knowed I was going to stay, I'd fix a canning house or a cellar—whatever you want to call it—that would be convenient. I'd dig it out in the bank like that. You can't hardly dig one on flat ground because it'd be hard to keep water out. If you want a good one, dig it out like that and line it with blocks—eight- or six-inch blocks would be the best.

That's the cooler [springhouse] over there. When you cook corn in the canner, and if you just set it down somewhere you have to wait and wait on it to get cool. But if you just take it and set it in that cooler water and go back every once in a while and stir it, it ain't but a little while that it's cool. Then you can put it in the cups [freezer containers] and put it in the freezer. It's a handy thing.

Now you take this later generation of people that's coming up. They don't know anything much about making a living. If all these old-timers was to drop out, they'd starve to death. They wouldn't know how to plant nothing. I hate to say such a thing, but it's the truth. They've got an education and went to school, but it takes more than that to make a living.

Pickles, Relishes, Chutneys, and Sauerkraut

Pickles and relishes are sliced, chopped, or whole fruits or vegetables preserved in a brine or a vinegar-sugar mixture. Chutneys are relishes that are made of fruits or vegetables or both. They may be hot, spicy, sweet, and sour all at one time. Ginger, fresh or crystallized, is a common ingredient in chutneys.

The earlier method for pickling involved using wooden tubs. Gladys Nichols remembered using them:

People didn't used to have cans [glass canning jars]. The old-time way they made it back when this world here was settled was to pickle in [crockery] jars and wooden tubs and things like that. My daddy made wooden tubs to pickle beans and make kraut in. He'd cut a big old hickory tree, split it out, and then shave them staves about that wide. He put that thing together, put a head on it, and fixed it to where it'd hold water. Then we'd chop up cabbage in there and put the salt in. Done pickled beans the same way.

Many of our contacts followed the signs of the zodiac when they performed certain tasks. This was especially true when making pickles and relishes, as explained to us by Addie Norton:

I don't pay so much attention to it in cooking, but I do in pickling beans and putting up things like that. You can make kraut, pickled beans, and things like that, and I go with the signs all the time to do that. I avoid the heart and the head, anywhere from the head down to the waist. After the signs gets down in the legs, it's better, but it's better to wait till they get below the knees to pickle beans. In the new of the moon when the signs are below the knees is the best

time you'll ever make pickled beans and anything else that you work in vinegar with [laughter].

Many of our contacts use canning manuals and pamphlets as aids to perfect canning results. They are of especially good use in helping with the particulars of canning pickles. One of our contacts suggested using the instructions given by the *Blue Book*, published by the Ball Corporation.

Brined pickles, also called fermented pickles, go through a curing process of two to three weeks. The curing process changes cucumber color from a bright green to a yellow green and the white interior becomes uniformly translucent. Pickle-making begins with the brine, and carelessness in making or maintaining the brine is the reason for most of the soft and unfit pickles. Fresh-pack or quick-process pickles are brined for several hours or overnight and then drained before continuing with the recipe. Use only sound, tender, freshly gathered fruits and vegetables. If purchasing fruits and vegetables from the store, use a fir brush or other available object suitable for scraping off wax because the brine solution will not penetrate through the wax. Always use fruits and vegetables as soon as possible after gathering or purchasing them.

Soft water makes better brine than hard water. To soften hard water boil it for fifteen to twenty minutes. Let it stand for fourteen hours and then remove the scum that has accumulated on top. Be very careful when dipping water out from the kettle so the sediment at the bottom is not disturbed. Add one tablespoon of vinegar per gallon of boiled water before using.

Using the correct type of vinegar is important. A high-grade cider or white distilled vinegar of 4 to 6 percent acidity (forty to sixty grain) should be used. It is wise not to use vinegars of unknown acidity. Cider vinegar gives a nice blending of flavors but may darken white or light-colored fruits and vegetables. White distilled vinegar is used when a light color is desired. The two vinegars do have different tastes—cider vinegar with its mellow acid taste and the white vinegar with a sharp acid taste. If a less sour product is desired, adding sugar rather than decreasing vinegar is suggested.

Non-iodized table salt may be used for the pickling process, but pure granulated salt should be used if it is available. The non-iodized table salt has materials added to prevent caking, which may cause the brine to become cloudy. Iodized table salt should never be used because it will darken the pickles.

For the fermenting or brining process a crock, a churn, a glass jar, or an enamel-lined pan should be used. A heavy plate should be used to fit just inside the container to cover the vegetables in the brine. A heavy board, rock, or other heavy object is used to hold the cover down and keep vegetables below the surface of the brine. The time for fermentation will vary. It is complete when no bubbles rise to the surface when the side of the crock is pounded with the hand.

Special utensils such as enamelware, stainless steel, aluminum, or glass should always be used for heating pickling liquids. Never use copper, brass, galvanized, or iron utensils because these metals cause color changes in the product as a result of acid or salt reaction. Canned pickle products require processing to prevent spoilage. Our contacts advised us to follow the instructions for processing with each recipe.

SAUERKRAUT

Sauerkraut, or "sour kraut," is eaten year-round in our part of the country, but because this is a good way to preserve cabbage, it's served often throughout the winter. Willie and Bessie Underwood demonstrated their method for making kraut. They use a small wooden box for chopping their cabbage. It is about eighteen to twenty inches square and twelve inches high, just made of scrap wood. The small chopper is actually a garden hoe that has been straightened and wired to a short handle. The cutting edge is sharpened each year before kraut-making time.

To make kraut, use freshly picked cabbage (three large cabbages, ten to twelve inches in diameter, will make two gallons of kraut) and non-iodized table salt (three-fourths to one cup per gallon of chopped cabbage). Equipment needed: an earthenware churn of five-gallon (or more) capacity, a wooden box or other container to chop the cabbage in, and a kraut chopper.

Trim off and discard the outer leaves of several heads of cabbage. Wash the cabbage thoroughly, drain off excess water, and cut from the stalk. Discard stalks and chop the cabbage into fine pieces, one-quarter inch or smaller.

Measure one gallon of chopped cabbage and place in a large churn. Spread one-fourth to one cup salt over the cabbage and pack the cabbage down firmly. Do *not* add water to the cabbage in the churn. An accumulation of water from the cabbage itself will appear.

Add a second gallon of chopped cabbage, spread one-fourth to one cup salt over it, and pack it down. After two to three gallons of cabbage have been packed down in the churn, water will rise above the level of the cabbage.

Keep adding a gallon of cabbage and one-fourth to one cup salt until the level of water is at the mouth of the churn. At this point, put clean cabbage leaves over the chopped cabbage in the churn. Clean and scrub a smooth stone and lay it on top of the cabbage leaves. This will prevent the chopped cabbage from floating to the top. Cover the top of the churn with a clean white cloth and tie securely with string.

Let the churn sit seven to ten days in the kitchen. The higher the temperature at which the cabbage stays, the faster it will ferment. The kraut may remain in the churn indefinitely, with the amount needed to eat being taken out and the churn re-covered with the cabbage leaves and stone. It will become saltier as it gets older if left in the churn, but it will still be suitable to eat throughout the winter. The Underwoods pack their kraut in clean canning jars and heat them in a boiling water bath on the stove to seal. They store the jars of finished kraut in a cool, dark place.

SAUERKRAUT

MARGARET NORTON

You make your kraut when your cabbage is tender. You wash and dry your cabbage and chop them up. I've got a little chopper that my husband made for me that looks like a little hoe. I've got a small churn jar that's great big around and holds about four gallons. It's good to chop in. I put my cabbage in there and chop it up. Then I pack it in a big jar and put a layer of cabbage and a little salt, more cabbage and more salt. Then you may need to add a little water to cover the cabbage and let it set in there nine days. You taste your kraut along (while it's in the churn) and when it gets just right, like you want it, you put it in canning jars. It gets too sour if you leave it in that big churn

jar and don't can it. Then you set the jars in a pan of water on the stove. Let it come to a boil and can the kraut. Then just set them out in the can house.

PICKLED CUCUMBERS

GLADYS NICHOLS

"You can also pickle green tomatoes and bell peppers this way; onions may be added. Wash and slice vegetable to desired size. Put in container. For six to eight quarts add a handful of salt, cover with water, and let sit overnight. Pour off salty water and rinse with cold water. Pour boiling water over them; drain and pack into cans."

Prepare vinegar solution by mixing:

3 cups vinegar

1 ½ cups sugar

1 cup water

1 tablespoon mixed spices

Bring to a boil. Pour over pickles in jars. Seal. Process 15 minutes in boiling water bath.

THIRTEEN-DAY CUCUMBER PICKLES

MARY PITTS

2 gallons fresh, firm pickling cucumbers

10 percent salt solution by mixing ⅔ cup salt with 1 ½ gallons water

1 ounce alum

2 quarts vinegar, not too strong

¾ cup water

1 box stick cinnamon

1 tablespoon whole celery seed

2 tablespoons whole mixed spice

8 cups sugar

1st day: Wash cucumbers, drain thoroughly, cover with salt solution strong enough to float an egg.

2nd to 7th days: Let pickles stand, removing scum and stirring about every other day.

8th day: Drain; cover with boiling water; let stand.

9th day: Drain; cover with boiling water to which alum has been added.

10th day: Drain; cover with boiling water; let stand until cold. Drain well, then cover with hot syrup made of the vinegar, ¾ cup water, spices tied in a bag, and 2 cups of the sugar.

11th day: Drain off syrup and add 2 more cups sugar. Heat and pour over pickles.

12th day: Repeat.

13th day: Repeat, adding last 2 cups of sugar, only this time pack pickles in jars, add syrup, and seal.

CUCUMBER
OR GREEN TOMATO PICKLES
BELLE LEDFORD

7 pounds cucumbers or 7 pounds green tomatoes
2 gallons water
9 cups pickling lime

Soak for 24 hours, then rinse by letting cucumbers soak in clean water for 4 hours. Drain well between each change in water, and after final water. Bring to boil the following syrup:

5 pounds (10 cups) sugar
3 pints (6 cups) vinegar
1 teaspoon each of whole cloves, ginger, allspice, celery seed, mace, and cinnamon

Once mixture comes to a boil, pour it over the cucumbers or tomatoes and let stand overnight. Next morning, simmer for 1 hour. Pack in sterilized jars and seal. Process 20 minutes in boiling water bath.

SWEET DILL PICKLES
RUTH CABE

3 cups vinegar
6 tablespoons salt
1 cup sugar
3 cups water
30 to 36 cucumbers
Fresh or dried dill
Garlic cloves
Mustard seed

Make a brine of vinegar, salt, sugar, and water. Bring to a boil. Place a large handful dill, ½ to 1 clove garlic, and ½ tablespoon of mustard seed in each jar. Add cucumbers. Pour boiling brine over the cucumbers in each jar and seal. Process 5 minutes in boiling water.

SWEET PICKLES
CLYDE BURRELL

1 bushel green and red bell peppers
8 medium-sized onions
1 head cabbage
Vinegar to cover
3 cups sugar (reduce to 2 cups for sour pickles)
Whole hot peppers to taste (optional)

Grind or chop into small bits the peppers, onions, and cabbage. Salt the mixture (about 2 tablespoonsful), and let it sit 2 or 3 hours. Pour off the juices that accumulate. Put vegetable mixture (along with hot peppers, if desired) into a large metal dish pan or saucepan . Add the vinegar and sugar and cook until the mixture changes color; it will have a brownish tint. Bring to a boil. Then pack in canning jars. Process 5 minutes in boiling water bath.

Margaret Norton describes the steps in making icicle pickles:

First thing you do is gather a peck of cucumbers. Try to get some that are small and tender. Don't peel them. Just cut them up longways and put them in a churn jar. Add one-half cup salt and fill the churn to the top with boiling water. Put a plate over the churn, cover with a white cloth, and place a weight over that. Let them set one week. Then pour off the salty water and add a fresh batch of boiling water without salt. This will remove excess salt from the pickles.

Next day melt a lump of alum the size of a walnut in a small amount of boiling water. Add this to the churn of pickles to crisp them. Leave this on the pickles overnight. Then prepare a mixture of three quarts of vinegar, eight pounds of white sugar, a cinnamon bar, and two tablespoons pickling spices. Bring to a boil and pour over the pickles. Each morning, for four days in all, pour this mixture back into a pan, bring it to a boil, and pour it back over the pickles.

You see, they're not any trouble. I just pass by and fix mine while I'm doing something else, because I'm always working in the garden or something. That will make about twelve or thirteen pints of icicle pickles. The recipe says they're guaranteed to keep in an open jar, but I don't want them setting there in an open jar so I put mine in pint cans and place the cans in some water on the stove and bring them to boiling, and that seals them and then I've got my cucumbers.

ICICLE PICKLES

2 gallons cucumbers
2 cups coarse salt
1 gallon boiling water
1 walnut-sized lump of alum
2 quarts apple cider vinegar
16 cups sugar
1 grain (pill) saccharin
2 tablespoons celery seed
1 tablespoon pickling spice
3 tablespoons cinnamon sticks

Split the cucumbers lengthwise, no matter how small. Add salt to the gallon of boiling water. Pour over the cucumbers. Let stand 1 week. Drain. Cover with boiling water. Let stand 24 hours. Drain, dissolve the alum in boiling water, then pour over pickles. Let stand 24 hours. Drain the pickles. Boil together the vinegar, sugar, saccharin, and spices; pour over the pickles. Do this for 4 consecutive mornings (boil what liquid was poured off and pour back on mixture again). Then seal in cans—but they *will* keep in an open jar.

CUCUMBER, SWEET BELL PEPPER, OR GREEN TOMATO ICICLE PICKLES

This is a process that takes 14 days, but is actually much easier than it sounds. Select and cut up a peck of the above, peeling and all. Cut cucumbers into 6- to 8-inch strips. Leave the tomatoes whole if they are small ones. Put vegetables in a crock and over the top add boiling water to fill the crock. Add ½ cup salt per peck of vegetables. Let this mixture sit for 9 days. At the end of 9 days, pour out the liquid, wash the pickles, put them back in the jar, add 3 tablespoons of alum (to make pickles brittle), and fill again with boiling water. Let this mixture sit for 24 hours. After 24 hours, empty the liquid again, wash the pickles again, and replace them in the jar.

Meanwhile, be cooking together the following mixture:

9 cups sugar
2 quarts vinegar
3 sticks cinnamon
1 tablespoon pickling spice
4 to 5 pieces ginger
1 tablespoon celery seed

Cook this mixture until it boils, then pour it over the pickles and let it sit for 24 hours. Then pour the liquid into a container, reboil it, and pour it over the pickles again. Repeat this procedure for 4 consecutive days. On the fourth day, the pickles are ready to serve. Keep them in the open jar in a cool place or can them for convenience.

When pickling the above, the old-timers in the area would usually let them sit overnight in a crock in salty water, then remove them the next day, boil them in vinegar, sugar, and spices to suit taste, and can them immediately. Grape leaves were often added while the pickles were sitting overnight in the crock. These had approximately the same effect as the alum. For spices and added flavor, they used pickling spice, strips of sassafras, and spicewood. These were called "bread and butter pickles."

BREAD AND BUTTER PICKLES
GLADYS NICHOLS

"I never have knowed of nobody fixing them like I fix them until I give them the recipe. It's not so hard to do, and they *are* good. Soak twenty-five cucumbers and twelve onions in salt water one hour and drain off. Add one box mixed pickling spices and one and one-half cups sugar. Cook together until cucumbers are tender, and can."

CANNED PICKLED SWEET PEPPERS
ARIZONA DICKERSON

"Quarter and seed as many peppers as desired. Cover with salt water and let come to a boil. Drain and put the peppers in canning jars. Make a solution of vinegar and sugar, two cups of vinegar to two cups of sugar. Bring to a boil and pour over the peppers and seal."

PICKLED GREEN TOMATOES

Wash and quarter green tomatoes. Pack raw into pint jars, adding to each jar 2 or 3 small whole pods of hot pepper and 1 quartered pod of bell pepper. Make a brine of 2 parts vinegar, 1 part water, and 1 part sugar, and heat it until the sugar melts. Pour into the packed jars, leaving ½ inch at top. Process 15 minutes in a water bath.

FLORENCE BROOKS: *We made tomato pickles—you've got to take them green, when they're good and green, just before they go to turning. I always soaked mine overnight in salt water and then took them out, and made my brine with sugar and vinegar—have to taste to know when you've got them as sour or sweet as you want them, and put it all in a pan and let it get to boiling and just as quick as the tomatoes turn white looking, put them in the can.*

RIPE TOMATO PICKLES

3 pints tomatoes (peeled and chopped)
¼ cup chopped red pepper
1 cup celery
¼ cup chopped onion
2 cups vinegar
¼ cup salt
6 tablespoons sugar
6 tablespoons mustard seed
½ teaspoon cloves
½ teaspoon cinnamon
1 teaspoon nutmeg

Place the vegetable ingredients in order given into a stone jar. Mix together the remaining ingredients and pour over vegetable mixture. Allow this uncooked mixture to stand a week before using.

ICEBERG GREEN TOMATO PICKLES

7 pounds green tomatoes
Pickling lime*
2 pounds sugar
3 pints vinegar
1 teaspoon each of cloves, ginger, allspice,
    celery seed, mace, and cinnamon

Soak the tomatoes in a mixture of 1½ cups lime to 1 gallon water, making enough to cover the tomatoes. Drain and soak for 4 hours in fresh water, changing it hourly. Make a syrup of the sugar, vinegar, and spices, and bring it to a boil. Pour it over the tomatoes (after the last change of water has been drained off) and let stand overnight. Then boil for 1 hour and seal in jars.

*Be sure lime is pure enough for cooking use.

LIME PICKLES

7 pounds cucumbers or tomatoes, cut up
3 cups pickling lime*
2 gallons cold water
3 pints vinegar
5 pounds white sugar
2 tablespoons pickling spice

Combine cucumbers in the lime and cold water mixture; let soak 24 hours. Drain and then soak in clear water for 4 hours, changing water every hour. Bring vinegar, sugar, and spices to a boil. Add the cucumbers and let stand overnight, then boil 1 hour. Pack in glass jars or a large crock. Seal. Process in a boiling water bath for 10 minutes. Yield: 7 quarts or 14 pints.

*Be sure lime is pure enough for cooking use.

SCHOOL GIRL PICKLES

NANCY SEWELL

Make a brine strong enough to float an egg (1 pint salt to 1 gallon water). Let cucumbers soak whole for 2 to 3 weeks (do not cut up). Drain and soak in fresh water overnight, then cut up the cucumbers. Soak in alum water (7 teaspoons alum to 6 pounds cucumbers) for 6 hours. Then take out of alum water.

Heat enough apple cider vinegar to cover cucumbers. Add pickling spices (about 1 heaping tablespoon in a cheesecloth bag) and let stand 25 hours. Take out of vinegar. In a churn put in a layer of sugar and a layer of cucumbers (using 8 pounds sugar to 12 pounds of cucumbers). Let stand 3 days after which they are ready to use. May be covered to stand in stone jars for years.

Variation: When you bring vinegar to boil, put loose pickling spices in vinegar.

BEET PICKLES

GRANNY GIBSON

"I make beet pickles. You have to boil your beets until they're tender, and then you have to peel that skin off of them. Then you just slice them up, put vinegar and sugar in them, and boil them a while and can them."

PICKLED CORN

MARGARET NORTON

"Shuck and silk corn that is in roasting ear. Boil on cob. Cool with cold water and pack in clean churn jar, sprinkling a little salt over each layer as you fill jar. Some prefer to line the churn with a white meal sack and tie at the top. When corn is pickled it will keep without canning. You can eat as is off cob or cut it off with a knife and fry in bacon grease. Pickled corn is good mixed with pickled beans and fried in bacon grease or in butter. Some people even pickle them together, first slicing the corn off the cob."

WATERMELON PICKLES

4 pounds watermelon rind

3 quarts cold water

1 tablespoon pickling lime

2 tablespoons whole cloves

2 tablespoons whole allspice

1 quart cider vinegar

4 pounds sugar

10 pieces (2 inches each) stick cinnamon

Remove all the pink pulp from the watermelon rind. Peel the outside peeling from the rind. Weigh. Cut in 1-inch circles or cubes. Combine 2 quarts of the cold water and the lime. Pour over rind. Let stand 1 hour. Drain. Cover with fresh cold water. Simmer 1½ hours or until tender. Drain. Tie the spices in cheesecloth. Combine the vinegar, remaining 1 quart water, and sugar. Heat until the sugar dissolves, then add the spice bag and rind. Simmer gently 2 hours. Pack the rind in clean, hot sterile jars. Fill the jars with boiling hot syrup. Seal. Process 10 minutes in boiling water bath. Yield: *About 12 half pints.*

PEPPER RELISH

"Grind up twelve pods of [sweet] red pepper, twelve pods of green pepper, and twelve onions together. If you have the vinegar-spice mixture left over from icicle pickles, you can use that. Otherwise, make up a vinegar-sugar mixture to pour over them. Use about a pint of vinegar for that many peppers and onions. I don't add any other spices because you'd be chewing on them when you eat the relish. The vinegar mixture I used on the icicle pickles has been strained, and there's always more than I need to put up those pickles so I save it, and the flavor of the spices is in there but nothing to bite down on."

MR. SHORT'S PEPPER RELISH

BELLE LEDFORD

3 pecks sweet red peppers

1 peck sweet green peppers

1 gallon onions

1 stalk celery

5 pounds sugar

2 quarts vinegar

3 tablespoons pickling salt

Grind peppers, onions, and celery. Let stand 30 minutes and then drain. In a 6-quart kettle combine the sugar, vinegar, and salt; cook, drain. Process 10 minutes in boiling water bath.

PEPPER RELISH

ARIZONA DICKERSON

1 gallon red sweet peppers

1 gallon green sweet peppers

1 cup diced celery

2 cups diced sweet apples

1 cup diced onion

2 cups sugar, 2 cups vinegar, 3 tablespoons salt, and spices if desired

Dice the peppers. Pour boiling water over the peppers, celery, apples, and onions, and let stand for a few minutes. Drain off. Add sugar, vinegar, and spices and cook until apples, peppers, and celery are tender. Stir often and blend well. Seal in jars. Process 10 minutes in boiling water bath.

GREEN TOMATO PICKLE RELISH

8 pounds green tomatoes, chopped fine

4 pounds brown sugar

1 quart vinegar

1 teaspoon mace

1 teaspoon cinnamon

1 teaspoon cloves

Boil the tomatoes and sugar for 3 hours. Add the other ingredients and boil 15 minutes more. Let cool and seal in jars. Process 10 minutes in boiling water bath.

WHITE HOUSE RELISH
ARIZONA DICKERSON

12 sweet green peppers

12 sweet red peppers

12 onions

1 head cabbage, ground fine

2 cups vinegar

2 cups sugar

3 tablespoons salt

Chop the peppers and onions up into small pieces. Add the cabbage and cover with boiling water. Let stand 5 minutes. Drain. Add vinegar, sugar, and salt. Boil 5 minutes. Seal in canning jars. Process 10 minutes in boiling water bath.

MUSTARD PICKLE RELISH
MARGARET NORTON

1 cup salt

1 gallon water

1 quart cucumbers, chopped fine

1 quart green tomatoes, chopped fine

1 head cabbage, chopped fine

4 sweet peppers, chopped fine

6 tablespoons dry mustard

1 cup flour

1 tablespoon turmeric

2 quarts vinegar

Make a brine of salt and water, and let the next 4 ingredients stand in brine for 24 hours. Drain. Make a mixture of the last 4 ingredients, add to the first mixture, and cook for 3 minutes. Seal in jars. Process 10 minutes in boiling water bath.

SQUASH RELISH
BELLE LEDFORD

Chop very fine by hand or in blender:

12 cups squash (6 to 8 medium-sized squash)

4 cups onion (6 to 8 large onions)

1 sweet green pepper

1 sweet red pepper

5 pounds salt

Mix and let set overnight. In the morning put in colander and run water over it. In a large saucepan mix:

2 ½ cups vinegar

6 cups sugar

1 tablespoon dry mustard

¾ teaspoon nutmeg

¾ tablespoon flour or cornstarch

¾ teaspoon turmeric

1 ½ teaspoons celery seed

½ teaspoon black pepper

Let this cook until it begins to thicken, then add the squash mixture and let boil slowly for 30 minutes. Put in jars and seal. Process 10 minutes in boiling water bath. Yield: 8 pints.

CUCUMBER RELISH

12 cucumbers

4 green peppers

4 onions

½ cup salt

1 cup sugar

1 teaspoon celery seed

1 tablespoon mustard seed

1 cup grated horseradish

Vinegar

Remove the seeds and skin from the cucumbers and chop. Also chop the peppers and onions. Add the salt, mix well, and let stand overnight. Drain, add the sugar, spices, and horseradish and mix with enough vinegar to provide moisture but not make the mixture watery. Seal in jars. Process 10 minutes in boiling water bath.

PEPPER SAUCE

14 large onions
12 green bell peppers
12 red bell peppers
2 to 3 pints vinegar
2 cups sugar
2 tablespoons salt

Chop vegetable ingredients up fine, pour boiling water over them, let stand for 5 minutes, and then drain. Put ingredients back in a kettle and pour on more boiling water to cover. Let boil 2 minutes, drain, and then put back in kettle again. Add vinegar, sugar, and salt. Boil for 15 minutes. Fill jars and seal. Process 20 minutes in boiling water bath.

CHOWCHOW

1 peck green tomatoes
2 large heads of cabbage
2 quarts small white onions
1 peck string beans
2 quarts sweet green peppers
2 quarts sweet red peppers
¼ cup white mustard seed
2 ounces white or black cloves
2 ounces celery seed
2 ounces allspice
1 (1½-ounce) box yellow mustard seed
1 ounce turmeric
1 pound brown sugar
Vinegar

Chop the tomatoes. Let them stand overnight in their own juice. Drain well. Chop the cabbage, onions, beans, and peppers, mix together, and add the tomatoes, spices, and sugar. Put in a porcelain kettle, cover with vinegar, and boil 3 hours. When cool, seal in jars. Process 10 minutes in boiling water bath.

ADDIE'S CHOWCHOW

5 pounds apples
5 pounds sweet peppers
2 onions
1 pound hot peppers
2 quarts vinegar
1 cup water
3 tablespoons cinnamon
3 pounds sugar
½ box pickling spices
Salt to taste

Grind in food chopper, or chop up fine with a knife, the apples, peppers, and onions. Let set 10 minutes and drain. Combine remaining ingredients; simmer 10 minutes. Add the apples, peppers, and onions and let mixture simmer 3 hours. Fill immediately and seal. Process 10 minutes in boiling water bath.

MARGARET NORTON'S CHOWCHOW

"My chowchow has green tomatoes, peppers, onion, and cabbage in it. It's made like kraut. It isn't cooked. You just chop up all your vegetables and put them in your jar. It sets in there till it gets as sour as you want it. Then you can it. Some people put hot pepper in it, but I use sweet peppers."

CHUTNEY

6 green tomatoes

4 onions

2 green peppers

1 cup seedless raisins

2 tablespoons mustard seed

Hot pepper (optional)

2 tablespoons salt

2 cups brown sugar

2 cups white sugar

1 quart vinegar

2 tablespoons pickling spice (in bags)

12 very tart apples, cored, peeled if desired, diced

Chop all vegetables up finely. Put all ingredients except the apples into a kettle and cook 1 hour. Add the diced apples and cook until they become soft. Pack into jars and seal. Process 10 minutes in boiling water bath.

PEAR RELISH

1 peck pears, peeled and cored

6 large onions

4 red sweet peppers

4 green sweet peppers

3 stalks celery, chopped up finely

5 cups vinegar

1 tablespoon allspice

3½ cups sugar

Grind up the pears and vegetables in a food chopper. Add the vinegar, allspice, and sugar and mix together well. Let stand overnight. Cook for 30 minutes. Pack mixture in jars and process for 20 minutes in boiling water bath. Yield: *9 pints*.

SWEET PICKLED PEACHES

3 pounds peaches

4 cups sugar

1 cup water

2 cups vinegar

2 ounces stick cinnamon

1 ounce ground cloves

¼ to ½-inch piece ginger

Select uniform peaches and blanch in boiling water for 1 minute, or long enough to loosen skin. Chill by dropping in cold water for just a moment, then drain and peel. Freestone peaches may be cut in halves and the pits removed (a few pits may be boiled with the peaches and then removed). Clingstone peaches may be pickled whole.

Make a syrup by boiling 2 cups of the sugar, the water, vinegar, and spices (in bag) together for 5 minutes. Add the peaches and boil 3 minutes, if whole; 1 minute, if cut in halves. Let peaches cool in syrup. Add the remaining 2 cups sugar and cook until tender but not mushy. Cover and let stand overnight. Drain off syrup and reheat. Pack peaches in hot sterile pint jars. Cover with hot syrup. Process in water bath at simmering temperature (180°F) for 20 minutes.

PICKLED PEACHES OR APPLES

Peel apples or peaches, quarter, and put in a pot. Make enough brine of 2 parts vinegar, 2 parts sugar, and 1 part water to cover the fruit. Add ground cinnamon, nutmeg, and allspice to taste. Cook until tender. When done, lift the fruit out and pack into jars. Keep the brine simmering, and pour into jars over the fruit, leaving ½ inch at the top. Seal immediately. Process 15 to 20 minutes in boiling water bath.

TOMATO KETCHUP

RUTH HOLCOMB

1 gallon cooked tomatoes (approximately 1 peck)
½ cup sugar
2 tablespoons dry mustard
1 tablespoon ground allspice
1 pint cider vinegar
3 tablespoons salt
1 tablespoon black pepper
½ tablespoon ground cloves

Select good, ripe tomatoes. Scald and strain through a coarse sieve to remove seed and skin. When the tomatoes become cold add the remaining ingredients. Let simmer slowly for 3 hours. Pour in bottles or jars. Process for 15 minutes in boiling water bath.

Jams, Jellies, and Preserves

Nora Garland remembers picking cherries and wild strawberries as a child for canning purposes:

Law, yeah. That's all we had to can on. We had four big cherry trees and they were hanging just as full as they could be. They wasn't big ones, guess just as high as the ceiling. I was so little—I didn't weigh but about seventy-five pounds—that I was the only one that could get up in them [trees]. They'd put me up in the cherry trees. They'd be hanging just as full and red as they could be. I'd sit up there and pick cherries and eat my part of them. I'd pick a bucket full and then take them down and we'd can, I guess, seventy-five cans of cherries. And wild strawberries, the ground was just full of them just red with wild strawberries. I've knowed us to have fifty or sixty cans of wild strawberries.

When we asked cooks if there was any difference between canning jams and jellies on the wood stove and the conventional stove, most of them agreed that you don't do anything different except for putting the wood in the stove. Jams are made of whole crushed berries or fruits cooked with sugar to a soft consistency. Almost no other liquid is added. Jellies are the juice of berries or fruits boiled with sugar. Some of our contacts like to use Sure-Jell, a commercial pectin. Others refuse to use it, cooking their jelly the "old way": boiling it down with nothing but sugar.

ANNIE LONG: *I can here at home. I usually have pretty good luck with jelly. Lot of people prefer it flavored, but I like it just plain the best. You put your juice and your sugar on—I usually put a cup of each—and let it come to a boil, and then boil it for about fifteen minutes. You can stir it and let it stream to see if it's thickening like thread when it gets done. It's usually jelled by then. I don't like it when you add Sure-Jell. Tastes salty to me, especially if you keep it any time over a year.*

GRANNY GIBSON: *I used to make jelly without the Sure-Jell, but I haven't made none in a long time. For apple jelly you'd add a cup of sugar to a cup of apple juice. Then you'd boil it till—you can kind of guess at it. Lift it up and drop off a drop to see if it's done. It don't take long for it to make. Do grape or any kind the same way. I used to just can peaches and pears straight.*

MARY PITTS (remembering her mother using crab apples as a thickener): *I've seen my mother cut up crab apples and cook her up a pan full a many a time. She'd mix a little bit of that crab apple juice in with her blackberry juice and her apple butter. And you'd have to use some for peaches and pears and blackberries. It don't change the taste any. It just helps them jell. We had big crab apples, and you could take the core out and cook them.*

VIOLET "JAM"

Stella Burrell has never before given her recipe for violet jam to anyone, not even to the girls in her family; but since she is now unable to can because of arthritis in her hands, she decided to share the recipe with us for this cookbook. This is really a jelly, even though it's called a jam.

Years ago I had a little jelly and jam shop and I made violet jam from an old English recipe. It's the richest food we have in vitamins, and it's still in the drugstores in England. They call it "vitamin paste" there, and pharmacists use it for the vitamin content. You just take a little bit of it each day, like taking a vitamin tablet. Lemon juice has always been used in violet jam, and it does have the lemony flavor. This is the first time I've given the violet jam recipe out, but now I can't get out and pick the violets to do it with.

The blue or purple wild violets is what I always used. The purple violets will give the jam a pink cast; the blue violets come out a little clearer. There is a little dark red-purply violet and it will give your jelly or jam more of a reddish-purplish cast. I've had a lot of people to buy it just to sit in the window to look at.

> 1 package Sure-Jell
> 2½ cups water
> ½ cup lemon juice
> 3 cups sugar
> 1 cup violet blooms, packed

Mix together the Sure-Jell, water, and lemon juice. Bring to a boil, add the sugar, and boil for 3 minutes. Stir in the violet blooms and remove from the heat. Pour into hot sterilized jars and seal. Stella continued:

People didn't used to have Sure-Jell, and we would take crab apples—they're real sour—and use that as pectin for our juice. There're certain fruits that just don't jell as well as others, and you need this added pectin. Some people used a little vinegar to make their jellies jell. You need something sour for any juice from a sweet fruit. In my jelly recipes I've used Sure-Jell because that's the way I make it now, but years ago you wouldn't have had the Sure-Jell and you would have substituted that sour crab apple juice. [To make plain crab apple jelly] just boil the crab apples and take the juice off like you would for apple jelly. It's maybe not as good as apple jelly, but it's edible and it has its own flavor. It's more of a novelty.

I put wax on everything that I sold in the shop. If you're going to store it for a while, you need to put paraffin on it. If you're going to use it within two or three months, you don't need to put the paraffin on. People used to use beeswax a lot to go around the outside as well as on the inside like paraffin.

CORNCOB JELLY
STELLA BURRELL

"To make a run of corncob jelly, you need twelve red corncobs. You wash these, break them up, and cover them with water in your pot. Let them come to a boil and then boil them for thirty minutes. You strain this broth with a cloth to get the particles from the cob out of it so that it will be clear. The red cob has its own color. Mix three cups of the juice with a box of Sure-Jell, and when that comes to a rolling boil, add three cups of sugar. Let this boil for two minutes. Pour into sterilized jars and seal."

MISCELLANEOUS JELLY RECIPE
BERTHA WALDROOP

"Pick your berries—blackberries, blueberries, huckleberries, whatever kind are available. Wash them and put them in a pan with a small amount of water. You don't want to add more water than just enough to keep them from scorching, because as they cook they will have lots of juice. Cook the berries until they are soft. Then allow to cool. Strain the juice through a good strong cloth that's not too thick. Cheesecloth is good if you double it. Also a cloth flour sack will probably do. Strain the juice and then squeeze the cloth to get all the juice out. Measure the juice and put into a pot to cook. Add one cup of sugar for every cup of juice. Bring to a slow boil, stirring often. Keep boiling until it makes jelly."

CRAB APPLE JELLY

Select sound crab apples. Wash and remove the blossom ends. Slice crab apples without peeling. Barely cover with water and cook until the fruit is tender. Strain through a jelly bag. Measure juice and boil rapidly until the jelly stage is reached. Skim and pour into hot sterilized glasses. Seal with airtight cover.

MAYHAW JELLY

Cook 1 pound mayhaws (part underripe) with 2 cups water until tender enough to mash. Strain the juice and add ¾ cup of sugar for each cup of juice. Cook rapidly to the jelly stage. Pour into jars and seal.

MINT JELLY FROM APPLE JUICE

Pour boiling water over 1 cup clean, finely chopped, tightly packed mint leaves. Cover and allow to steep for 1 hour. Press the juice from the leaves and add 2 tablespoons of this extract to 1 cup apple juice and ¾ cup sugar. Boil until the jelly stage is reached. Add green food coloring. Pour into hot glasses and seal.

MUSCADINE JELLY
BELLE LEDFORD

"I use the recipe that's on the Sure-Jell box for muscadine jelly. I think I just read the recipe for grapes and worked out what I thought would work, and it did. To prepare your muscadines, you punch out the inside. By the time you're through, your hands are black and sore as they can be. You cook the inside and then put it through a strainer or sieve. A colander is hardly fine enough to put it through, because if the seeds are small some of them will go through it. And then you put that and the hull back together and cook the hull and all."

Preserves are made from whole or sliced fruits preserved in a heavy sugar syrup. Nora Garland explained to us, "Well, preserves are made out of fruit cut into slices. The figs are used whole sometimes. I like mine split half in two. [Preserves] stick but jellies won't unless you got a real hot fire. I like to cook my jellies fast and my preserves slow."

PEAR PRESERVES

Peel and cut into quarters, then wash pears. Rinse and place a layer of sugar and a layer of pears until all the fruit has been used. Let this sit overnight. Put over moderate heat and cook until well done and syrup has been made from the mixture. Put into sterile jars and seal.

WATERMELON PRESERVES

Cut off all the red part. Cut in pieces 4 to 5 inches in size. Stand each piece on its side on the cutting board. Cut off the peeling and the soft side using one cut of the knife for each. Put into boiling water and boil 5 minutes. Cut the rinds in

any shape desired. Pieces 1½ by ⅞ inches are at-
tractive and pack conveniently. Thirty-six pieces
(1 pound or about 3 cups full) and 1 round piece
for the top fill one 12-ounce jar, and 16 round
pieces fill one 12-ounce jar. Soak in lime water
(1 tablespoon air-slaked lime to 1 quart water for
1 pound) for at least 4 hours. Freshen ½ hour.
Drain, weigh, place in the preserving kettle, and
cover with cold water. Cook 30 minutes, or until
tender. Then add ¾ cup sugar for each pound
of rind and cook until clear. Cool, plump, pack,
cover with syrup, and process for 20 minutes at
simmering. Seal. One pound rind yields 1 cup of
preserves on average.

Fruit Butters

Fruit butters are made by cooking fruit pulp
with sugar. After making jelly, butter may be
made using leftover pulp. Making apple butter
is customary after making a "run" of applesauce.
Because the article on "Making Apple Butter"
as it appeared in *Foxfire Book 3* (pp. 416–23) was
so concise, we decided to reproduce it for this
section on food preservation:

"It's so good that if you put some on your
forehead, your tongue would slap your brains
out trying to get to it!" Pat Brooks told us. Mr.
and Mrs. Pat Brooks still make apple butter the
old-time way. "Back years ago, you either made it
or you didn't eat it. This day and time everybody
has got enough money. They don't have to work
like us poor folks. Nobody wants to take the time
to make it, but they've all got their hand out for
a jar." Pat and his wife showed us how to make
apple butter the way the Brooks family has made
it for over forty years. Mrs. Brooks and Pat took
turns giving us directions.

It takes three bushels of apples to make a
stir. You can keep the apples for three or four
days before using them in the apple butter.
Mrs. Brooks explains, "I wouldn't have nothing
but the Winesaps. That's the only kind that
makes good butter. The other kind won't cook up
good. Sour apples do. An apple that has a sweet
taste to it [won't] make good butter.

"So first you peel the apples and cook them on
a stove for fifteen or twenty minutes. Then run
them through a colander. Clean the kettle with a
solution of vinegar and baking soda. Some people
use wood ashes. Brass is the only kind [of kettle]
I would have. It just makes better butter somehow. I don't like a copper kettle because it makes
the butter taste, I think."

Pat Brooks points out that "you can use any
kind of wood for the fire except pine, because it
would make the butter taste funny. Don't let the
wood touch the bottom of the kettle or the butter
will burn." Mrs. Brooks says to "pour applesauce
in the twenty-gallon brass kettle heated by an
open furnace." Pat made the butter-stirring stick
himself out of cypress. He says you can't use a
wood with acid in it because you'll be able to taste
the acid. He likes the yellow poplar best for it. Pat
explains, "When you stir, you go once on one side,
once on the other side, and once in the middle.
You see, the bottom is narrow and that way it
won't stick."

Constantly stir the applesauce until it's hot
enough to melt sugar. Then, using one five-
pound bag at a time, at regular intervals gradually pour fifty pounds of sugar in. Let it cook
for about two hours and keep stirring. After it
is taken off the fire, add four and a quarter fluid
ounces of imitation oil of cinnamon [which the

The apples must be washed and peeled (1). The apples are cooked on a stove for fifteen to twenty minutes, then run through a colander (2). The applesauce is poured into a twenty-gallon brass kettle, which is heated by an open fire. Note: The kettle must be cleaned with a solution of vinegar and baking soda before use (3). The applesauce is constantly stirred until it's hot enough to melt sugar. Then, using one five-pound bag at a time, in regular intervals, fifty pounds of sugar is poured in. The mixture must cook for about two hours, with constant stirring (4). "When you stir, you go once on one side, once on the other side, and once in the middle. You see, the bottom is narrow and that way it won't stick."—Pat Brooks

Mr. Brooks made the butter-stirring stick out of cypress. Wood with acid in it can't be used because it will taste. He likes yellow poplar the best.

Brookses use] for desired flavor. Then pour into jars. Each stir yields about seventy-five jars [of varied sizes].

There's still the emptying of the peelings and the cleaning up to do, but we considered sampling the first stir with hot homemade biscuits a higher priority. Mrs. Brooks says, "Sometimes [we sell it], but most of the time we keep it. The family likes it. They must, every time I turn around they're asking for more."

APPLE BUTTER
LUCY YORK

"Use tart apples, such as Nancy June, Horse apples, or Transparents, as they cook up more quickly than sweet apples. Peel and core; cook until tender in small amount of water. Mash. Add crushed ginger root or cinnamon, if available. Sweeten with sorghum syrup. It will be the consistency of thick applesauce. The Dickersons called this 'apple marmalade' if it was cooked down to a jelly."

QUINCE HONEY

3 quinces
2 pounds sugar
2 cups water

Grate the quinces. Boil the sugar and water and add grated quinces. Let boil 20 minutes. Seal in jars. (Pear honey is made the same way, substituting 3 small pears for the quinces.)

HUCKLEBERRIES IN MOLASSES

Huckleberries should be picked ripe. When ready to use, place the huckleberries in a smooth stone jar. Cover them over the top with molasses (homemade syrup). Cut brown paper, cover it with paste and fasten 6 or 7 layers over the top of the jar, and tie on. Put in a cool place.

CROCK GRAPES

Collect dry, sound fox grapes. Pack them in a churn and pour boiling hot fresh molasses or syrup over them. Then take 2 clean cloths. Dip the first in hot beeswax and the second in hot tallow and tie each cloth separately around the top of the churn. Make this in the fall when the grapes are fresh and ripe. Then set the churn in a cool place until winter. They can be eaten during the winter after they get mildly fermented.

SPICED GRAPES

GLADYS NICHOLS

"The old-timers picked grapes and put them in jars. They'd pour cane syrup over them to preserve their grapes." This relish is good with meat, vegetables, and bread.

7 pounds grapes (Concord or wine)
1 cup fruit vinegar
5 pounds sugar
2 teaspoons cinnamon
1 teaspoon cloves
1 teaspoon allspice

Wash, stem, and pulp the grapes. Put the pulp, with seeds, over the fire and cook until the seeds come free. Remove the seeds. Add skins and remaining ingredients and cook until thick, then can.

4 The Pasture

Daddy didn't think you had much if
you didn't have meat on the table.
—Billy Long

For many Appalachian families, hogs and chickens were the primary livestock raised on the farm. Chickens were set out in the yard each morning to forage for insects and plants and put up in a coop in the evening. Laying hens might be confined to a pen and coop so that their laying spots could be more easily managed. Hogs were free-ranging and would spend the spring and summer foraging in the surrounding forests for foodstuffs like acorns, mushrooms, berries, and wild tubers. The hogs' ears would be notched, helping farmers identify their herd when it was time to round them up in the late fall for slaughter.

Beef cattle rose in popularity in the latter half of the twentieth century and is now second only to chickens for livestock raised in southern Appalachia. Grass-fed beef cattle, pastured in picturesque, mountainous landscapes, is now commonplace throughout the region. Rare, but still present, are sheep for wool and meat, along with goats, most raised for milk but some for meat (perhaps due to the growing Hispanic population).

Pork

In previous generations, pork was an essential part of the overall diet, including traditional delicacies such as souse meat, scrapple, hog's head stew, and cracklins. Old-timers adamantly stood by their belief that virtually no part of the hog should be thrown away. This is evidenced by the recipes that follow, which include such things as the head, tongue, brain, snout or "rooter," ears, liver, heart, lungs or "lights," skin, intestines, feet, and even tail. Use of the entire hog is clearly reminiscent of the pioneer traditions of conservation and utility, as every part found both a creative and practical use.

Billy Long remembered when he and his father raised hogs in the mountains:

When I was growing up and when we was raising our family, we had plenty of scraps. Young'uns are all the time wasting stuff, you know. I can feed a good hog on scraps; I mean feed him good on things like potato peelings.

My daddy also had hogs out in the mountains all the time, and I had [them too] for several years after he died. We'd just turn them out to feed themselves in the woods and go to them all along through the year to look after them. We had them marked, and we knew our mark, too. We had it registered. It was a "over half crop" in the right ear and "split and under bit" in the left. An over half crop was a cut right straight down about halfway on the hog's ear—about two inches—from the end. And for the under bit, we'd just double the ear up and take out a nick—what we called a small form. Our mark was always pretty hard [to mistake] to me, and it was kind of unusual.

I never was much of a meat eater, but Daddy didn't think you had much if you didn't have meat on the table. I remember he'd tell about eating dinner one time with somebody. When they started eating, the fellow he eat with said, "We're out of meat here. It seems like when you're out of meat, you're just about out of everything." Another old fellow there said, "Yeah, and it's just about that way, too." I never did care that much for it, but when people ate a lot of pork they seemed to live longer than they do now.

Pork Recipes

Esco Pitts explains how the various parts of the hog were used in his family:

We always fattened our hogs in a floored pen and topped them off on corn. Of course, they could get fat in the mountains eating chestnuts, but the meat from chestnuts would be streaked and flabby. We didn't like it. So we would always catch our hogs and bring them in and pen them and top them off on corn. That'd make the meat solid and firm and produced more gravy, and we liked gravy. I was raised on meat and gravy and sorghum syrup and corn bread.

Then when we killed a hog in the fall, we would dress it and take the entrails out; and my daddy would slice it up into middlings and hams and shoulders, and salt it away in the smokehouse. My mother was a conservative person, and she didn't waste anything. So she would clean the head good—take the eyes out—and put that in a pot and cook it until all the meat come off the bone. She made pressed meat out of that. That was something good to eat. And when my mother would fix a mess of meat to cook, she would peel off the skin, I guess. I have seen her put a bunch of skins in the skillet and fry them good and crisp, and us children would just eat them to beat the band.

And I like hog's feet. We would take the hoofs off and clean the feet good and cook them. There was more bones in a hog's feet than there is in all the rest of the hog, but it's awful good meat. You can't get much out of it, but it has such a good flavor. You can suck the bone and get what meat you want.

My mother would also take a hog's entrails and split them open. She had a spout off the ground where the water was running down to the branch, and she would take them entrails and wash them off good and clean, put them in the pot, and boil them down

to what she called chitlins. And then she would sea-
son bread with cracklins and make shortnin' bread.
You take a pone of cracklin bread warm out of the
oven and a glass of sweet milk or buttermilk, and
you had a meal that was fit for a king.

For every part of the hog, there are as many favorite recipes as there are cooks. We begin our pork cooking section with the preparation of less well known pork dishes and conclude with more conventional ones.

THE HEAD

LETTIE CHASTAIN: *Hog's head is good.*
You clean the head, boil it, and get the good, lean
meat off it. Mother used to make pressed meat out
of hog's head and that used to be the best stuff.

Hog's head is also called souse, souse meat, head cheese, or pressed hog's head. Prepare the raw hog's head as follows:

Trim, scrape, or singe off any hairs or bristles that are left. If you intend to use the ears, brains, snout, tongue, or jowls for any purpose other than souse, remove them and set them aside to soak. Otherwise leave them on the head to be ground up. Note that the ears are gristly and when ground up into souse, they leave white flukes of gristle in the meat. This is not harmful, but some find it unattractive.

Cut out the eyes. The bulk of the head is now halved or quartered with an ax, or left whole—depending on the size of your pot—and while still fresh it is put in a pot of fresh water, usually to soak overnight. This soaking removes the remaining blood from the meat.

After soaking, rinse the head until the rinse water runs clear. Then put it in a pot of clean, salty water and cook it slowly until it is good and

tender, and the meat begins to fall off the bones. Then remove all meat from the bones and run through a food chopper. Seasoning depends on your own taste. Some use, per head, 1 tablespoon sage, ½ teaspoon ground red pepper, and salt and black pepper to taste. Others use 1 onion, 1 pod of strong red pepper chopped fine, and 1 teaspoon salt.

Beulah Perry uses a little red and black pepper, an onion, a little cornmeal, sage, and garlic to taste. Evie Carpenter adds a little vinegar, along with sage, black pepper, and onion.

The meat and seasoning are thoroughly mixed and then put into capped jars, in a mold, or onto a plate covered with a clean white cloth. Then, if it is not to be eaten immediately, it is put into the smokehouse, where the winter weather will keep it fresh. It can be eaten cold or hot.

Another method is to proceed as before through the seasoning step, then put the mixture in a skillet; place the skillet on the back of the wood stove until the grease is runny. Remove from the fire, put a plate on top of the meat, and apply pressure to remove grease. Repeat until all the grease is poured off. Remove the plate, put the meat on a clean plate, and keep in a cold place. Slice as needed.

SOUSE MEAT

DAISY JUSTUS
1 hog's head
Salt
4 teaspoons pepper
2 teaspoons red pepper
2½ teaspoons allspice
3 teaspoons cloves
Vinegar (optional)

Clean the hog's head by removing snout, eyes, ears, brains, and all skin. Trim off fat. Cut head in 4 pieces and soak in salt water (½ cup salt to 1 gallon cold water) for 3 hours to draw out blood. Drain off salt water and wash well in cold water. (Heart, tongue, and other meat trimmings may be cooked with head meat.) Cover meat with hot water and boil until all meat can be removed from the bones. Remove all meat from bones. Strain broth and measure. This will make about 6 pounds of meat. Add about 3 tablespoons salt, the other seasonings, and 2 quarts broth in which meat is boiled. Mix thoroughly. Add a little vinegar, if desired. Cook mixture 15 to 20 minutes. Pour into a large square pan or a big stone crock. Cover with a clean cloth and weight down. Refrigerate and cut into slices as needed. May be canned by putting into clean jars within 1 inch of top of jar. Seal and process in pressure cooker 1 hour 15 minutes at 10 pounds pressure.

MINCEMEAT

DAISY JUSTUS

1 hog's head
4 cups dried apples
1 pound raisins
1 dozen oranges, peeled and seeded
5 pounds sugar
1 to 2 quarts grape juice

Clean hog's head as for souse meat (see preceding recipe). Cook until tender, then strain off broth and remove bone. Put into a large pot. Cook dried apples until tender. Add to hog's meat, along with remaining ingredients. Cook as if making apple butter. Simmer and stir until thick enough to be used as pie filling, or eat as is with bread.

SCRAPPLE

Mrs. Mann Norton told us how to make scrapple:

Take the head and take the eyeballs out, and the ears. Then you got all the hairs off of it. You put it in a big pot and cooked it till the meat just turned loose of the main big bone. You lifted them bones out and laid your meat over in there and felt of it with your hands to see if they wasn't no bones in it. Then you strain your liquid through a strainer so the little bones would come out. Put your liquid back in a pot and put that mashed meat back in that liquid. Put your sage and pepper in there. Then you stir it till it got to boiling. Then you stick plain cornmeal in there till it's just plumb thick. Then you pour it up in a mold and cut it off and fry it and brown it. Tastes just like fish.

(See also a recipe for Hog's Head Stew on page 203.)

JOWLS

The jowls are fatty, so they are often removed rather than being combined with the souse meat. Some people salt them down and cure them just like hams or middling meat, then save them until warm weather to be boiled in with vegetables. Others grind them up with the sausage meat. Bill Lamb told us, "You fry it. Now you're talking about part of a hog that I love is the jowls. They ain't a better tasting bite of meat in a hog than the jowl is."

TONGUE

Clean by pouring boiling water over it and scraping it. Then boil until tender in a little salt water, with pepper added if you wish. Slice and serve.

BRAIN

Most of our contacts put the hog's brains in hot water to loosen the veil of skin covering them. Then they boil them in 1 cup water, adding salt and pepper to taste while stirring. When cooked, they are mashed with a potato masher and, usually, scrambled with eggs. Others let the brains stand in cold water for 1 to 2 hours, then drain them and remove any unwanted fibers. The brains are then cooked, as above.

SNOUT

The snout is often cleaned and roasted. Mann Norton said: "Lot of people throwed away what they called the rooter. Oh, I forbid that. I'd rather have that as any part of the hog. Oh, that's good eating."

LIVER

Most of our contacts used the liver for liver pudding or liver mush. They made it as follows:

1 hog's liver
½ to 1 cup sifted cornmeal to thicken
Salt to taste
½ teaspoon black pepper
2 tablespoons sage
Ground red pepper (optional)

Cut up the liver, wash it well, and remove the skin. Boil until tender in salted water. Remove and run through a colander until fine, or smash well. Mix the meat with 1 cup of the broth it was cooked in. Bring to a boil slowly, stirring in sifted cornmeal until thick. Also stir in salt to taste, black pepper, sage, and a little red pepper if desired. Pour into a mold and let sit until cold. Slice and eat. Some eat it as sandwich meat or sliced and fried in bacon fat. According to Lucy, "Liver mush serves as bread and meat for a meal."

HEART

None of our contacts used the heart by itself. Neither did any of them throw it away, though. Some cleaned it and canned it with backbones and ribs for use later in stews. Some boiled the heart, backbone, and lights—lungs—together for stew; and one boiled heart, tail, kidneys, and tongue together for stew.

LIGHTS, OR LUNGS

Nowhere did we run into as much difference of opinion as with this item. One participant said, "It's very good—*very* good." Another said, "Lots of folks like the lights, but I never did." Another comment was simply, "Feed them to the dogs!"

We did get a few recipes: Boil them in just enough salted water to cover them after cleaning them well. Don't use too much water or it will steal some of their flavor. If there isn't any water left when they're done, it's better. Cook them down to the consistency of gravy, mash, and serve. They cannot be kept. Another chopped up the lights with the liver and tongue. She added a chopped onion, red pepper, and salt and cooked until tender.

STOMACH, PAUNCH, OR PUNCH

Cut the stomach free of intestines, split, and wash out well. Scrape it down and put in salt water for 3 days. Then rinse, cut up, and cook like chitlins. Most of our contacts also removed the inside layer when cutting it up prior to frying.

INTESTINES (CHITTERLINGS OR CHITLINS)

Sections of the intestine are put in a jar of salt water and allowed to sit for 3 or 4 days. Then they are taken out, rinsed, washed, and rinsed again. In winter, they can be lightly salted, put up in jars, and kept for a few days before cooking. When cooking, cut up in small pieces and remove any unwanted layers of lining. Then boil in salt water with half a pod of pepper until tender. Dip in a batter of flour, water, and baking powder (and an egg, if desired) and fry; or roll in cornmeal and fry.

FEET

Rake hot coals out on the fireplace hearth. Put the feet on the hearth with the hooves against the coals. When very hot, the hooves can be sliced out of the meat easily, and the remainder of the hair scraped or singed off, and the meat scraped clean. Then put in a pan of salt water and cook; or roast. The feet can also be boiled in salty water until the meat slips off the hoofs. They can also be pickled.

Mann Norton said, "Doc Neville, now he always wanted the feet. I'd pack them in a shoebox just as full as I could get it and mail them to him."

BACKBONES AND RIBS

These can be put together and stewed like chicken parts or barbecued or canned with a teaspoon of salt per quart can.

TAIL

Often the tail was saved for use in stews. One contact made a stew of feet, ears, tail, salt, and red pepper, boiled until tender.

A black iron pot is used for rendering fat into lard and cracklins.

SAUSAGE

Use any combination of lean meat not used otherwise. This includes trimmings of lean meat from ham, shoulders, middling meat, and so on; it can also include the tenderloin, meat from the head, and, if you wish, the jowls. Some people parch their own red pepper in front of the fireplace, crush it, and then add it to the sausage.

10 pounds of lean pork
¼ cup salt
½ cup brown sugar
2 tablespoons sage
2 teaspoons black pepper
2 teaspoons red pepper

Run the pork through a sausage grinder, mix in the remaining ingredients well, and fry until browned but not completely cooked since it has to be reheated when served. Pack it into jars halfway to three-fourths full while still very hot. Pour hot grease over the top, close the jars, and turn them upside down to cool. When the grease cools,

The cracklins will be all that remain from this boiling pot of pork fat. These will be the main ingredient in the winter's cracklin corn bread.

it seals the lids shut and the sausage will keep until you are ready to use it. It is usually stored with the jars upside down.

FOUR OTHER WAYS TO KEEP SAUSAGE

1. Roll the sausage into balls, pack them in a churn jar, pour hot grease over the top, tie a cloth over the lid, and set the jar in the water trough of your springhouse.
2. Pack the sausage in sections of cleaned small intestine, tie the intestine off at both ends, and hang from the joists of the smokehouse for curing.
3. Remove the ear from a corn shuck. Wash the shuck thoroughly and pack the sausage inside. Tie the end of the shuck closed with string or wire and hang in the smokehouse.
4. Pack in small, clean, white cloth sacks and hang in the smokehouse.

A baked ham ready for Sunday dinner.

LARD AND CRACKLINS

The fat is trimmed from entrails, hams, shoulders, middling meat, and so on. It may be left out all night in the lard pot so the cold weather can solidify it, making it easier to cut. In the morning, the fat is cut into pieces about the size of hens' eggs and put in a pot containing just enough water to keep the fat from sticking to the sides when cooked. The pot is then placed over a fire and the fat is allowed to cook slowly. Stir the fat often. By evening, the grease will have boiled out, the water evaporated, and the hard residue, called "cracklins," will have fallen to the bottom. Add soda if you don't want many cracklins. The soda also keeps the fat from smelling while cooking and from tasting strong. The liquid fat is poured into containers, allowed to harden into lard, and used all winter for cooking. The cracklins are saved for bread.

FRIED FATBACK

RUTH HOLCOMB

"Try rolling fatback meat in cornmeal and frying that in grease until the meat is done. That's *real* good."

Chicken

Most of the people we talked to about poultry had raised and killed their own chickens for eating. None of them enjoyed the task of "dressing" them—the entire process from killing the chicken to cutting them up—but most of them agreed that poultry can add variety to the menu and is a delightful and economic alternative to beef and pork.

In this section, we show a basic method that can be used to dress most birds, and we present a variety of cooking methods. The South is famous for its fried chicken, but we found that the other chicken dishes such as dumplings, pies, and simple roasted or stewed meat are enjoyed almost as much. Fried chicken was served in summer when there were young fryers to kill. Chicken and dumplings were cooked in the winter when it was necessary to kill a hen or rooster. Their meat is tougher and requires a longer time cooking.

LINDA GARLAND: *On a cool foggy July morning my mother called to tell me she and my father were getting ready to kill chickens. I told her to get started and I would be there soon. I ate a quick bite of breakfast, knowing that the episode ahead could do strange things to one with an empty stomach, especially at seven o'clock in the morning. When I arrived at my parents' home, they had already killed ten of the fifteen chickens and were busily at work skinning them. I watched them kill the remaining five, as my two sons, Seth and Nolan, who are always entertained by unusual events, looked on.*

Marinda Brown comments on killing chickens:

In, I guess, the early forties, we grew chickens [fryers] and furnished some of the summer camps.

We furnished the Athens Y camp one time and the boys' camps. Then another time we furnished the girls' camp and some of the hotels around. We dressed sometimes a hundred at a time and took [them] to those camps.

My husband would kill them. We'd tie them up on a line, and he'd go along and cut the jugular vein and we'd let them hang till they dripped blood. That's the way they were killed. We'd hire some of the women in the community to come in on certain days and help dress those chickens. We'd scald them. We had a big old washpot out there to scald the chickens in, then we'd pull the feathers off and dress them out in the house. We did that for several summers. Sometimes we'd let people come in and dress their own chickens if they had a bunch they wanted to clean.

And then later we had this little building out here with running water in it, and we got a chicken picker to pick the feathers off. It was kind of a barrel-like thing, and it had little rubber things [suctions] on it that stuck up so far. And it would turn, and as it turned those suctions would pull the feathers off. It worked good. It would clean the feathers off. You had to be mighty careful and not get your scalding water too hot or it would bring the skin, too, but if you got them scalded just right it would take every feather off. 'Course there were lots of pin feathers that had to be picked off by hand.

My family likes fried chicken mighty good. That's something I guess we've eaten more of than any other one kind of meat. Since we killed chickens, you know, we could have all we wanted to eat any time we wanted them. I guess we ate more fried chicken and gravy on mashed potatoes or rice than anything. That was about their most favorite.

O. S. Garland wrings a chicken's neck.

Mr. Garland chops the chicken's neck for bleeding.

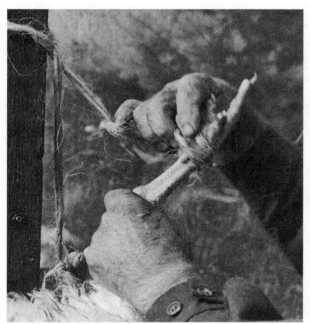

Using a piece of twine, Mr. Garland hangs the chicken up by its feet.

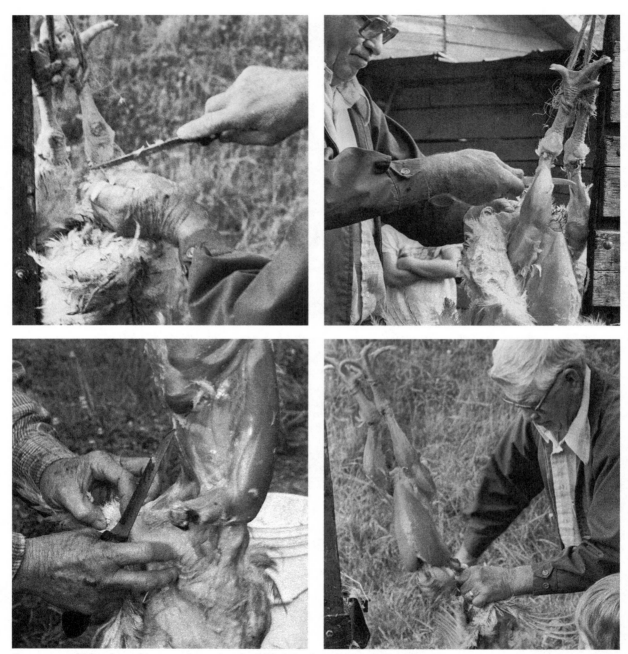

To prepare a chicken for cooking, start by cutting the skin away where the feet and legs connect, pulling the skin away and down the body of the chicken, using a knife to cut it away from the joints of the chicken's body where it is connected, and cutting it off at the neck.

When the skinning is completed, cut through the joint where the legs and feet connect, leaving the feet to throw into a bucket for feet, feathers, heads, and entrails.

Blanche Harkins adds: "We used to raise our chickens and we'd kill them, scald them, and dress them. We singed the hair off of them using paper. You have to use a paper bag; if you use paper with dark ink it will smoke and darken the chicken. A paper bag won't do that. Then rinse the chicken good and dress it."

The following method is what most of our contacts call the "old-timey way" of cutting up a chicken. Following these instructions will yield the reader four separate pieces of breast: the pulleybone (wishbone), center breast, and two side breasts. For a family that loves white meat, this helps to stretch the supply. Mary Ellen Means describes how to use this method in the following illustrations:

AUNT ADDIE NORTON: *Chicken is good fried in a lot of ways. If you buy the chicken at the store already cut and fixed, you thaw it out, naturally. If it's never been frozen I always just salt mine good. Not too much, just enough to make it salty like. Roll it in flour. I use flour or meal. I love my chicken fixed in meal a lot of times instead of flour. Dampen your chicken good before you roll it in meal or flour or whatever you're rolling it in. You got to get it damp so it [the meal or flour] will stick to it, you know. Dampen it with water, milk, anything you want to put in it. Make a paste if you want to fix it that way. A lot of folks do it that way. Just like making a batter and rolling your chicken in that. Then you use salt and pepper. I just guess at it and put whatever I think that it needs. Then you put it in your grease to fry or you can fry it in the oven. Put in just a little bit of grease and put it in and bake it. 'Course I use Crisco lard. It won't soak into it. I never was very good about frying chicken, I didn't think. Most people said I always had good chicken, though.*

BLANCHE HARKINS: *We had a black thick frying pan. Some people called them skillets but they're frying pans. Just put your grease in there. I use to use just pure lard. We'd cut up the chicken, roll it in flour, and have your grease hot enough to fry it when you put it in. Let that side brown, turn it over, and brown it. I put a lid on mine. I don't just fry it open. It takes about an hour to fry chicken and not fry it too fast. It won't be tender if you brown them too fast.*

EXIE DILLS: *Roll it in meal and gosh it is good! It don't take as much grease to fry it thataway as it does flour. [Gladys Nichols remembers using meal made by grinding up chestnuts.] Pepper it just like you do your flour and roll your pieces in it and lay it in your hot grease. It's good. Then make your gravy in there. Gee, that makes good chicken gravy, I think. Not ever'one has a taste like someone else. I like that.*

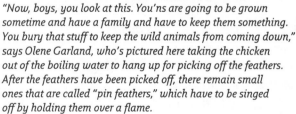

"Now, boys, you look at this. You'ns are going to be grown sometime and have a family and have to keep them something. You bury that stuff to keep the wild animals from coming down," says Olene Garland, who's pictured here taking the chicken out of the boiling water to hang up for picking off the feathers. After the feathers have been picked off, there remain small ones that are called "pin feathers," which have to be singed off by holding them over a flame.

MARY ELLEN MEANS: *Salt and pepper the chicken; roll in flour. Fry in lard with three table-spoons of butter added to make the chicken brown well. Brown both sides, cover with a tight lid, and cook on low temperature for thirty minutes. Check in ten minutes to see that it's not burning. After thirty minutes, take the lid off and remove top pieces that have not been submerged in grease. Turn heat up to medium and fry until remaining pieces get crispy. Take out and drain on paper towel and serve.*

Wash the chickens well, and they're ready to start cutting up. Using a sharp knife, cut through the skin of the abdomen along a straight line from the end of the breastbone to within half an inch of the vent. Keep the vent small. Insert your forefinger into the opening and circle your finger around the intestine, leading back to the vent. Lift the intestine up, then cut the skin about three-fourths around and completely encircling the vent. Holding the carcass with one hand, insert your other hand through the opening and locate the gizzard near the center of the cavity. Grasp the gizzard and draw the entrails out of the cavity. "You have to soak the cut-up chickens in salt water to draw the rest of the blood out of them. I always soak mine about an hour."

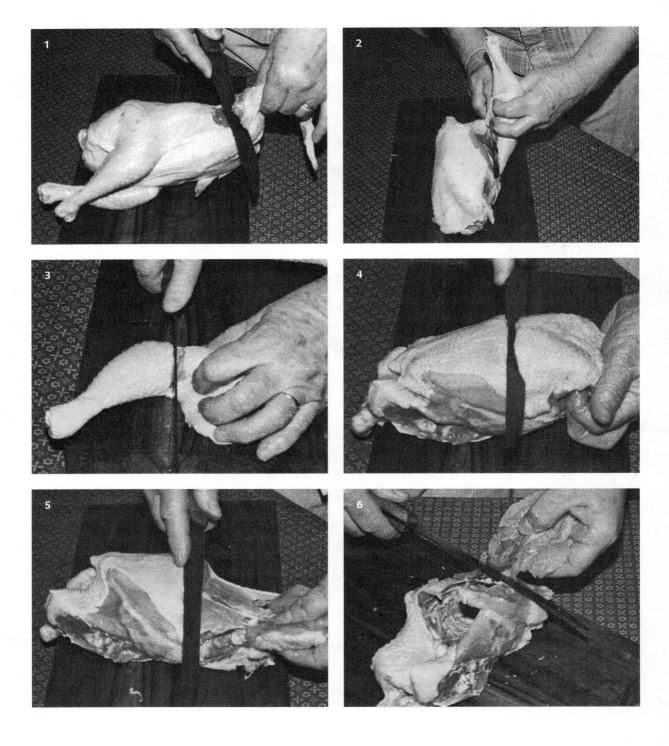

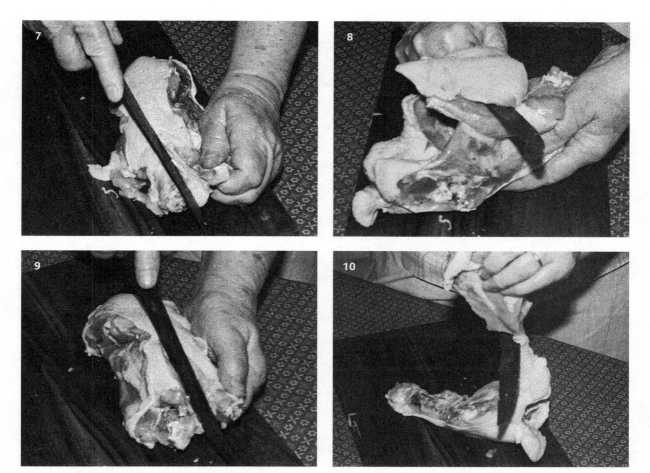

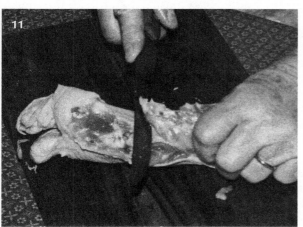

Pull back the wing, cutting away from the thigh toward yourself with a sharp knife, removing the wing (1). Repeat with the other side. Turn the chicken on its back and, grasping the drumstick, cut the thigh off at the joint (2). The thigh and drumstick will be cut off together. To separate, sever at the joint (3). With the chicken breast side up, grasp at the wing end and cut straight down about one third of the way through the body from the wing end (4). The incision will be approximately one inch deep. Then cut back until you meet your hand grasping the end. Pull back the "pulleybone" (or wishbone) and break off at the joint (5). Still holding the wing end, cut straight back toward your hand under the cartilage of the breastbone until you reach two joints left from the wings (6). Pull this center breast up and break it off at these joints (7). Turn the chicken over. Cut under the two knuckles exposed at the neck and down the neck to the ribs on the back of the chicken (8). Turn the bird back over and split the exposed cartilage (left-over from the center breast) down to the center (9). Turn it over again, grasp the knuckles one at a time and pull them toward the tail of the chicken (10). This will remove each side breast. Back, ribs, and neck remain. Cut at the back of the ribs to make two pieces: neck and ribs; and back (11).

During our visit with Ione Dickerson, she was cooking fried chicken in an iron skillet on her wood stove. We forgot about it while we were talking and it almost burned. She pulled it away from the heat and placed a stick of wood under one side of the pan, arranging the chicken on the raised side so that the grease would drain off. She said disgustedly, "Well, pot can't call the kettle black for they're both black!"

FRIED CHICKEN

For each pound of chicken mix together the following flour mixture to dip or shake chicken in.

¼ cup flour
1 teaspoon paprika
½ teaspoon salt
¼ teaspoon pepper

Put the flour mixture in a pie plate to roll chicken pieces in or in a paper bag to drop chicken in and shake until coated. Leftover flour can be saved for gravy. Drop chicken pieces into a hot skillet with a ¼-inch layer of lard, shortening, or oil. Turn pieces to brown evenly. Once the pieces are lightly browned, cover, then reduce heat and fry slowly until tender—30 to 45 minutes, depending on size of chicken pieces. Turn often but carefully, being careful not to pierce the chicken with the fork.

BROILED CHICKEN

Lay split bird, skin side down, on a broiler rack or in a shallow pan. Brush well with melted butter or other fat. Place under preheated broiler. Broil slowly, regulating the heat or changing the rack position so chicken just begins to color lightly after cooking for 10 to 12 minutes. Turn then brush with melted butter about every 10 minutes as browning increases. Broil until tender and evenly browned, 30 to 40 minutes, according to size. Season to taste.

STEWED CHICKEN

Cover chicken in a pot with water and bring to a boil; lower heat and let cook until tender. Pull the meat off the bone, putting the meat back into the broth. Stewed chicken may be eaten plain, poured over mashed potatoes or dressing, or used for making dumplings.

BARBECUED CHICKEN

Cut chicken in half sections or into serving pieces. Place aluminum foil in a shallow pan; place chicken on foil and pour your favorite barbecue sauce over it (try the recipes in our Gravies and Sauces section, pages 207–9). Add salt and pepper to taste. Pull aluminum foil over chicken, making sure it is covered tightly and there are no holes for juice to boil out. Bake in 325°F to 350°F oven until chicken is tender.

OLD-FASHIONED CHICKEN PIE

OLENE GARLAND

3 cups chicken broth

2 tablespoons flour

1 fryer, boiled and boned

2 hard-boiled eggs, chopped

Salt and pepper to taste

Biscuit dough

Thicken broth with flour. Add chicken, chopped eggs, and salt and pepper. Pour into a large casserole dish. Make up a recipe for biscuits; roll and cut out thin with a biscuit cutter or a glass. Place the biscuits on top of the chicken. Bake 15 to 20 minutes in a 400°F oven.

Variation: Leftover vegetables may be added to the broth mixture. Peas and carrots are used by most cooks.

CHICKEN AND DUMPLINGS

ARIZONA DICKERSON

1 chicken

¼ cup rendered chicken fat

3 to 6 tablespoons flour

Salt and pepper to taste

Stew the chicken in water to cover, then remove from the broth; cut it up. Mix other ingredients together and pour into 3 or 4 cups of the broth, stirring constantly until it thickens slightly.

DUMPLINGS

¾ cup sifted flour

2½ teaspoons baking powder

½ teaspoon salt

1 egg

⅓ cup milk

To make the dumplings, mix dry ingredients. Add egg and milk and beat. Drop by small spoonfuls into the boiling chicken gravy. Cover pot tightly and cook 15 minutes. Do not remove the lid while dumplings are cooking. The steam is necessary for them to be light. To serve, spoon out dumplings and gravy together into dish.

Beef

In the context of the first edition of this cookbook, beef was already an established staple for most families. At least one cow was kept for breeding in order to raise a few calves each year. Area cattle sales were and remain popular events where local farmers trade and sell their cattle. Programs through local chapters of the Future Farmers of America and 4-H introduce young prospective cattle farmers to the processes of husbandry and cultivation of beef.

Slaughtering beef was once done by families with the help of neighbors and friends. Today, local slaughtering houses do much of the meat processing, relieving families from the once all-day affair.

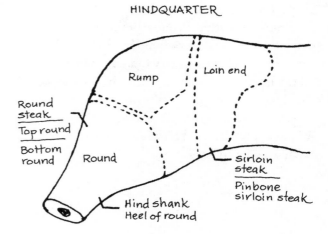

HINDQUARTER

Garnet cuts the round and rump portions in eight to ten pound chunks, removing the bone and fat.

As with pork, when slaughtering was done at home, some of the beef was salted down and put into the smokehouse to dry and cure; and much of the remainder was canned. Garnet Lovell's wife, Blanche, told us how she prepared dried beef. Slice off a little piece the thickness of a fifty-cent piece. Let it soak just a little, until it is soft. Roll the beef in flour and fry it; you have a piece of regular steak. Or lay it out in the hot grease and cook it until it is tender and make milk gravy on top of that. She said, "That is the way they used to do it fifty years ago, and still do it that way today. If you are going to stew it, just throw it in water with vegetables in it."

The fat from the meat may be used in several different ways. Some of it was made into tallow. Garnet said, "We don't do anything with it [ourselves, but] it makes good shoe grease, [and] old people used to grease the bottom of kid's feet and chests with it for croup."

Beef Recipes

GELATINED BEEF

Simmer together a couple pounds of beef from the neck and some soup bones from the shin, until the meat is very tender. Take it out of the broth, remove all bone, skin, and sinew, and place in a bowl. Pour the broth over the meat. Place a weight on it, and let it all congeal. When ready, slice and serve cold, or rub slices with butter and broil.

MEAT LOAF
GLADYS NICHOLS
"Now that's a cheap meat loaf."
1 pound ground beef
1 pound ground pork
1 cup cracker meal or bread crumbs
7 ounces tomato sauce
1 or 2 eggs
1 small onion, chopped
Salt and pepper to taste
Mix together all the ingredients and put into a baking dish. Bake in a 350°F oven for 45 to 60 minutes.

ARIZONA DICKERSON'S MEAT LOAF VARIATIONS

- Make your ground meat into patties and wrap a strip of raw bacon around each one. Fry them until they're well done. Serve for breakfast.
- Shape your ground meat into pyramid-shaped cones and bake in a 325°F oven until they're done.
- Make cones of your ground beef and roll in dry, uncooked rice. Place in a shallow pan and cover with a mixture of tomato juice and stock from chicken. Bake in a moderate oven until done.

COW'S TONGUE

Boil the cow's tongue until tender. Then peel off the outer skin, and boil in salt water until very tender. Slice thin, and serve with mustard or relish.

SUPPER ON A PIECE OF BREAD

MARGARET NORTON

1 ½ pounds ground beef

1 teaspoon salt

⅛ teaspoon pepper

2 eggs

½ cup bread crumbs

¾ cup sweet milk

1 onion cooked in butter

Bread dough for 1 loaf

Cheese, Swiss or cheddar, cut in strips,
    enough to decorate

Mix all (except the bread dough and cheese) together, and shape into an oblong (or to fit whatever baking pan you use). Make bread as if you were making white biscuits, but roll out oblong a little larger than the meat loaf. Place meat loaf on top and bake. If edges of bread get too brown, put aluminum foil under bread and bring up over the edge. Bake 45 minutes in a 325°F oven. Ten minutes before taking out, decorate top with cheese. You can crisscross the cheese and make it really pretty. This is a whole meal in itself—with milk, coffee, or tea.

ROAST

DOROTHY BECK

"In my roast I always flour it good and put it in the roaster. I usually wrap it in aluminum foil. I put a whole onion in with it and I put about a cup of Coca-Cola and a little water over it and cook it slow [250° to 300°F] in the oven."

SWISS STEAK

2 pounds round steak, 2 inches thick

½ cup flour combined with 1 teaspoon salt
    and a dash of pepper

¼ cup bacon or ham drippings

2 cups tomatoes, boiled until tender

Pound flour mixture into both sides of steak. Heat fat in large skillet or casserole dish and sear the steak. Add boiled tomatoes, cover casserole closely, and place in a slow 275°F oven about 2 hours until done. Make a gravy of drippings and pour over steak. Yield: 6 servings.

BEEF STEW

1 ½ pounds short ribs, shank, neck, flank,
    plate, rump, or brisket

¼ cup flour

1 ½ teaspoons salt

¼ teaspoon pepper

1 pint stewed and drained tomatoes

2 small onions

1 cup cubed carrots

4 cups potatoes, cut in quarters

Remove meat from the bone, cut in 1½-inch cubes. Mix flour with salt and pepper and roll cubes of meat in it. Heat some of fat from meat in frying pan. Add cubes of meat and brown. Place meat with browned fat into a stewing pot. Add the pint of tomatoes. Simmer until tender (about 3 hours). Add onions, carrots, and potatoes the last hour of cooking. Yield: 14 servings.

PAN-FRIED LIVER

Remove the skin and veins from young beef liver and cut it into ½-inch slices. Season the slices of liver with salt and pepper, then coat with flour. Fry quickly in shallow hot bacon drippings until done. Serve with crisp bacon.

Milk and Butter

In the past, every home in this area probably had at least one milk cow. Families depended on the cow for milk, buttermilk, butter, and cottage cheese. To get the butter and buttermilk, one had to churn. Although there are those who still do churn in this part of the country, it is quickly becoming a thing of the past. Inez Taylor is one of the few who still enjoys keeping a milk cow:

You see, Mama had four girls and five boys. None of the boys learned to milk. I guess I was about twelve or thirteen when I learned. She'd go to milk, and she'd have a cow there that was dry, and I'd get in there and play with it. Mama'd tell me to pull on the cow's tit to learn how to milk and that's the way I learned how.

I churn about once or twice a week, and I enjoy it. I have two cows, but I just milk one because one is dry. I get a gallon of a morning and half a gallon at night. You know, there's a man that buys milk and butter from me, and I told him, "I wish I had a place big enough and all the cows I wanted and that all I had to do is just fool with cows, because I love animals."

Tammy Ledford's grandmother Ruth Ledford remembers learning to churn and still enjoys it:

My mother taught me how to churn. It really wasn't hard when I was learning, but churning is never easy. Some milk is harder to churn than others. It is according to the kind of cow it is, I reckon. My mother churned a lot—about every other day. I churn about three times a week. My grandmother had a churn and it was square. It had two big dashers of the thing that went in the middle of it and it had a wheel-like thing and you turned it around and around. It had pedals on it like bicycle pedals that you turned with

your hands. Gosh, I loved to churn for her 'cause man you could just fly and it didn't take you long to churn. My daughter Liz used to churn all of the time and I was like her. I used to go to Granny's just to get to churn.

After you milk the cow, bring the milk in and strain it into a jar. Let the milk stay in the refrigerator for a few days to let the cream "rise on it." Inez Taylor told us what she does after the cream rises: "I take a spoon and run it around that cream, and I take it off and put it in a separate jar till I get what I need for a churning. And then I wash and scald my churn out real good and put that [cream] in it."

You need to have the churn at least half full, "about two to three gallons for a good churning," according to Gladys Nichols. After pouring up the cream, let it stand until it gets thick. The time required for the cream to clabber is determined by the temperature of the cream. Ruth Ledford said, "[In the summer] I let it set that night, and then the next morning it's ready to churn." Rittie Webb added that if it's hot weather, pouring a little buttermilk in it will start it to souring. Others told us that in winter it may take as long as three days if it is warmed on alternate sides by the fireplace. Gladys Nichols instructed us to "let it stay where it's warm till it sours, and then it'll clabber and be thick. Then it's ready to churn."

The clabbered cream must be churned as soon as it has thickened. If it is left too long, it will curdle and separate and making butter will not be as successful. On the other hand, good butter will not be made if it is churned too soon—while it is still "blinky milk," or sour milk.

Inez Taylor showed us how to test the cream for churning: "You can tell when it's ready to churn when you pull your churn to the side and it's thick and pulls away from the churn. A lot of people will go ahead and churn it before it's ready, but then their buttermilk is thin. I want mine thick."

Mrs. Ledford told us, "It's according to the temperature of the cream as to how long it takes to churn. The cream can be too cold or it can be too hot. It has to be just right. If it's just right, then it don't take but about twenty minutes [for the butter to start forming]. If the cream is real cold the butter doesn't gather, and you'll have to place [the churn] in a tub of warm water." Otherwise the butter will form small balls, which will not stick together. A small amount of hot water, stirred into the cold liquid with the dasher, will also help to gather the butter.

Inez Taylor explained what to do in warm weather: "Put your churn down in a bucket of ice. I do because I like all the water worked out of [my butter]. When it's warm weather it won't work all the water out without you do that." If the clabbered cream is too warm the result will be soft white puffy butter. To start churning, Rittie Webb suggested: "Take your dasher—it has to be scalded before you put it in there—and churn it just 'round and 'round like this." The more cream you have the more butter you get. Mrs. Ledford said:

The milk actually doesn't make the butter; the cream does. The butter comes to the top when [the cream] is churned. After you take the butter off, the milk that's left is the buttermilk. You make both butter and buttermilk at the same time. I don't ever churn the whole milk. I just have my cream and churn the cream. You won't have much buttermilk that way but you will have lots of butter.

Once churning is complete, butter can be molded and buttermilk "poured up."

Ruth Ledford scoops butter out of her churn with her hand and into a bowl of cold water.

Mrs. Ledford packages butter into a mold.

You'll know that the butter is starting to make when you see these little specks coming out of the top. I learned that from watching my mama, I guess. You turn the dasher as you take it up and down. I don't know if everybody does that or not, but I do. I think it helps the butter to gather. I don't know how long it takes after you see the specks but it usually takes about an hour and a half to do it all. It gets harder to churn when the butter starts to gather, too. You know that the butter is finished making because it all comes to the top.

After the butter is made, Stella Burrell said to "dip the butter off the top [by hand or with the dasher], and put it in a bowl in cold water and you wash the milk out of it. Some people use their hands, and some use a wooden paddle. I still have a wooden paddle I used. Work it out till it's firm. You mix about a half teaspoon of salt in it, and

Molded butter ready to store in a cool place.

Inez Taylor pours buttermilk into jars.

then while it is still soft, you mold it or put it in dishes." The buttermilk is "poured up" into jars for storage.

Besides using the clabbered milk for making butter, some people found other uses. Many of our contacts talked about eating the clabbered milk. Terry and Arizona Dickerson have eaten it often. Others dotted it on cobblers for an added flavor.

By placing the butter in the refrigerator, it will get cold and hard. Before refrigerators, contacts remember storing butter and milk along with other foods in their springs or springhouses or in water troughs inside their homes. Gladys Nichols described the function of a springhouse: "Where they had a spring, the old-timers would build a little house. And they built a box through that house that would hold water. And they put their milk and butter in containers in this box of water that continually run through there, and that's the way they kept it cool. They didn't have no refrigerator. Mama and Daddy had a springhouse over yonder, and I went and got butter and milk many a time."

IONE DICKERSON: *We just had a spring; we didn't have a [springhouse]. We had a spring about two hundred yards downhill from the house. It was cold water, and we put milk and butter in there.*

Cheese

Mrs. Monroe Reese and Mrs. Thelma Earp are both expert cheese makers. This section begins with interviews with Mrs. Reese and Mrs. Earp and incorporates material from Tedra Harmon, Harriet Echols, and Aunt Nora Garland.

The first person we talked with was Mrs. Reese. She showed us the process she follows for making blocks of cheese that she and her husband like best. On occasion, she has sold some to bring in a little extra money. She begins with two and a half gallons of refrigerated whole milk from their cow. She pours this all into a large pan and heats it on her wood stove until it is a little past lukewarm. She prefers a wood stove, as it gives a slower, steadier heat.

When the milk is warm, she takes the pan off the stove and adds one-fourth Hansen's cheese rennet tablet dissolved in one teacup of water and one-eighth Hansen's cheese color tablet dissolved in one teacup of water. Both these tablets are available in drugstores, and directions for their use are listed on the containers.

She lets the milk stand from fifteen to thirty minutes until it stiffens and gets jelly-like. Then she cuts it with a knife or spatula into tiny squares, also running the spatula under the surface as if cutting it into layers. Letting it stay there briefly, she then works the mixture until it is all broken up into pieces that are about the size of grains of corn. She works it gently, squeezing the custard-like substance until it is completely broken apart. Then she puts the pan back on the stove and heats the mixture slowly until it is almost as hot as the touch can stand, although not boiling. While reheating, the mixture is stirred constantly so that the curds will stay separated and not melt back together. She then removes the mixture from the stove and lets it cool from fifteen to thirty minutes. Next, she strains the contents through cheesecloth in the colander she has ready on her sink. She does not squeeze the mixture dry—she lets it drip naturally; and then she returns the mixture to the pan, adds a heaping teaspoonful of salt, and massages it in well.

Mrs. Reese starts her cheese-making process by heating the milk.

Finally, she puts the contents of the pan into a homemade press, which she has lined with cheesecloth. Adding weights in stages, she leaves it in the press overnight, or up to twelve hours, to press the cheese down into a firm block. She removes it from the press and dries it for a week in the open air with a cloth underneath the cheese to absorb any additional moisture. She turns it two times a day during this drying process, during which the cake of cheese forms a dry crust on the outside. It should not spoil for a month or more.

Before rennet tablets were available, cheese of this sort was still possible to make. Tedra Harmon remembers that when they killed a cow for butchering, they would get the stomach out, cut it open, and clean it well. Then they would stretch it out in one piece to dry like a banjo hide. After it was thoroughly dry, they rolled it up and hung it in a bag from a convenient rafter. Whenever his mother made cheese of the sort just described, she would use a tiny piece of the stomach lining (about the size of a thumbnail) to curdle the milk, just as the rennet tablets are

used now. He also remembers his mother using a small piece of the stomach lining when making light bread. He remembers it giving the bread a sour taste. The cheese his mother made was pressed into wooden hoops that were from twelve to fourteen inches in diameter. The cheese would be placed up in the attic to dry for six to eight weeks before being cut, and he remembers that the older the cheese got, the better it tasted.

Mrs. Thelma Earp makes a different kind of cheese. It can be eaten right away. In fact, it was so good that we wound up taking half a cake with

us in the car and nibbling on it all the way home. Before we got to her house, she had clabbered the milk and had it waiting in the refrigerator. To do this, she took whole milk, allowed the cream to rise, skimmed it off, and made butter. Then she added two to three tablespoons of buttermilk per gallon of skimmed milk and let it sit out for two days to sour. She put this in the refrigerator to await use.

When we arrived, she went right to work, pouring two gallons of the clabbered milk into a pan and heating it on the stove until it was a

little hotter than lukewarm. She said it should be pretty hot, but not boiling, and not so hot that it would burn your hands. Once the clabbered milk was thoroughly heated, she poured it into a strainer made with a cotton cloth pinned over a bucket with clothespins. She then gathered the corners of the cloth and squeezed the whey through the cloth, leaving the curd. "The best thing to do with the whey, now, is feed it to the hogs," she said, laughing.

She then put the curds in a bowl and added one and a half teaspoons of salt and a raw egg. (She prefers barnyard eggs to store-bought ones, as they make the cheese yellower.) She mixed it all in with her hands, readying it for cooking. Then she put a lump of butter about the size of a large hen egg into a big iron frying pan and melted it. She prefers a wood cookstove because it heats more evenly and slowly. When the butter was melted, she added curds and kept turning them in the pan over medium heat. When all the curds were melted enough to form a cake, she put them into a dish to cool. As they cooled, they formed a cake.

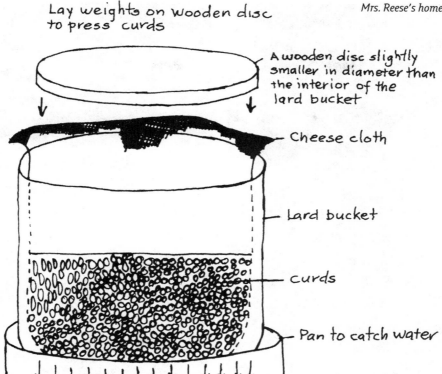

Lay weights on wooden disc to press curds

Mrs. Reese's homemade press.

A wooden disc slightly smaller in diameter than the interior of the lard bucket

Cheese cloth

Lard bucket

curds

Pan to catch water

HOLES IN BOTTOM OF LARD BUCKET ALLOWING WATER TO RUN OFF.

COTTAGE CHEESE

We asked Mrs. Harriet Echols to tell us how she makes cottage cheese. Below are her directions, with some additional comments from Mrs. Nora Garland.

To begin the process of making cottage cheese, pour about a gallon of raw (unpasteurized) whole milk into an enameled or metal pan. Any amount of milk may be used. The amount used here is what is preferred by Harriet Echols for her family. Mrs. Echols puts her pan of milk on the back of the wood stove in the winter or on a kitchen table during warm weather, so that it can sour slowly. This process may only take 1 day, or perhaps 2, according to the temperature. Mrs. Echols does not heat the milk at all before it clabbers. When on the stove, it is not over direct heat—only in a warm place.

After the milk clabbers, the cream is lifted off and refrigerated. The cream may be used later as sour cream in any recipe. The skimmed, clabbered milk is then heated over a low fire until it curdles. It is removed from the heat and poured into a colander or cheesecloth to drain all the water.

Mrs. Earp mixes the ingredients for cheese.

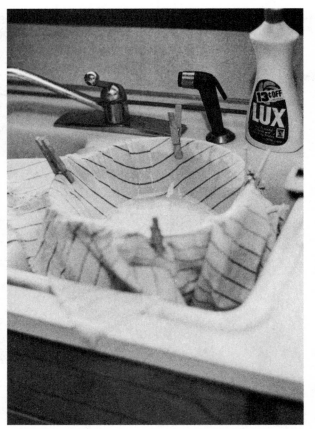

Mrs. Earp's strainer.

Final stages in making Mrs. Earp's cheese.

This usually takes a couple of hours. It may also be hung in a cloth overnight. Mrs. Nora Garland remembers that she put the curdled milk into a clean flour sack and let it drain overnight outside.

Both Mrs. Garland and Mrs. Echols told us they would work the cheese by putting it back into a pan or bowl and squeezing it with their hands or a spoon or spatula, getting out any remaining water. Mrs. Echols warned us not to work the cheese too vigorously or get the curds too fine. A little salt may be sprinkled into taste, and to make the cheese creamier some of the sour cream may be mixed in with it. The cottage cheese is then packed in small containers and refrigerated. It will keep several weeks in the refrigerator.

Cheese Soufflé

CHEESE SOUFFLÉ

MARGARET NORTON

3 eggs, separated
½ cup grated cheese
Salt and pepper to taste

Beat egg whites with an electric mixer until peaks are formed. Set aside. Mix together grated cheese and egg yolks. Add salt and pepper to taste. Fold the whites into the egg yolk mixture. Pour into a buttered baking dish and set the dish in a pan of cold water to keep the milk and egg mixture from burning. Bake at 350°F for 15 minutes. Yield: *4 servings.*

MACARONI AND CHEESE

1 cup macaroni, boiled
1 cup grated cheese
⅔ cup milk
1 to 2 eggs
Salt to taste
¼ cup soft bread crumbs

Place alternate layers of macaroni and cheese in a buttered baking dish, reserving 2 tablespoons of the cheese for the top. Beat the eggs; add milk and salt, and pour over macaroni. Sprinkle top with remaining cheese combined with the bread crumbs. Bake in a 400°F oven until well browned. Yield: *4 to 5 servings.*

Eggs

Naturally, with chickens come eggs. Although eggs appear in a number of recipes throughout this book, we thought it would be fun to point out a few Appalachian favorites where eggs take center stage.

BAKED EGGS

Break number of eggs desired into a buttered baking dish. Cover eggs with cheese, mustard, or curry sauce, etc. Bake in a 350°F oven for 10 minutes. Buttered crumbs may be placed on top before or after baking.

SOUFFLÉ

This soufflé is especially good using broccoli or spinach. Also good served with cheese, tomato, or mushroom sauce.

3 tablespoons butter
3 tablespoons flour
1 cup liquid (milk, stock, vegetable water, or cream)
1 cup minced meat, fish, or vegetables
3 eggs, separated
Salt and pepper to taste

Make a sauce out of the first 3 ingredients by first making a paste from the flour and a small amount of the liquid. Gradually mix paste into remaining liquid, add butter, and place over heat. When mixture comes to a boil, add minced ingredients. Bring to a boil again and remove from heat. Beat in egg yolks. Cook and stir over low heat until slightly thickened. Remove from heat and add salt and pepper. Cool. Beat egg whites, and when stiff fold into egg yolk mixture. Pour into an ungreased ovenproof dish and bake in a 325°F oven for 30 minutes. Serve immediately. Yield: 6 servings.

Variation: Substitute ½ cup cheese for the minced ingredients.

DEVILED EGGS

6 eggs, hard cooked
¼ cup mayonnaise
¼ teaspoon salt
1 tablespoon vinegar
Sliced olives, chopped pickles, chopped parsley, diced pimiento, or paprika for garnish

Shell eggs, and once cool, cut in even halves lengthwise with a sharp knife. Carefully remove yolks with teaspoon into a bowl; mash with a fork until very fine and crumbly. Add mayonnaise, salt, and vinegar. Mix well until smooth. Refill hollows in the whites with the mixture. Garnish with olives, pickles, parsley, pimiento, or paprika.

Mary Pitts elaborates:

For deviled eggs, first boil your eggs. If you'll put them under cold water and lay them to one side, I find it's easier to peel the shell off right then. After you cut that egg in two [lengthwise] you take the yellow out and put it in a dish. I put in mayonnaise and chip up a little cucumber pickles, or if I have some relish, I'll use that. Sometimes the vinegar in your pickles is not strong enough, so I add a teaspoonful or more of vinegar—taste it and you'll know how to do it. You can use pickle juice if you want to, but sometimes it makes the yellow too mushy. And then you put salt and pepper in it. Mix all that up good with your egg yellow and put it back in your eggs.

5 The Smokehouse

Like its cousins the springhouse and the root cellar, the smokehouse played an important role in food preservation before refrigerators and freezers were widely available. To call it a smokehouse is a bit of a misnomer, as it was used more often without smoke as with it. Generally speaking, the smokehouse was a space for storing salt- and sugar-cured meats. Curing was restricted to cooler months, from late fall to early spring, to minimize the chance of the meat spoiling or becoming infested with insect larvae. Smoking the meat wasn't necessary but rather a matter of taste. For those who liked to use smoke, hickory wood was the most common choice, but folks would also use wood from fruit trees such as apple or cherry. The smoke acted as both a flavoring agent and as a natural insect repellent, which was especially useful because the smoking process was more often performed in the spring.

For the structure itself, our contacts were split on their preferences for design. As noted in *The Foxfire Book*, some folks constructed their smokehouses to include slatted sides, leaving three-quarter-inch cracks between each slat to encourage ventilation. Others argued that a sealed smokehouse, chinked with mud, was the best option because it helped keep insects out and provided insulation to keep the meat from freezing in the winter months or getting too warm in the spring. Nearly all agreed, however, that a shelf system was the best means of storing the meat. Only those who liked to smoke their meat preferred to hang or skewer it on a pole.

During interviews conducted in the 1970s, some of our contacts remarked that smokehouse curing couldn't be done anymore because of how much the climate had warmed. In 1975, for instance, Carl Rogers noted, "You can't cure anymore; it's just too hot." Twenty years later, J. C. Stubblefield remarked, "You can't do that now. It's not cold enough. The way it is now, it's cold for a few days and then it gets warm again. That's when your meat would spoil—it's cold and then turns warm. We never had no meat spoil." Some modern inventions have addressed these temperamental weather issues through more controlled processes, but we are seeing a resurgence in interest around the older methods. In response, we've put together this chapter as a collection of some of our favorite interviews on smokehouses and salt- or sugar-curing of meats. We also invite you to pick up a copy of *The Foxfire Book* and check out the section on curing and smoking pork.

Buck Carver on Curing and Smoking Meat

Of all our interviews on the topic curing and smoking meat, the most complete comes from Buck Carver, conducted in 1983. Buck's descriptions of the process are thorough and provide great insight on the subject of preserving meat in this manner. For that reason, we've included the entire interview, conducted by Foxfire student Chet Welch.

> Buck: No, I don't smoke nothing no more [but I used to] years ago. The doc stopped me from eatin' pork, I don't know, fifteen or sixteen years ago. It's still hard for me to do without one. It's rough on your blood pressure [. . .]. To avoid temptation, I just quit having any hogs around. I used to raise Cain with the old lady if we didn't have meat on the table three times a day. It's still that way with me. It seems like to me if you ain't got meat on the table, you just ain't got nothin'.

A smokehouse.

> Chet: How did you go about smoking your meat?
>
> Buck: I used hickory wood. I worked with the Dillards several years over there—back when they growed and slaughtered and cured their own meat. And they used applewood most to smoke their meat with. The Morton sugar-cure salt was pretty expensive. They tried to be pretty conservative if they can—they have to, I guess, in order to make any money to make ends meet and clear a profit, too. But, they would buy a five-pound sack of sugar and a five-pound pack of salt t'make it equal—50 percent of one and 50 percent of the other—and use that to cure their meat with. And, they'd pack tight in boxes. They called it "pickling

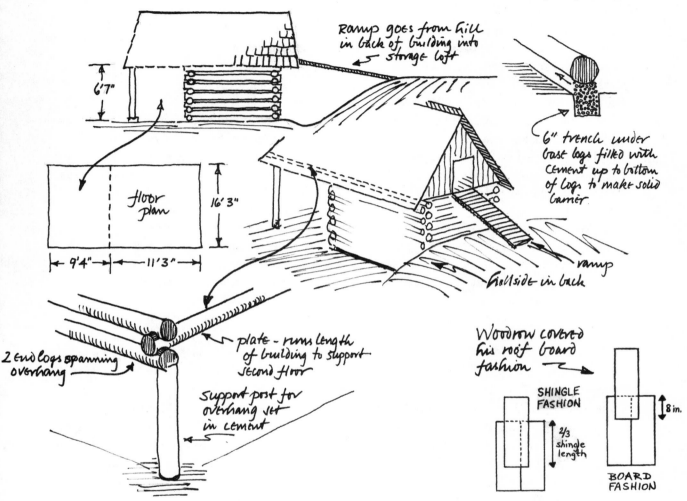

Text within the diagram:

Ramp goes from hill in back of building into storage loft

6'7"

floor plan

16' 3"

9'4"   11'3"

2 end logs spanning overhang

plate - runs length of building to support second floor

support post for overhang set in cement

6" trench under base logs filled with cement up to bottom of logs to make solid barrier

ramp

hillside in back

Woodrow covered his roof board fashion

SHINGLE FASHION

2/3 shingle length

BOARD FASHION

8 in.

---

it in its own juice." It'd stay packed in them boxes for, I believe, about three weeks, if I remember right. Garrison helped me fit one of mine over there one time. I left it in their cooler, I believe, three weeks.

The way I usually cure is by the Morton smoke sugar-cure salt and on the benches of the smokehouse. Spread a very liberal amount on them boards—that's for the skin part of the meat to lay on, you know. I'd simply pour it on the rest of it.

Chet: Do you rub it in?

Buck: Rub it in with your hands, that's right. And you can't just buy pure salt—it probably, possibly set too much of it. [usually] use that prepared preparation. There ain't no danger of you putting [too much] on there. The more, the better.

Let that stay on there on over in November or December. In February, scrape it off. Your smokehouse should have—if it ain't got, should have—an earth floor in it. Set you a big old fire and dishpan, or something similar to it, right in the center of the room. Hang your meat up on the nails and rafters overhead, along the walls, too. If you got it hanging and out over these rafters, smoke can set all over in and around the stuff.

I know the last one I killed—the old girl was Bonny Gillespie's Hampshire [pig], I believe it was the name of that. It's been so long since I had one, but she dressed out about 450 pounds. Her middlins was just about that thick [holds up hands to indicate size]. And I cured it with that Morton sugar-cure salt, let it stay on till over February. [. . .] I'd take small pieces [of hickory], anywhere from small to medium, and lay them on top of that, in that, dishpan—set it right in the center of the room. That was back in old man Linus McCoy's lifetime. He said it looked like that dern smokehouse was a-fire, the smoke boiling out of the cracks of it. You don't want them to be tight—you want 'em to where they can set plenty of air. And, it might be a good idea to screen the inside–nail screens over it—so where the flies won't set in, but leave it to where plenty of air can set in there. But, I never did screen mine. That smoke would boil out and it looked like the smokehouse was on fire every time you looked that way . . . maybe three weeks that way, at the first

part of March. You talk about good eatin'. I raised Cain with the War Department [Mrs. Carver] if there wasn't some meat on the tables three times a day. Go to the table, "Are you too dern lazy to walk up to smokehouse and get a ration or two of meat?" That would boil her over and she'd go and get two or three rations. What's the use in having it if you're not a-goin' to use it? I was raised on the stuff and I've never got tired of it yet. Once in a while, I break down like a shotgun and eat a mess of it anyhow.

Chet: How did you get your smoke into the smokehouse?

Buck: You had your fire in the center of the smokehouse and that smoke would come up and boil all over that smokehouse.

Chet: What did you have it in?

Buck: Had it in an old discarded dishpan. Where you got an earthen floor, if you want to you can—and if you don't mind getting your dirt floor messy—you can just build it on the ground and there's no danger of catchin' it a'fire. But, if you got it in a pan, it sure-as-heck ain't goin to catch. If it's on the ground, a piece might accidentally roll down against the wall and set it a'fire.

Chet: Would your fire not be a fire? Just smoke?

Buck: You didn't want no blaze a'tall hardly, if you could help it. Just a continuous smoke. But, don't think it don't make a difference in the meat—it really does.

Chet: How long does it take to smoke?

Buck: Well, a week or ten days would do. I always like to be sure, so I always smoke mine about three weeks.

Chet: A continuous smoke all that time?

Buck: Yeah, then after you do that, get you some saltpeter and ground red and black pepper [and] sprinkle that all over your meat and place it back on your benches. I usually used two sticks of stove wood (we used a wood cookstove). The sticks would be around one and one-half to two inches thick. Lay that on the meat benches so air could get under it, you know, over it and around it.

 I never lost but one piece of meat in my life. There was a hole in the windowpane—it was stacked on a table right in front of this window—and wind blowed rain in through that window. I had to carry that thing and throw it out. That was back during World War II, when you couldn't buy lard hardly, for love or money or both. Then, it was tough. I believe I lost both of two hams, I'm pretty sure I did. It's been so long ago, my mind's gettin' so shaky I don't remember clearly like I one time could. I believe it was two of 'em. I know it made me awful sick to have to carry them pretty things off and bury 'em.

Chet: So, you have meat laying on benches?

Buck: You have you some benches built up about waist high, around the walls of the house. It don't have to be one single row, you can double deck 'em if you want to.

Chet: How would you set the smoke all around the meat?

Buck: I'd lie wire, strings, or something and have it up on the rafters, you know. That way the smoke got around it.

Chet: When you're sugar-curing it, you just put it on the bench and rub it all over it?

Buck: That's right. When you first kill the hog, you got to lay it down flat on the bench so you can put that salt all over it. Rub a good portion of it in that skin side—just rub it in there good. You'd be surprised how much it would take. When you lay your meat down, really pour it to it. Then after, it quits drippin'—that salt draws the blood and water and stuff out of it, you know. That's what spoils it. If you don't draw that out good, your meat will go bad. After it draws that out good, then you can set it up—lean it up—against the wall, you know, on the benches. Let it drain down good. Then, put your sticks under where air can set in over and around the stuff. It's an easy thing to do. There's some work in it, like there is with everything else that's worthwhile.

 My father used to have hogs and goats in the woods. That was back when they had the free range. We tried to pasture them goats in the pasture, but the only way you can pasture the blame goat is to put brush on top of the fence. We had rail fences, you know, and them sons of guns would set up on top of them rail fences and walk them rails like a squirrel. There weren't no trouble for them to jump over the dern thing, but we lost a few anyhow out of the woods.

Chet: When you're smoking your meat, do you need to sugar cure it before you smoke it?

Buck: Used to, in older times, people didn't know of such a thing as sugar cure.

Chet: They just hung it up in the building and smoked it?

Buck: That's what they called the meat storage house, that why they called it the "smokehouse." That's where they built their smoke.

All most everybody had a smokehouse– there were other things you could use 'em for, you know, put junk and so forth in it. That's all that's in mine now.

Chet: Does it have to be wintertime before you can smoke it?

Buck: No, it don't necessarily have to be. You can smoke it anytime of the year you want for that matter. To keep skippers and things off of it, we usually smoked it in February or March, then go to the store and get this black and red ground pepper and saltpeter, and give it a doggone good coatin' of that. And [that] keeps what we call the skippers off of it and the green flies, too.

Chet: Does it have to be winter to sugar cure it?

Buck: It has to be cool weather or got to have a cooler or something to put that in. In the summertime and springtime, the weather is too doggone warm. No, in the fall of the year is hog killin' time. If you have two or three weeks of rainy weather is sure rough on that meat. There's been many a piece of meat had to be thrown away on account of the atmosphere being too damp, you know, and too warm. A lot of meat has been lost on that account. I don't want it to be freezing cold because it's wet, nasty work, anyhow—hog killing is. I like the temperature to be reasonably cool. If it's too darn cold, your meat will freeze and it won't take that salt. It's got to penetrate through and through.

Chet: How long does it take for that?

Buck: Lord, it takes a long time—more than a month to cure good from that salt. See that salt penetrates slow. Go back every few days and rub salt on the naked spots. If you ain't got extra salt, take some off a thicker spot or pick some up off the bench and rub it in right good. It's got to penetrate the whole thing. It ain't done overnight.

I used to have another way to do it. I told Paul about that yesterday—it's been so long ago I forgot. If you kids talk to Earl Vinson's wife, she'd probably remember the last one I cured that way. I went to her—her husband run a little store there in Dillard—and buy these things. She knew right quick . . . some of it was brown sugar, ground red and black pepper, saltpeter . . . I don't know, different kinds of spices and things. And, you make that up in a soupy paste—get you a clean white cloth and roll it about that far [indicates with hands] up a stick—a stick about so long [indicates with hands] and roll that cloth around it and make what you call a swab, or you can use a paint brush. I would use nothing but a brand-new paint brush. I wouldn't want one that's been used. Use that swab to baste that stuff all over your meat. I remember I didn't have to tell her what I was fixing to do. Her daddy and her brother had butchered so many hogs and them girls had a hand in everything. They really worked—there wadn't no two ways about it. Everyone of 'em worked. [Mrs. Vinson] said to me when I went to buying them things, "You're fixin' to have some awfully good meat!" What all they was, I don't remember, but you can ask Earl Vinson's wife. I believe they live just across the line in North Carolina—first house on the left, I believe. If you ask her, she could probably tell you [. . .] . She knew exactly what I was fixin' to do—she didn't have to be told.

Chet: What did you do—just rub it on the meat?

Buck: Yeah, it's just like the salt—it penetrates in there. Old Man John Bell learn't me that trick in 1935—'35 or '36. Old Man Bell was from down around the Cornelia-Baldwin area down in there.

Chet: It's just like sugar curing—it's just put on there?

Buck: Paste, it was what we called it.

Chet: How would you do that?

Buck: Take that swab stick, put it in the bowl where you got that mixture, and saturate it, rub it, and roll it into the meat. Make sure you cover the whole thing with it. I wish I could remember what all was in that recipe.

You could cure your meat with that old-fashioned damp salt, you know—regular salt. We used to buy it in twenty-five-pound bags. You could cure with that pure white salt and use that mixture I was telling you about . . . Old Man Bell . . . and, brother, it made all the difference in this world. Smokin' it will, too.

It's real good eatin'. Make sure you use Morton sugar cure—use plenty of it, though. So, use it generously. Don't be stingy with it. Pour it to it. The ends of the bones—you know, where you cut the meat off—be sure you rub a whole good portion in there. Be sure you rub it in there good.

Them bones is what usually spoils your ham. I got to talkin' about what they call the log bone of there. That's the one that usually does the spoiling. It's the one you cut loose from the backbone, and it's not very much trouble. And there's nothing wasted. You might leave meat on that bone, but put it in a pot of bones and season your beans and you've got some doggone eating on that bone, too. Pour that place full of salt, also. You won't have nearly as much trouble with your meat if you take that bone out of there. [talking about the paste-cured ham] You had something that would make your tongue slap your brains out. It was awful [good] pickens. I get awful hungry just talking about it.

A Few More Words on Smokehouses and Curing

Throughout our archive are little jewels of knowledge on the topic of smokehouses and curing meat, though none as extensive as Buck Carver's knowledge on the subject. In these interviews we find broad consensus on the essentials but small differences in the minutiae of how folks approached the process.

In an interview with Arie Carpenter in 1969, Foxfire students inquired how she and her husband, Ulysses, would cure meat and, specifically, if they smoked it:

Don't want no ol' smoked meat. You might, but I don't. See that little house right out there? Well, that's the smokehouse. Well now, we always, we'd kill as high as four big hogs at one time. [. . .] We have killed four big hogs at one time. Take and cut it all up. Just like this is. We always salted ours the day that we cut it up. Some people waits till the next day, but I don't like that. Take it and spread it out on the bench—Ulysses made benches in there—and spread it all out, take salt and pepper and mix it all up in a pan. We always did and we'd always let it lay out there till it got cured. And, then, see, that black pepper keeps the flies off of it, and that preserves it—that salt preserves it.

She was then asked again whether she smoked the meat:

No sir. Well, now, if the flies come . . . if they smell fresh meat, if you do it too soon and they smell fresh meat, they'll come and they'll brew it. You know, they'll lay eggs there and they'll make worms. Well, now, you'll hear 'em when they come. We've got an old [Dutch] oven that we use to bake bread in. We'll put coals and set the fire and set it down under the meat to run the flies off. [. . .] The oven's iron, you know, and it won't burn the floor.

Sallie Beaty noted that they used the same curing processes for all of their meats, including beef:

We cured it out in a smokehouse. That was just a house with a dirt floor—no ceiling or nothing. And we had strips of wood across there that we hung it up on or shelves that we left the meat laying on. Uh, they cured beef the same way. Dried out our beef instead of canning. Back then, they used salt with red pepper and black pepper in it and rubbed it on the meat on both sides and, uh, then put it out on a shelf. And, put corncobs between each layer. Like, sometimes, they would make it like three layers high. And then, they would go back like in a week or two weeks and turn it over so all the water that had drained in there and was settling would run out.

As part of their process, Bertha Dawkins's family cured their meat by wrapping it in cotton cloth and hanging it in the smokehouse.

They cured it and wrapped it in this cheesecloth, hung it in the smokehouse. They call it dried meat—they call it jerky in the West. We ate what we could fresh, and dried the rest. That's th'way they used to do it. Hogs now, they'd put up just kind of a shoat

Cutting out the "middlins" from a hog.

Simmie Free preferred sugar-cured pork to anything else:

You kill your hog. Let the heat go out'a your hog. Lay it down on a table durin' the night and let th'heat of the hog get out of it. Then, take your sugar cure and just rub it all over—you know—just plumb over both sides of it. Then you got it and, boy, it'll go all through that meat. I hung mine up over yonder in the crib. [. . .] When you sugar cure it, ain't nothin' else'll ever happen to it—just good all the way through. It makes some awful good breakfast eatin'. Good!

The 1970 Spring/Summer issue of *The Foxfire Magazine* contained an extensive article on slaughtering and preparing various types of meat. We've excerpted it here to wrap up our discussion on curing meat.

Taylor Crockett preferred eight pounds of salt for each hundred pounds of meat. He mixed the salt with one quart of molasses, two ounces of black pepper, and two ounces of red pepper. Then he smeared the mix on the meat, allowing it to stay six to eight weeks depending on the weather (longer if it got very cold). "Valley John" Carpenter used simply five pounds of salt for a two-hundred-pound hog, while Lon Reid used ten pounds of salt per hundred pounds of meat. Lake Stiles, rather than putting the meat in a smokehouse, would take it to his cellar, which had a dirt floor. He would put the meat right on the floor with the flat side down, and allow the earth to draw the animal taint out of the meat, keep it cool, and prevent souring or spoiling.

If meat was needed during the winter months, the family simply cut what they needed off the curing pork, washed the salt off, soaked it overnight, parboiled it the next day, and then cooked

Placing meat in a cotton sack to be hung in the smokehouse.

in th'pen—'bout a hundred pounds—then kill 'em in November. And, had to pack his meat in a big old box, salt all of it, and let it stay there 'bout two months, and he'd take it out then and wash it and hang it. Let it drip from November to 'bout March, and he'd wash it and let it dry and put it in any kind of cotton sack. Put that down in, tie it up real good. Most th'time just hang it back up.

Fanny Powell shows students middlins and hams hanging in the smokehouse.

it. If it was left all winter, it would go through a second operation in the spring.

When the weather began to get warm (usually when the peach trees bloomed), the second phase of the operation began on the meat that was left. It was taken out of the salt mix, washed, and then treated by any of the following means:

Cover the meat with a mixture of black pepper and borax to keep the "skippers" out (skippers are the larvae of the skipper fly). The meat is then hung in the smokehouse. Wash the meat thoroughly and coat it with a mixture of brown sugar and pepper. Then put it in a bag and hang it up in the smokehouse.

Turner Enloe washes the meat, and then uses a mixture of one package of brown sugar, two boxes of red pepper, and one box of saltpeter per hog. He adds enough water to the mixture to make a syrup, coats the pieces in the liquid, and then sets them in a box to age. Lizzie Carpenter shells a bushel of white corn. She puts some in the bottom of a wooden box, puts the washed middling meat on top of that, skin side down, covers it with corn, adds another side, and so on until finished. The corn draws the salt out, keeps the meat from tasting strong, and gives it a good flavor. Bill Lamb puts a mixture of borax and black pepper on the washed meat and *then* smokes it.* Lake Stiles washes the meat and then buries it in a box of hickory ashes. He claims it never tastes strong this way since the ashes keep air from getting to the meat. His grandmother would bury it in cornmeal, which would do almost as well.

Many, however, prefer the taste of smoked meat. Holes were poked in the middling meat, white oak splits were run through the holes, and the meat was hung from the joists of the smokehouse. Hams and shoulders were done the same way. Then a fire was built inside the house. If it had a dirt floor, the fire could be built right on the floor. Otherwise, a washpot was set in the middle of the room and a fire built in that. The fire itself was made out of small green chips of hickory or oak, pieces of hickory bark, or even corncobs in some cases. Using this fuel, the smoke was kept billowing through the house for from two to six days, or until the meat took on the brown crust that was desired for both its flavor and for its ability to keep flies and insects out of the meat.

If you intend to cure and smoke your own meats, you might want to write to the Cooperative Extension Service of the College

*The safety of borax for consumption is debated by many sources but was common during this time period. Please conduct research and evaluate yourself prior to any usage.

of Agriculture at the University of Georgia in Athens and ask them for their booklet *Curing Georgia Hams Country Style*.** It gives specific instructions, such as:

- The best slaughtering weight for a hog is from 180 to 240 pounds.
- Kill hogs only when the temperature is 32°F to 35°F. Souring bacteria multiply rapidly at temperatures above 40°F. Cure meat immediately after slaughtering.
- Do not cure a bruised ham as it will spoil.
- A good curing mixture is eight pounds of salt, three pounds of sugar, and three ounces of saltpeter. Apply the mix at the rate of one and a quarter ounces per pound. Use a third of the mixture on first day, another third on the third day, and the last third on the tenth day. Rub it in thoroughly each time.

- On a ham, good salt penetration requires seven days per inch of thickness. Bacon requires fourteen to sixteen days.
- Add another day to the curing schedule for each day the weather is below freezing.
- Then, wash the outside coating of salt off and leave the meat at a temperature below 40°F for another twenty to twenty-five days for salt equalization.
- Then, smoke the meat, if desired. Don't allow the temperature in the smokehouse to exceed 100°F. Use hickory, oak, or apple as fuel.
- Smoke hams until they are amber or mahogany in color (usually about two days). The smokehouse should be sealed and ventilated with fans, or completely screened for natural ventilation.

**The University of Georgia now offers much of this information online, made available by the National Center for Home Food Preservation (https://nchfp.uga.edu/).

6 The Woods

People say I make good squirrel dumplings.
—Gladys Nichols

The history of wild foods in Southern Appalachia is long and rich. Though the region is often regarded as the nation's apothecary for its abundance of medicinal herbs, Southern Appalachia may also be viewed as the nation's most abundant cupboard of wild edibles. From berries and grapes to greens and mushrooms, there is no shortage of native plants to eat, which may be part of the reason why humans have inhabited Appalachia for more than sixteen thousand years.

Wild foraging is enjoying a bit of a come back as folks have become more interested in organic and natural foods. This renewed interest in foraging, however, highlights the ethics and dangers surrounding the harvesting of wild foods. Resources about ethical foraging are easily accessible, and we encourage anyone interested in wild foods to review them before going out into the woods to forage. There is also a risk associated with eating anything that grows wild if one doesn't know what to look for. These issues should be taken into consideration—any and all wild food harvesting should be done responsibly.

Wild game has also played a significant role in Southern Appalachian culture. Deer, wild hogs, rabbits, squirrels, game birds, and even raccoons have found their way into the regional diet at one time or another. Though hunting has largely evolved from necessity to sport, folks' appetites for cuts of wild meat haven't subsided much over the years. Unlike wild plant foraging, game hunting comes with well-established rules and regulations set by local, state, and federal government agencies. Be sure to check with your state's department of natural resources before setting out to hunt.

Wild Greens

Greens are among the foods best loved by adults—and sometimes most carefully avoided by children. In the spring, before garden greens could be picked, many women would take to the woods and creek banks to locate wild greens. Ethel Corn was one of these:

I'm bad for wild salads [greens]. You could cut crowsfoot—it grows in the mountains on branches and streams. And sochan grows all up and down these branches, and people'd eat that. It made a delicious salad. People always cooked poke salad and eat it, too. I have even knowed people to pick briar leaves, peppermint, and pepper grass and cook it together. Now, I never did try that because that didn't sound too good to me. And then there's this white rabbit plant and that groundhog plant that they'd cook back when I was just a young'un. Old people went for wild salads more than they did raising salad.

Mountain people have used wild greens since pioneer days, when wild plants were necessary supplements to the daily diet. Nowadays the consumption of wild plants is a matter of choice rather than need, but many folks still insist that everybody's system needs the personal "spring cleaning" offered by wild plant foods. Others argue for the high vitamin and mineral content of most wild plants. Here we include a few of the favorite and most talked about greens. A more complete discussion of wild plant foods grown from spring through fall may be found in *Foxfire Book 2* (pp. 47–94) and *Foxfire Book 3* (pp. 274–353).

POKE

It is sometimes misleading when people from other areas of the country hear southerners speak of poke "salad." Poke is not usually used as

A mature pokeweed plant.

a raw salad ingredient. Because of the wild taste of this green, most people parboil it and rinse it well before cooking it. Poke shoots resemble asparagus and are probably eaten more frequently than any other wild food in the mountain areas. Many country doctors supported the theory that "poke salad eaten in the spring revives the blood." Dr. Neville said to be sure to eat at least one mess of poke each spring, and Dr. Dove said, "Anybody that gets sick from eating poke, I'll treat them free." Local people tended to follow the advice, and, as Carrie Dixon said, "My ma used to send us young'uns looking for it as soon as the frogs started croaking in spring."

It is a fact that parts of the plant are toxic, however, and readers would be well advised to avoid the root, the berries, the stalk, and the leaves of the mature plant, cooking only the young shoots (four to six inches high) as they first emerge from the ground. These are safe when cooked, and generally prized.

BESSIE BOLT: *My mother told me that an old doctor said that if you eat three messes of poke in the spring it would doctor you free of any fevers. It killed* all the poison from the stomach and body. *The way I cook poke is I boil it, squeeze it out, and put oil in it. I don't use lard or meat grease. Cut an onion up and put it in there and just turn it over a few times so the onion cooks, and it's ready to serve. It's good, too. I like poke salad. When I was a girl I knowed where all the poke stalks growed, and mother'd send me to get the poke salad. I used to didn't care so much for it, but I got to liking it. Now I'd rather have it than most anything on the table—chicken stew, eggs, or any kind of meat.*

RITTIE WEBB: *Boy, I've eat a lot of poke salad. You put your poke in a pot and hard-boil it. Then take it up and run some cold water over it. Mash the water out of it, and put it in a pan of grease. Let it start to fry, and when it's about done, break an egg in it, stir it up, and fry it some more. That poke is so strong that if you don't wash it good and cook it till it's done, it will make you sick.*

BOILED POKE
RUTH GIBBS
"Collect tender young shoots of poke in the spring when they are six to eight inches high. Do not cut them below the surface of the ground, as the root is poisonous. Wash and cook the leaves and stems together, parboiling two times (pouring off the water each time after boiling a few minutes). Boil in third water until tender, salting to taste. Drain and top with slices of hard-boiled egg."

FRIED POKE AND EGGS
LOVEY KELSO
"Cook two pounds fresh tender greens by bringing them to a hard boil for ten to fifteen minutes. Drain and wash well. Put three table-spoons grease in an iron frypan, and add salt.

Fry greens. You can scramble three eggs in it, serve hard-boiled eggs over it, or cook with a streak of fat and some streak of lean."

POKE AND ONIONS
MRS. DILLARD THOMPSON
"Cook in boiling water the same as turnip greens. When tender, take the dark green leaves, chop them up, and add little spring green onions."

ZESTY POKE SALAD
ADDIE NORTON
"Wash well and parboil for ten minutes. Rinse three or four times and then fry in fatback grease until tender. Season with salt and pepper or add pepper sauce or apple vinegar. The young stalks are also eaten. They are sliced and peeled, rolled in cornmeal or flour, and fried until tender. You may also pickle stalks in warm vinegar and spices."

SOCHAN
Sochan (or tall coneflower) is another popular wild green. Its leaves are edible when young and tender, and it is prepared much like poke. Lizzie Moore is an authority on sochan:

Sochan is a wild [plant]. You'd say it was a weed [laughter]. But it grows out on the branch banks and in real rich ground. It has a forked leaf, and it's always great long. After it gets grown it has a yellow flower on it like this Golden Glow. Some people likes it and some don't.

I was the one that used to fix the sochan dinner for ten or fifteen or twenty. I guess you seen that in the [Clayton Tribune] if you ever used to read the Tribune. I used to fix it for Irene Bynum and Connie Green, Vera Mincemoyer, and all those people. Their

Kenny Runion holds a newly gathered mess of sochan.

water off, and put some more water back in it. It's got a kind of flavor, you know, and when you drain that [water] off, it's much better. And what they always wanted to eat with that was little tender onions, corn bread, and pickled beets. I've had a crippled arm this time, and I can't get out and pick it, so I haven't fixed a sochan dinner. It takes a long time to pick that much when you have to get out on the branch banks or somewhere like that.

CREASES

Granny Gibson told us, "Creases is another salad-like stuff that grows out mostly in the cornfield. You cook it just like turnip greens." The leaves of creases are sharp-tasting, very like watercress, and can be cooked or used raw in salads. It is gathered young, within days of its appearance.

BOILED CREASES

ARIE CARPENTER

"Put in a piece of middling meat in the morning to boil. Boil for at least two hours or as long as it takes to get it tender. Take the grease off the meat, add it to a pot of water, and bring to a boil. Add cleaned creases and boil for thirty minutes."

FRIED CREASES

NEAROLA TAYLOR

"Fry fatback meat in a heavy pot, preferably an old black dinner pot. Have crease clean and washed. Take meat out, leaving grease in pot. Shake out creases and drop in hot grease, stirring and mixing thoroughly with grease. Add just enough water to keep from burning or sticking to pot. Add salt as desired, and cook about twenty minutes, or until tender. Stir often."

mother always cooked that sochan for them when they were children, and they liked it so good they always wanted me to fix it. We kept it up for years.

We always had the sochan dinner here in about April or May. I'd get out and pick a half a bushel or just as much as I could. I'd put it in the cooker, slice fatback or streak-of-lean meat, and put it in the sochan and, after I got it cooked down some, put salt in it. Let it boil about thirty minutes, drain that

RAMPS

Some people much preferred the taste of ramps to any type of cultivated onion, and the controversy continues even today. It seems that people either love or hate the strong-scented plant. One gentleman said, "They're not for ladies or those who court them." And Ethel Corn said, "Now a lot of people still go into the mountains and get ramps to cook and eat. I don't see how they could because you can smell anybody that's took a bite of one a half a mile away before they get there. But some people are crazy about them. They'll even get them and put them up for the winter and freeze them. Down in South Georgia they's sights of these old wild onions. Now they smelled *good* to what a ramp does. Ramps stinks worse than what wild onions does." Others, as Maude Shope noted, "go crazy for a mess of ramps in the spring of the year."

Ramps—onionlike wild plants—are eaten by some brave folks as a cold remedy.

LESSIE CONNER: *Wash them clean, cut them up fine just like you would onions, put them in some grease, salt them, and fry them. When they get about done, break you two or three eggs in them and scramble them. I like them, but they'll knock you down. You can smell them in the house for weeks! Minyard's got about fifteen quarts of ramps out there in the freezer now.*

Minyard Conner says, "Every time I get sick I always eat them." But Addie Norton argues, "I never could stand them, and I never did gather them. There was plenty of wild onions just a mile off. You can boil them, and they just nearly make you sick they're so strong. And they say ramps is lots worse."

You may want to try them for yourself, using the following recipes.

FRIED RAMPS

NORA GARLAND: *There are red ramps and white ones. White are best. Put them in a pan with water and cook until tender. Drain and fry in grease along with tuna fish and eggs.*

Other suggestions include coating with bread crumbs and frying in butter, boiling with a piece of fatback, or adding to soups and salads.

CLIFFORD CONNER: *To clean them, pull off the outer skin around the bulb. Chop a good bit of ramps with about five eggs into a frying pan, and fry them with about three heaped tablespoons of grease. Fry them hot and fast because of smell. Add a little salt, pepper, eggs, or potatoes in with them for flavor to your own fancy. Most important, go into solitary in the woods somewhere and stay for two or three weeks because nobody can stand your breath after you've eat them.*

Other Wild Greens

Wild lettuce, dandelion, lamb's-quarters, dock, sheep sorrel, and watercress are common spring greens that may be found in damp woods or by streams. When cooked, their preparation follows the basic salad and greens variations of other wild plants we've mentioned. These greens are sometimes cooked together, and sometimes eaten raw in salads.

TURNIP GREENS AND CORNMEAL DUMPLINGS
DOROTHY BECK

"We used to take the turnip greens out of the crock and set them to boiling. We would make a dough out of cornmeal and onions just like you do hush puppies and drop them in that turnip green broth like a dumpling."

Wild Herbs

Wild herbs are prevalent in the Appalachian Mountains. People used herbs to create teas and tonics to cure a variety of ailments. People gathered roots or barks, then dried and stored them for later use.

Spring was the time to refresh the spirit and tone up the system with a tonic. Spicewood, sweet birch, and sassafras were common spring tonics. The spicy, distinct flavor of sassafras made it a particularly popular tea served hot or cold.

Pearl Martin had a field behind her house that she kept cleared of brush to allow sassafras to grow freely. Left alone, this native plant grows into a medium-sized tree with an irregularly shaped trunk, but when Pearl's sassafras reached bush height, she would dig it up for tea. Pearl told us that she could gather the roots any time of the year without affecting the taste of the tea, but roots should be gathered young when they are tender. They can be used dried or green. She brings the roots to a boil in water. The longer they are boiled, the stronger the tea. To make a gallon of tea, Pearl boils four average-sized roots in a gallon of water for fifteen to twenty minutes. She then strains it and serves it either hot or iced, sweetened with sugar or honey.

Herbal Tea and Tonic Recipes

SASSAFRAS TEA

In the spring, gather roots and tender twigs of sassafras. Pound the roots to a pulp if they are very big, and wash them with the twigs. Boil them, strain, and sweeten.

Pearl Martin harvests young sassafras from her woods.

Back at home, Mrs. Martin takes the ax to the limbs and removes the roots she requires for tea.

Cold mountain water is used to clean the sassafras roots.

Scraping the roots adds a further degree of cleanliness.

Mrs. Martin stirs the boiling roots.

Pearl also shared her recipe for sassafras jelly, which is made from the tea itself. To make the jelly, follow the steps for making tea and then mix 1 package of Sure-Jell with 8 cups of tea in a large saucepan. Bring quickly to a hard boil, stirring occasionally. Now add 8 cups sugar and bring to a full rolling boil. Boil hard 1 minute, stirring constantly. Skim off the foam with a metal spoon. Pour at once into hot sterilized jelly jars and seal with paraffin.

SPICEWOOD TEA

The spicebush (*Lindera benzoin*) grows along branch banks. It is best to gather the twigs in early spring when the bark "slips," or peels off easily. Break the twigs, place them in a pot, cover with water, and boil until the water is dark. Strain and serve hot. Sweeten if desired, with honey or molasses. Mrs. Hershel Keener claims the tea is especially good with pork and cracklin bread.

MINT OR WHITE HORSEMINT TEA

Gather mint leaves in the summer when the plant is young, just before or just after blooming. Boil the leaves in water, strain, and sweeten with honey. This is used both for an exceptionally pleasant tea and for a cold remedy.

GROUND IVY TEA

This vine can be gathered in the summer and fall. Make the tea by boiling 6 or 7 leaves in a pint of water. Strain and sweeten to taste.

Ethel Corn said, "Ground ivy does make a pleasant tea for anybody to drink, and old people was bad to give it to babies for colic."

Catnip.

CATNIP TEA

It is best to gather catnip in the spring when it is flowering. Catnip tea is also often given to a fretful child to make him sleep.

Pour a pint of boiling water over about ½ cup of broken stems and leaves. Let stand several minutes, then strain.

Boneset.

BONESET TEA

Boneset grows in swampy places, and it is best if gathered in the summer while in bloom. It is quite bitter. Three or four leaves boiled in a cup of water will make a strong tea. Strain, sweeten, and drink.

As Icie Rickman said, "You see that yellow weed that grows—boneset? You make tea out of that. My daddy and mother did that all the time. They would get yellowroot, rabbit tobacco, boneset, and all that stuff and boil it, and that is the way they treated us. That's good for a cold."

YELLOWROOT TEA

The plant grows along branches, and it can be gathered in the summer and fall. The roots are brilliant yellow and very bitter when tasted raw. Put the roots of a medium-sized plant in a pint of water and boil them until the water is colored. The tea will need a good bit of sweetening for most people. It is essentially a remedy.

Peppermint.

Wild Game

In *The Foxfire Book* (pp. 266–73), there is a collection of methods for killing and dressing wild game. Others have since provided more information. Glenn Worley, from the Turnerville Community in Habersham County, is well known in this area for his hunting skills. We visited with him and his wife, Sara, both of whom graciously shared with us their knowledge of how to dress and cook deer, frogs, rabbits, squirrels, ground-hogs, and possums:

It's a matter of choice how you cut deer up, but most people take all four legs off or either quarter it. If you quarter it, it has to be cut up in smaller pieces later. But most people like to take the legs off. With that they have a big rib section with half the back attached to each piece. And then if you cut that in half you've got two sides. You cut it crossways, making four pieces, two front quarters and two hindquarters. Then it's up to you how you want to cut it. Most people remove the rib section. With that they have split the backbone down the center so they get either rib steaks or filet mignon. It's a section of choice lean meat. Then they usually steak the hind legs and the front legs, and the remainder they make into roasts or barbecue ribs. The neck is a very choice piece—it is all solid meat. The backbone continues on up the neck and that's the only bone in the neck section. From there it's best then to take the meat and put it in a cooler. I would stress to age your deer a little—hang it in the cooler for one to five days—and a lot of the wild goes out, and it becomes drained and it's choice venison.

You have a butcher carve your venison. If you prefer steaks, you tell him the thickness and the section you want, and if you want large roasts, he'll do that. Most all people who are in butcher shops know professionally how to prepare deer and will cut it up for you in thirty minutes. They cut it, wrap it, and give you a little basket of scraps that's left. They'll freeze it and package it for you and mark it all, identifying each piece.

It is not true that deer is tough! The preparation of the deer from the hunter's workpoint to the skillet is really one of the big success factors to having good venison. Most people who cook venison can really do a good job if the dressing and aging has been properly done. I believe that's true in the preparation of all wild game.

My preference of venison of course, is steak and roast and barbecued ribs. I never eat boiled deer. Some people make mulligans or stews, but I just don't eat mulligans from anyone's deer. That's one of my peculiarities. Too much goes in mulligans and stews. But I like fried steak primarily. It doesn't take a lot of sauces or additives to make good deer steak; normally they are fine. Fried steak is my choice. Normally deer steaks are cut about a half inch thick and the size will vary just like any other kind of steak—whether it's rib, round, sirloin, T-bone. It all depends on the size of the animal. Cooks usually take them and flour them a little with white flour and put them in a skillet and cook them rather fast over a hot fire.

Sara: Put a little grease in the pan and add pepper and salt—lots of pepper. They're best to eat while they're hot. Deer gets cold real fast.

Glenn: The meat is very firm so it's best cooked and eaten immediately. And cook it at a little faster pace than you cook chicken. Keep the fire up a little bit.

Sara: I'd say medium-high. Now with a roast, it's different. I always marinate my roast overnight.

Glenn: Usually with some wine.

Sara: Or some vinegar water. And put some salt—all wild game needs some salt in the vinegar. It all depends on the deer. If it's an old one I marinate it and then use a lot of onions in it when I cook it to remove some of the wild game taste. When I put it in the oven, I cook it about thirty minutes per pound. If you was cooking a four-pound roast you'd cook it two hours at about 400 degrees. You'd just sorta have to test to see how done it is.

Glenn: Test it occasionally toward the end of that time period, and when it's exactly right call your family together and enjoy.

Sara: You can easily pressure-cook deer. For people who like pressure cooked, that'd be a faster way. I'm sure it'd help to make it tender a whole lot. A lot of people use all the scrap parts to make hamburger from deer. They mix some pork [or beef] with it and grind it up in a sausage grinder. But our favorite way is steaks, and we put all we can in steaks because we just like them best.

Glenn: Now about the only organs people eat is the liver. Fried liver is choice—either just fried alone or with onions. Most hunters will eat that in the woods unless they've brought beef with them. But this is fresh—it's very choice. And some people here eat the heart—it's a firm, muscular organ—but there's nothing else eaten from a deer that I know of other than the heart and the liver. Those are the two organs. Leave the rest for a bear or a possum or whatever comes along—one of the scavengers. They'll hunt the entrails up and they won't be there very long.

Glenn continued by telling us how he dresses and cooks his other favorite wild animals:

Rabbits are my choice, I guess, next to venison. Wild rabbits are delicious. When you've been hunting in the woods with a pack of beagles or something to jump them and run them by, you bring them home. They still have their intestines and everything still in, so you take the rabbit out and you put him on your dressing block. Most times, I take a sharp knife and cut him off right at the base of his neck. Then I clip off the feet above the footpads. Just clip them off entirely. Then I reach over to the back and make about a two-inch cut crossways in the skin—just the skin.

The skin on a rabbit is rather loose, and you just pick it up and pull it away from the meat. Then insert two fingers in that two-inch cut pointed toward the shoulders and two toward the tail. Then you pull that little cut open, and the skin just gives freely and comes right off the shoulders and tail at the same time, and most times right on down over the legs. You can pull it off at one time—half goes toward the head and half goes toward the tail—and you've got a totally skinned rabbit.

Then you clip the tail off as a rule, and that's all there is till you open him up. There's very little meat attached to the skin. He's just clean and beautiful. If there's any hair or if you dropped him or something, you wash him off. Next you turn him over on his back and open him up. Remove all his vital organs. The liver in a rabbit is absolutely delightful, and that's one of my choice pieces. So you open that rabbit up from the base of his neck all the way. His head has been removed in the first operation. You open him up and clean him out good. His organs are exactly like a deer or bear's. They're all attached in a sack, and you pull those out. Split his hind legs apart and split his front legs apart and cut him up into

Glenn Worley with a rabbit he killed. Make about a two-inch cut crossways in the skin—just in the skin. Then, insert two fingers toward the head and two toward the tail, and the skin just gives freely and comes off both ends at the same time. "He's just clean and beautiful. If there is any hair or if you dropped him or something, you just wash him off."

about eight pieces. If he's a big wild rabbit we take a knife and cut crossways through the biggest area of the hind legs about one inch apart. That eliminates the toughness and breaks down the muscle tissue a little bit for frying. And when you flour him to put him in the skillet, you rub a little flour in those cuts and that makes him more tempting. Cook him

just like you would fried chicken. He is my favorite! The first time I get a rabbit, I'll bring him by and I'll do it for you.

I use the same procedure with a squirrel, but I somehow have difficulty with squirrel. Whereas I can skin a rabbit and never get five hairs from the skin on his body, I sorta wrestle a squirrel pretty much. He's

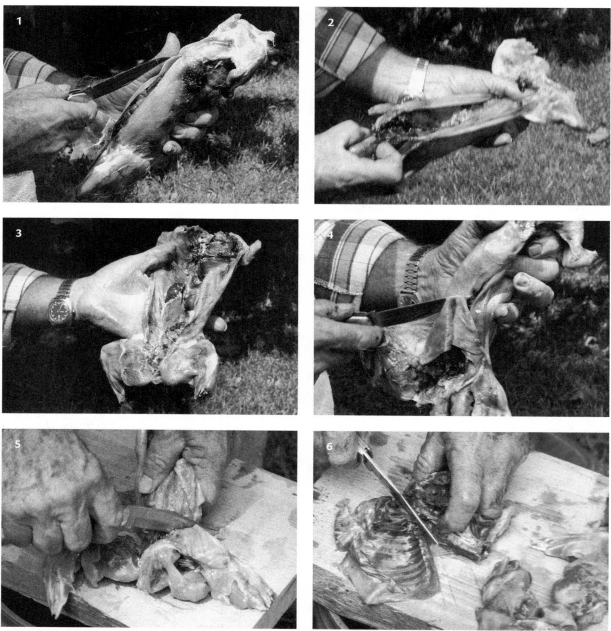

"Then you turn him over on his back and open him up (1). Remove all his vital organs (2). The rabbit liver (the two dark patches inside [3]) is absolutely delightful, and that's one of my choice pieces." Cut the unwanted skin from the torso of the rabbit (4). Mr. Worley separates the leg from the ribcage (5) and cuts the ribcage in half (6).

very tough. He's just got the toughest skin of any little animal I've ever tangled with, but I skin him precisely the same way. When you open up the back crossways with the first cut, you tuck your fingers in that skin and pull both ways. You've already removed his head and his feet and sometimes the tail, but when you start pulling that skin on them back, boy, you've gotta have some muscles for that, because he doesn't give easily! But once you do get him skinned out you fry him precisely the same way as a rabbit. The meat is a little tougher, but he's good. Somehow I just don't feel that a squirrel is quite worth the trouble, but there's lots of squirrel hunters in the state that would surely disagree. I love squirrel meat—I guess it's just skinning the squirrel. It's tough for me.

My family has also eaten lots of groundhog, and we like it very much. I first hang him up by the hind feet and I skin him just like the deer or the bear. Cut inside of each leg and cut around his legs, and then I peel him down sorta like a small blanket-type operation. Pull down all the way around him till he's totally skinned out to the front of the shoulders. Throw the neck and the head away. Open him up, and cut all his innards out. As a rule they have a couple of glands, I believe, up in the front shoulder. If you can find them, it's good to remove them. If not, those two pieces of meat won't be as tasty, but he is delightful. He's roasted as a rule—baked whole or roasted. You usually put him in a covered vessel and put some margarine in with him in a roasting pan. You can use a cover or heavy aluminum foil. Baste and bake until it's brown, and then he's delightful.

I've eat many possum in my time, too. I used to trap and I've caught big possum. Sometimes I'd put them up in a pen and feed them three or four days and get a little of the wild out of them. Again, just catch them and dress them the same way. Yes, I've eaten lots of possum. They're good. You bake all of them.

Almost all of our other friends in the community have had experiences cooking wild game. As Lizzie Moore said,

My mother and I cooked a lot of wild meat 'cause my daddy was a man that killed a lot of wild game. And then when I married my husband, why, he was a man that hunted a lot. Back in those days you could just get out around here and kill anything that you wanted to and bring it in, you see. They'd kill a lot of squirrels, and when the snow was on was when you generally killed a rabbit. You'd find them sitting in a bed in the snow. They hide, you see. One time my husband [Emory] found a rabbit sitting back in the snow, and it was so much snow on he couldn't find a rock. So he just took his knife out of his pocket and throwed it and killed that rabbit in the snow. They killed coons, possum, deer, turkeys, anything like that.

Many of these friends shared their cooking methods with us.

RACCOON

LIZZIE MOORE: You know you've got to have raccoon all skinned and dressed first. Then you wash it and cut it up into small pieces, put it in a pot and put cold or warm water over the top. [Bring to a boil] and then you put in two pods of hot pepper and let it cool for an hour in that water. Then you drain all that water off, put water up over it again and put a teaspoonful of vinegar in it. Vinegar is what tenders them and takes that old wild taste out of them. And then you put salt in it, and let it [boil again and] get as tender as you want it to. Stick the fork into it to see if it's as good and tender as you want it.

Then you take it out of that water and roll it in meal or flour. I always prefer meal. Just roll it in your meal, have your grease hot in your [frying] pan, and lay that meat all in your pan. Then put some pepper on it, salt it to suit your taste, and let it stay in [the skillet] till it gets as brown as you want it. Take it out, and it's ready to eat. It's lean, dark meat, and it's good.

WILL SINGLETON: *Take one coon any size and clean it. Cut it up and put it in a pressure pot with two cups of water. Then take one-half onion and cut it up on top of the coon along with one pod of hot pepper. Pressure it till it is well cooked, then take it out and put it in a frying pan with grease and put sage and pepper on it. Fry it for about ten minutes and then it is ready to eat.*

POSSUM

SAMANTHA SPEED: *Put them on the stove in water and boil them for a long time. When they get tender, take them and roll them in flour or meal and fry them good and brown.*

GRANNY GIBSON: *You usually boil possum a while to get it tender and then slice up sweet potatoes and put them around it. Put your possum on top and let it bake with sweet potatoes. Now that is good.*

LIZZIE MOORE: *Most people like sweet potatoes and carrots around possum. Just put it in and bake it. I always put a spoonful of vinegar or pepper in with it 'cause then it doesn't taste too wild. A possum is fat. It's not as lean as raccoons. If they're tough, it takes longer to cook them; if they're tender, it doesn't take so long.*

SQUIRREL

GLADYS NICHOLS: *People say I make good squirrel dumplings. You just boil your squirrel like you would a chicken. Get it good and done and put your seasoning in it. Then make up your flour like you're going to make biscuits. Squeeze you off a little dough and roll it or cut it out. Have your squirrel boiling and just drop the flour dough in there, pepper and salt it, and boil it till it's good and done. I have got a lot of compliments on my dumplings. And then you can make gravy in your squirrel with just a spoonful or two of flour mixed with milk. Pour it in your pot and cook it. Most people, I think, like the gravy even better than they do the dumplings.*

MARGIE LEDFORD: *I like squirrel dumplings and Virge [Margie's husband] likes them. I fix my squirrel dumplings just like chicken dumplings. I stew my squirrel and put seasoning in it. When I boil squirrel I put a piece of fat meat in it, and then when I get ready to make my dumplings I take that fat meat out. The fat meat seasons the squirrel. Roll out your dough and drop it right in the pot with your squirrel.*

RABBIT

INEZ TAYLOR: *I have cooked wild game, but I won't eat it. I don't want nothing wild. Not deer, not rabbit—no sir. If rabbits are old you have to boil them, but if they're young and tender you can fry them like chicken. I usually boiled mine till it got tender, then I took it out and let it cool. I roll it in flour, pepper it, and fry it like chicken.*

MIKE CANNON: *After you kill the rabbit, skin and clean it. Bake it in the oven at 350 degrees with butter and wine on it. You can fry it too, like chicken. Dip it in flour and fry it in grease.*

WILL SINGLETON: *Take the [rabbit] meat, put it on a cutting board, and cut it as thin as you can get it. Put the meat in a pressure pot with two cups of water and pressure it till it's done. Then take it and roll it in flour and put it in a frying pan with shortening and fry it till it's brown on both sides.*

LIZZIE MOORE: *You dress a rabbit and when you've got it washed and all, just cut it up into small pieces. I always rolled it in flour or meal—just whichever one you prefer—and put salt and pepper on it to taste. And have your grease hot and just lay that in there, and if you cook it slow it tenders better. I think it's good eating.*

DEER

STELLA BURRELL: *I've cooked deer like a steak. We would beat it good like chopped steak and then roll it in flour and fry it. You can smother deer steaks with onions or something just like you do beef steaks to help take away the wild taste. But I've never used the tenderizer on deer, so it would maybe come out a little tough. It would depend on the age of the deer, I guess.*

Game Birds

ROAST WILD DUCK

1 wild duck
Stuffing of choice
⅔ cup undiluted canned consommé

Prepare the bird for cooking. Fill with preferred stuffing and place on a wire rack in covered roaster. Pour consommé in bottom, cover, and bake in a slow (250°F) oven for 2½ hours, or until tender.

WILD TURKEY

Wild turkey is prepared much like the domesticated turkey. After cleaning, some people cut off the legs and breast (saving them for frying like chicken) and stew the rest. Others rub the outside with lard, sprinkle it with 2 tablespoons of salt and 1 teaspoon of pepper, replace the liver and gizzard, and bake it for about 3 hours on low heat. After roasting, 2 cups of the resulting liquid are sometimes mixed in a saucepan with 2 tablespoons flour and ¼ cup water and heated to make gravy. Chopped liver and gizzard can be added.

Gladys Nichols adds: "Now I like the old-fashioned way of cooking wild turkey. And that's to cut it up, parboil it real good, and get it good and done and take it out and put it in an oven and bake it just a little. Or leave it in the pot and make gravy with it, either one. I like them that way better than I do the way they bake them now."

Lizzie Moore continues,

You prepare it just like a tame turkey. I prefer taking the broth out and making my dressing out of biscuit and corn bread. I bake my corn bread, and I bake my biscuit and make as much dressing as I want to. Now generally I think that a wild turkey is not as fat as a tame turkey, and you don't have as rich a broth. But I always put some butter in my broth when I'm making dressing. Then, of course, you've got to put salt, pepper, and sage in. Now some people like the dressing put in the turkey, but I put mine in an extra pan and have the dressing to itself. Then I cut it and set it on the table. And we used to take a wild turkey and slice the meat off its breast in big pieces, roll it in flour, and fry it. Now that's delicious. Next time you have a turkey you slice some off and try it. It'll fry just as brown like chicken, but it tastes different.

Lon Reid's family used to cut off the feathered wings, spread them out, and dry them in front of the fire. When stiff, they were used as fans for the fire.

ROAST QUAIL OR PARTRIDGE

1 quail or partridge
Butter
½ cup water
Salt and pepper to taste

Prepare the bird for roasting. Spread with butter, lay breast side up in an uncovered roasting pan, moisten with ½ cup water; season with salt and pepper. Roast in hot (450°F) oven for 5 minutes, then reduce the heat to 350°F and roast for 20 to 30 minutes longer. Baste frequently. Serve with gravy.

ROAST PHEASANT

1 pheasant (2½ to 3 pounds)
Stuffing of choice
Oil

Prepare the bird for roasting. Fill with preferred stuffing. Place on a wire rack in a covered roaster. Bake, uncovered, in a hot (400°F) oven for 20 minutes. Baste breast generously with oil; cover and bake at 250°F for 2 hours longer, or until tender.

Lizzie Moore claims, "The pheasant breast is the best eating there is."

BROILED QUAIL

Quail
Melted butter or margarine

Prepare the quail and split down the back. Brush each one with melted butter. Place, breast side down, on rack in broiler, broiling 6 to 8 minutes on each side. Brush once again with melted butter. Serve with juice from broiler pan.

FRIED QUAIL

2 quail
2 tablespoons flour
1 teaspoon salt
⅛ teaspoon pepper
2 tablespoons fat or oil
¾ cup light cream

Prepare the quail for cooking and split down the back. Mix the flour, salt, and pepper and roll the quail in the mixture. Brown in hot fat in a covered skillet. Add cream; cover and cook over low heat 20 to 25 minutes longer, or until tender. Make gravy from leftover fat.

PIGEON

BESSIE UNDERWOOD

"We used to cook pigeons. When we was children, we lived on a farm where they was lots of pigeons and you know, they multiply real fast. And they would kill maybe, oh seven, eight, or ten, and we would just fry them."

7 The River

They was plenty of fish in the river.

—*Minyard Conner*

Southern Appalachia is watered by a network of vibrant creeks, streams, rivers, and lakes. The region boasts one of the most complex and robust hydrological systems on earth, including a groundwater supply from which more than half the population draws drinking water. These aquifer systems also feed aboveground waterways. In addition, much of the region is part of a temperate rainforest, which means lush forests and a LOT of rain. Runoff careening down mountain slopes finds its way to thousands of creeks and streams, which feed the rivers, which feed the many lakes. As you might guess, fish and other water-based animals, such as turtles and frogs, are in abundance and have played a key role in the Appalachian diet for generations.

Fish

Minyard Conner: "One time I was camping in the mountains, and was starving to death! We didn't have nothing to eat but fish. I had my frying pan frying a fish and had one side cooked. I turned it over on the other side to cook, and reached in that pan and pulled that side off and ate, and left the side that was cooking in the pan. I pulled the bones out and ate the other side of that fish when it got done. I was that hungry! Couldn't wait!"

For people who enjoy camping, hunting, and fishing, it is customary to cook fish at the campsite or at least attempt it, as Buck Carver tells us: "When you go fishing and don't take anything to eat and you're depending on catching fish, I bet you're going to learn how to catch them darn things. Most of the time, when we went camping, we would take meat to fry, to make grease so the fish wouldn't stick to the pan. Most of the time we had a few fish to eat, but sometimes we wouldn't have so many. We always managed to make out with whatever we had, though."

Leonard Jones remembers: "I've camped out many a night. A whole bunch of us used to go together to Fontana [North Carolina]. We'd take a bunch of stuff and cook it. The camping was worth more than the fishing, almost."

Trout is the favorite fish in this area as told to us by many of our contacts, like Minyard Conner, who said, "I think speckled trout is the best eating fish I've had." Bream, catfish, bass, perch, and pike also rank high on the list as "good eating" fish in this area of the South.

"Stocked" fish, however, are not too popular here. Lawton Brooks echoed what several of our contacts had to say about stocked fish: "I don't eat them stocked fish. I just don't like [those that have been fed in the hatchery]. I like fish that's never had nothing to eat except just what fell in the creek. Then you got something! You can tell a difference in a fish that ain't never been hatchery fed and the stocked fish any time."

Preparing Fish for Cooking

The technique used to clean fish depends upon the kind of fish it is. Several people shared their techniques with us.

CATFISH

LEONARD JONES: *You have to skin a catfish. It ain't got no scales on it. Cut it around the neck, split it down the back and stomach, and take a pair of pliers and pull that skin off. You can skin 'em just about as quick as you can scrape 'em. If I catch a great big fish of any kind, I skin it. Small ones, I don't.*

WILLIE UNDERWOOD: *I clean big catfish by cutting around the head, and then pulling the skin off with a pair of pliers. Small catfish clean pretty easy. Just pour boiling water over them and the skin will turn loose. Then pull it off with pliers.*

TROUT AND BREAM

BUCK CARVER: *The rainbow and the brown trout and bream have scales and you have to scrape them. Though the speckled trout has scales, they're so fine you needn't try to scale him. All you do is rub that slime off with some sand. (Blanche Harkins takes the slime off with a scrub pad or a dishrag or luffa-gourd.)*

PERCH

BLANCHE HARKINS: *You skin perch. They have scales, but you just cut their heads off and get them started. The skin will just come off to the tail. You cook them the way you do trout. They're really good fresh fish.*

PIKE

LAWTON BROOKS: *A pike's bones lays exactly like a trout's. You fix them the same way, only you skin a pike. Generally when you catch a pike, he's a pretty good size, and you just cut around [his neck] and split him down the back. Then take your pliers and you can just pull that skin right off there.*

Lawton Brooks.

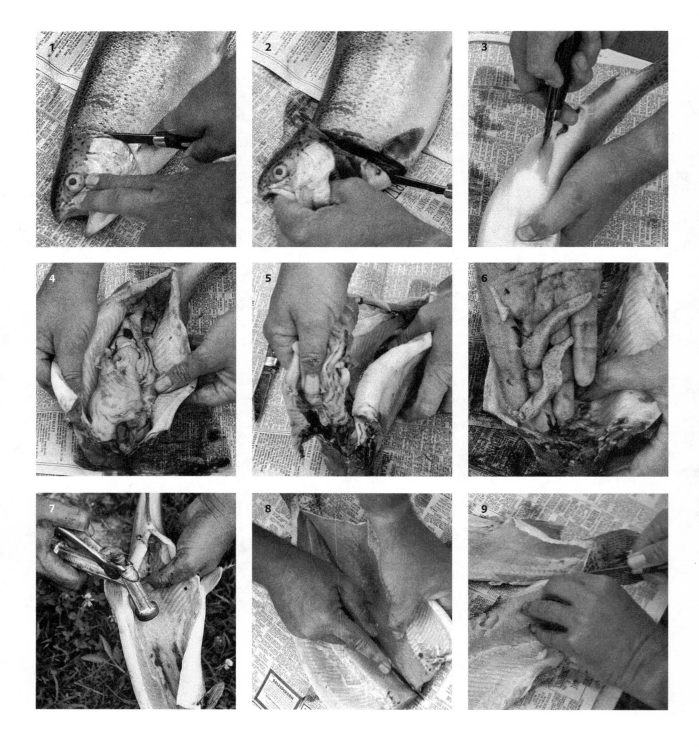

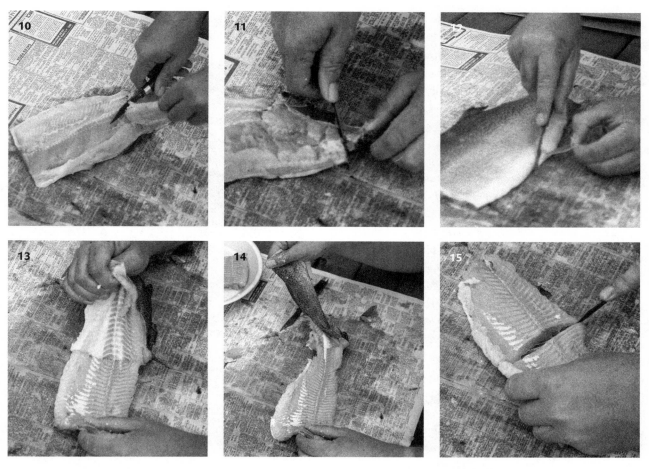

After washing the fish, lay it on a clean work surface—newspapers are good. Insert knife behind the gill and start cutting the head off (1). Pull on the head by inserting your fingers through the mouth (2). Holding the fish, belly side up, cut forward from the anal fin (3) and pull apart, exposing the entrails (4), and begin pulling them out (5). Fish eggs come out with the entrails (6). Wash out the inside using pressure from your fingers to scrape out the slimy remains. The pressure from a water hose is a good aid for doing this step (7). Slice through the middle of the two sections (8) until you have sliced completely through it to the caudal (tail) fin (9). Then cut one portion off where it is connected at the tail fin. Cut away the backbone (10). Cut off the tail fin and other fins (11–12). To skin the meat portions, pull up the skin on one end, being careful not to pull meat with the skin (13–14). Slice into fillet pieces (15) and you are ready to cook them (16).

Cooking Fish

There are several methods for cooking fish in this area. The South, being well known for "southern fried foods," is proud to include fried fish as a southern specialty and probably a favorite with most people in the area. Willie Underwood told us that almost all the fish "we catch around here can be fried."

Minyard Conner.

LEONARD JONES: *After I take their innards out and cut their heads and fins off, I salt the fish. Then I roll them good with cracker crumbs or cornmeal. I think cornmeal makes a better flavor. Then I put them in the shortening to fry. It's important to have your shortening pretty hot. Then turn them over and let them brown on the other side. I always turn my heat down and cook 'em slow so they get really cooked all the way through. One thing I don't do is to put a top on the skillet. The reason is because it makes the cornmeal soft and easy to come off. Leave the skillet open after you've turned your heat down. I cook stocked fish about twenty-five to thirty minutes, because they're not usually tough or hard to cook. If a fish is real wide, I slice it in two down the back. If you like crisp fish, just slice 'em and cook them quickly.*

MINYARD CONNER: *There are a lot of ways you can cook trout—bake 'em, fry 'em, or stew 'em. Now these stockers [stocked fish]—I'd stew 'em and take the bones out and make fish patties out of them because their meat's too tender to hold together to fry.*

Minyard's wife, Lessie, elaborated:

Take a mess of fish—ten trout or stockers—and boil them with a little grease and salt. When they are real tender, let them cool. Remove bones. Save a little of the juice in which the fish were boiled and add to a cup of flour. Mix in fish, two eggs, and one onion, chopped fine. Make mixture into patties and fry in hot grease until brown on both sides.

To bake fish, you coat them with a little grease and lemon juice. Heat your oven to about 350 and cook 'em about thirty minutes. And I've eat fish eggs. I've caught a lot of big fish with big rolls of eggs under them. Boy, I like them! That's caviar. That's good. That's extra good! Talk about burning you in grease! They'll pop and bust when you're frying them, and they'll burn you, buddy! I have never ate the liver out of a fish. I bet that would be really good, too.

SALMON CROQUETTES
MARY ELLEN MEANS

2 eggs
¼ teaspoon baking powder
¼ cup flour
¼ cup cornmeal
1 (8-ounce) can salmon (undrained)

Mix ingredients thoroughly and drop from teaspoons into hot fat to fry. Watch closely and turn to brown other side. Fry about 2 to 3 minutes on each side. Yield: *8 to 12 croquettes.*

Preserving Fish

Minyard Conner tells about preserving fish in the old days:

Well, I was raised with the Indians. They wouldn't do like the white man does—you know, catch too many of anything and have to throw them away. They'd just catch what they could eat, and that's all they took. If they could eat ten, then that's all they took. They didn't usually try to preserve them.

They was plenty of fish in the river. And it's always been a puzzle to me—we lived on the Oconoluftee River [in Cherokee, North Carolina]. They was over there on the other prong, and where they lived was the Indian territory. When I was a boy, there was what I called "chubs." That was a fish that was five or six inches long. When you'd catch one, he'd say, "Rooork, rooork," and start making a fuss. There was plenty of chubs in both forks of that river, but later on you could hardly catch them in the area where we'd lived, and there was still plenty in that part of the river that was Indian territory. (I guess they were more careful not to catch too many of them at one time, and the white man would get all he could catch, whether he was going to eat them or not. Just fished them all out.)

Well, the Indians would catch them chubs and fry 'em good and brown—just as hard as they could fry 'em—and put 'em in flour sacks and fill up those flour sacks. Just cook them in a frying pan right there by the river where they'd caught them, and they said those would last them two or three weeks. Now that's the only way they preserved them. They'd cook every bit of the grease out of the pan, and get 'em just as brown as they could get 'em, and they was good, too! You didn't have to worry about the bones because they were all cooked up. They'd just cut the heads off and pull out the backbones and ribs. The little ones that were left would just break up. They wouldn't hurt you to swallow.

JAKE WALDROOP: *[Before we had a freezer] we had some cool springs, and we would put any fish we weren't going to cook right then in a bucket or half-gallon jars and stand them under those springs where the cold water would run over them. We could keep them for four or five days or more.*

BLANCHE HARKINS: *To prepare fish for freezing, you first clean the fish and cut out their insides and wash them. Don't salt them before you put them in the freezer. Generally, I put enough in one plastic bag—and some people use half-gallon cardboard milk cartons—for one meal. Then I cover them with clear water and seal them up. Being packed in water keeps them from being freezer-burned. When I'm ready to cook them, I thaw them in cold running water. I wouldn't think about thawing them in hot water because they would tear all to pieces, they're so tender.*

Turtle

The origins of this section go back to the mid-1970s, when students Keith Head, Vickie Chastain, and Eddie Connor, along with staff members Suzy Angier and Pat Rogers, took a live mud turtle to Mrs. Vergil Lovell, who had agreed to show them how to clean and cook it. They spent the day there, tape recording and photographing the proceedings, and that evening, before returning home, they all sat down with Mrs. Lovell to a turtle dinner.

As sometimes happens, however, the students graduated before they could work up their material into publishable form. Years later, Pat Marcellino and Kenny Crumley uncovered the fat file folder labeled "turtles" and decided to finish

Lilly Lovell cleaning a turtle.

the article. They transcribed the tapes, printed the photographs, and, finding that some information they needed was missing, tried to contact Mrs. Lovell again, only to discover that she had died in the intervening years. Here is what she said:

[My husband] always got them by the tail. He'd just catch them. Keep their head away from you, though, because they'll bite you, and they are mean, too. And we've caught them with a hook. But now we had mud turtle hooks—great big ones. I ain't seen one of them in a long time. You can use a regular fish hook, but you have to be awfully careful because they'll get loose from that now. They'll snap it so quick you'll [lose them]. I guess they still have mud turtle hooks in fishing stores, but I ain't seen none since Daddy used them.

Now Verge always, when he was living, I'd go with him and he'd catch a chicken out of the chicken house—just a small little old chicken—chop it in two, and put one half on each hook good. Go back the next morning and he had two mud turtles.

Once we had a man that worked here, and we had a pipe almost like a stovepipe that carried water from the pond to the chicken house. Well, the water kept being cut off, and he'd come to the house and say, "I can't get nothing out. The water's gone and them chickens is starving to death."

So Verge said, "They's something in the pipe up there." So they went up there and worked and piddled and couldn't do nothing with it. So Verge just went in the pond and got down in there, and it was a mud turtle about the size of a dinner plate had stopped the hole up!

Now I like to cook these turtles when I clean them, unless I'm going to cut them up and freeze them like you would chicken or any other meat. When I cook them, I put them on and cook them till they're tender in salt and water. If you want to, you can put a little pod of pepper in. It won't hurt them a bit. Gives that whang to them that they ought to have. Now if you boil the meat too long, it'll just come all to pieces and I don't like it that way. I like to still have the pieces whole where you can pick them up just like a piece of chicken. It's pretty meat, and I don't want it to come off the bone if I can keep it on.

The boiling part doesn't take as long. It depends on the size of the turtle. One great big one I cooked took me nearly four hours, but they usually don't take that long. I always take my fork and test it and see if it's tender enough. When it is, I take those pieces out and fry them in a frying pan—brown them up nice.

Lots of times I've found thirty and forty eggs in them. You know the size of a partridge [grouse or pheasant] egg, don't you? Like that size. The last one I cooked had thirty-five or forty in it. I took them out and put them in a bowl in there and they filled a pretty good-sized bowl up. I don't care for them too much, though. You can't hardly cook them. They're a kind of rubbery—kind of a watery thing. They don't taste right to me. But now they say they make the best cakes there are, but I ain't done that now.

You'll get enough meat off an average-sized turtle for supper and two pieces left over to give to the cat! There's plenty of meat in them. I guess two pound and a half in one with any size to it. Lots of times you can't eat a whole hind leg by yourself. There's plenty of eating in it, and it's good meat, too.

Frogs

Large frogs also found their way into the Appalachian diet. Frog gigging was a popular pastime for many, especially young boys looking for something to do. Frog legs were most often battered and fried. Glenn Worley noted,

I caught bullfrogs for years when my father worked for Georgia Power. We always could get them out on the lake or in the river. We gigged them and caught them with our hands. They are delightful. We've had frogs all our lives.

Most times you just lay them out on a board and take a large butcher knife and cut them right above the joint of the hind legs against the backbone. You just cut them totally in two crossways. Just sever the two legs from the rest of the body. Then you take a knife and cut a slit down either leg. Take pliers or pullers and the skin will pull off in one piece down to the web feet. Then you take the same knife and cut their feet off, and the legs are totally dressed. You don't do anything further. There's no organs or anything attached when you cut them loose from the rest of his body. Just get two legs, that's all you want, and that's all you eat.

Then you just dip them in flour and put them in the skillet or pan and fry them in the same temperature you normally would chicken until they become brown. The meat is perfectly white and tender. Add just a little flour and perhaps pepper if you like—but lightly of both. The meat is very delicate and very choice. We always eat frog legs. I would now if I could find them!

Lizzie Moore had this to add on preparing frog: "Well you just dress them, put some salt and pepper on them, roll 'em in your meal, put 'em in your hot grease. Now they'll move and that's the reason I never could eat 'em. But it's the nature of it . . . being in water I guess. And you know whenever you put it in that hot grease it just moves. And I never did like it. If I had somebody else to cook 'em, I might eat 'em."

8 The Gristmill

*He's married a woman that can't
even cook corn bread.*
—Belle Ledford

After the invention of the gristmill, people could take the grains of corn, wheat, and rye, which they grew themselves, to be ground into meal for bread making. Although wheat and rye could be found in this region, the most common and versatile meal commodity in the kitchen was cornmeal, introduced to European settlers by Native Americans.

Cornmeal, grits, and hominy are all made from corn that is not harvested until after autumn frost, when the husks and kernels of the corn are hard and dry. The ears are either gathered and stored or shucked (husked) and the kernels shelled off the cobs. The kernels can be made into hominy, or they can be stored in cloth sacks in an airy area through the winter until they are ground. If left on the cob, they can be shelled at the time of grinding.

When going to the mill, most people preferred to take one or two bushels at a time so that their meal or grits did not stay on the kitchen shelf over long periods. If not used, the meal could become stale or infested with weevils.

Up until about thirty years ago, many folks raised their own corn for grinding. At the time of the first printing of *The Foxfire Book of Appalachian Cookery*, several water-powered gristmills were still in operation. Most had been somewhat modernized, such as the one Ruby Frady operated in the Persimmon Community in Rabun County. Mrs. Frady agreed to talk with Foxfire about her mill, and when we went to see her, she had her mill in operation. The following section came from that interview, which was conducted in 1984.

In 1955, Mrs. Frady and her husband, Lon, began operating the mill that he had built over a stream in the Persimmon Community. Together they ground cornmeal for the people of the surrounding area until Lon died in 1967. Since then, Ruby has continued to run their mill alone, serving a handful of customers who "don't come regular." Some days she doesn't grind any meal; on other days she might grind two or three bushels or perhaps only one "turn," which, Ruby tells us, is a bushel—the smallest amount she'll grind. A sixty-five-pound bushel of corn weighs, after grinding, about forty-eight pounds. For grinding this amount, Ruby charges a dollar and a half. "Some of them," she says, "want to pay first, but all of them don't want to pay. They want me to take a toll out, or take out so much meal for running it."

With her small fees, Ruby has to buy both gasoline and diesel fuel for her mill, which is run by two motors. She starts on gas and then turns over onto diesel, using a switch similar to a Jeep ignition. While getting the motor to crank is sometimes a chore, Ruby says that the most difficult part of the job is pouring the corn into the hopper. She says, "It's a pretty hard job grinding a whole lot at the time, but I don't mind it too bad when it ain't cold, just for a few turns."

Lester Baker told us about a gristmill that once operated in the Oak Grove Community:

The gristmill down here on the creek was last run in the early 1960s. Jimmy Howard bought it and was the last one to run it, and that's been fifteen or twenty years ago. My dad ran it, but my granddaddy and my uncles were the main ones that ran the mill. We had all these mills down here, and all except for the sawmill and shingle mill were pulled by water power. They were pulled by steam engine. When we lived down there we'd go grind corn any day anybody came. We didn't have no certain day to grind. We would take the toll out, and that was the way most people paid. An eighth of a bushel is what we got for grinding a bushel. We had a little box [down at the mill], and it'd hold about a half a gallon. Take that out twice for a bushel, and if they had a half a bushel we'd only take it out one time. If anybody wanted to pay with money they would, but I don't remember how much. People came from all over the community and some from over the mountain to have their corn ground here. They'd bring five or six bushels of corn in a wagon.

(For more information about gristmills, see *Foxfire Book 2*, pp. 142–63, and *Foxfire Book 6*, pp. 285–86.)

Corn Bread

Practically every contact Foxfire students interviewed for the first edition of this book gave a recipe for corn bread. Like most other older people in the area, Rittie Webb's grandparents cooked their corn bread in a Dutch oven in the fireplace: "I remember my grandpa used to get my grandma to make corn bread in the fireplace. It'd cook good if you got good [hot] coals and a good fire. We used to eat corn bread every day, and older people lived on it. My daddy lived on it and he lived to be ninety-three years old. It's got good stuff in it. We used to take corn bread and put buttermilk over it and eat it."

Later, of course, there were wood cookstoves, and corn bread remained a staple—and one item all women had to know how to cook. As Margie Ledford said, "The first thing I learned to cook was corn bread. There was about ten in our family altogether, and it took a pretty good pone of bread to fill them up with just 'taters, butter, corn bread, meat, and milk. I think corn bread tasted better cooked in a wood stove. Maybe that was just my belief, but I really do think that if you had a good hot wood stove and put your corn bread in there, it seemed like it tasted better."

During hard times, families depended on cornmeal for their main source of food when other products were unavailable. We heard several stories much like the one Stella Burrell told us: "I can remember during the Depression when we wasn't able to have flour, and my mother was sick in the hospital. I can remember having corn bread for breakfast, and my daddy would fix cornmeal gravy oftentimes. We did eat a lot of gravy; we called it 'sawmill gravy.'"

Gladys Nichols told us about one of the earliest methods for making bread: "We used to dry the corn for roastin' ears. Then we shucked it and baked it in the oven. Then you could grate it off the cob, put you a little soda and salt and a little buttermilk in it and bake it. That's called 'roastin' ear bread.'"

Another contact gave us instructions for making gritted meal chestnut bread, another old recipe that is seldom used today: "Gather the corn just past the roasting ear stage. Grit the raw corn on a meal gritter. Remove the chestnut meats from the hulls, scald, and remove bitter skins. Cook in water until tender. Pour boiling chestnut meats and water into gritted meal (be careful with the amount of water lest dough become too soft), fashion into hand-sized pones, wrap with corn blades or hickory leaves, drop into a pot of boiling water, and cook until done (an hour or so)."

CORN BREAD ON A WOOD STOVE

RUBY FRADY

3 cups freshly ground cornmeal
½ to 1 teaspoon salt
½ teaspoon soda
½ cup milk

Sift freshly ground (not self-rising) cornmeal into a large bowl. Add salt and soda, mixing well, and then the milk. Mix thoroughly and pour into a greased pan. Bake in a 450°F oven until golden brown (approximately 20 to 30 minutes). When brown, take out of the oven, let cool for a few minutes, and turn out the bread by inverting the pan. Yield: *6 to 8 servings*.

CORN BREAD

ANNIE LONG

2 cups cornmeal
1 teaspoon soda
1 teaspoon salt
1 egg, beaten
2 cups sour milk [buttermilk]
*2 tablespoons melted lard**

Sift cornmeal to get bran out. Measure the cornmeal, soda, and salt and sift together. Mix in beaten egg, milk, and melted lard. Pour into a hot greased iron skillet and bake in a 425°F oven. Yield: *6 servings*.

*Melt the lard in the skillet and this leaves the pan ready for baking.

QUICK AND EASY CORN BREAD

BERTHA WALDROOP

2 cups self-rising cornmeal

1 egg

Milk or water

Mix cornmeal and egg together. Add enough milk or water to make a thick batter and beat. Grease a pan and bake at 425°F until brown. Yield: *4 to 6 servings.*

CRACKLIN CORN BREAD

To add a different flavor to corn bread, cooks learned to use cracklins. Granny Gibson told us: "You can put cracklins in it. That's what I like—cracklin bread. You know when you kill a hog you've got all kinds of fat and stuff. You have to cut it up and put it on the stove and cook it out to make your lard. You have to keep it stirred, and it'll fry down to the cracklins. That's where your cracklins comes in at. Put them in with your corn bread whenever you go to cook it. That makes it good."

QUICK AND EASY CRACKLIN BREAD

RUTH HOLCOMB

2 cups self-rising cornmeal

1 cup cracklins

1 cup milk

Mix cornmeal, cracklins, and milk together. Pour into a greased pan and bake in a hot (425°F) oven until done, 20 or more minutes.

BUTTERMILK CRACKLIN BREAD

2 cups cornmeal

2 teaspoons salt

1 teaspoon soda

½ teaspoon baking powder

1 cup buttermilk

½ cup cracklins

Lukewarm water (optional)

Mix together the cornmeal, salt, soda, baking powder, and buttermilk. Mix cracklins into the mixture. If it is too dry, use some lukewarm water to make it the right consistency for corn bread. Bake in a 425°F oven for ½ hour, or until brown.

Cornmeal Recipes

Belle Ledford told us about learning to cook and the ways she has learned to use cornmeal through the years:

I couldn't even cook corn bread when I was married. Doc Page's mother came to visit me, and she was talking about cooking. I said, "Why, I can't even make corn bread." And she went up to Howard's [Ledford, her brother-in-law] and said, "I'm sorry for John Ledford. He's married a woman that can't even cook corn bread!" And I couldn't, but I just kept trying. I got recipes and tried to follow them and I eventually learned. [Now] I use cornmeal for other [cooking, too]. In cooking my fish, I roll the fish in it. And I use it in making potato croquettes. I dip my squash in cornmeal when I fry it; [and when] I make potato soup, I put cornmeal in it. I use corn bread in making my turkey dressing and chicken dressing.

Another use for cornmeal is in making cornmeal mush, most often used as a breakfast cereal. Stella Burrell remembers when her mother made mush: "My mother used to make cornmeal mush sometimes at night, too, and as a child I've helped her stir that over a fire in the fireplace, but that'd be when she was the supervisor, you know [laughing]. It was mostly made with just water and meal, and I'm sure she salted it. We ate it with milk, but I've known people to put sugar or butter in it. It'd be something similar to grits."

CORNMEAL MUSH

RUTH HOLCOMB

1 cup cornmeal

2 cups water

Pinch of salt

Sift meal. Bring water to a boil. Add a pinch of salt. Pour meal into the boiling water and continue cooking. Stir until thick. Put mush into a cereal bowl. Serve with sweet milk or buttermilk, and if desired add butter and sugar. Yield: *3 to 4 servings*.

CORNMEAL DUMPLINGS

RUTH HOLCOMB

"Use beef broth to cook these dumplings in. Remove the stewed beef and have only the liquid. Bring it to a rolling boil. Add salt to taste. Make up a cornmeal dough, the same kind you would for corn bread. Roll it into little patties, about two tablespoons to each. Drop these into the boiling broth, one at a time. Bring the broth back to boiling and cook the patties—or dumplings—for fifteen minutes. Stick a fork into them to test for doneness. They are ready to serve when cooked."

GOOD OLD-FASHIONED CORN LIGHTBREAD

ADA KELLY

1 quart cornmeal mush

Salt to taste

Cold water

¾ cup sugar

¾ cup lard

Cornmeal

Cook cornmeal mush until thoroughly done; add salt to taste. Remove from heat and add cold water until cool enough to stick a finger in without burning. Then add sugar, lard, and enough cornmeal to make a good, thick batter. Set aside until it ferments (overnight). Add enough meal to make a stiff batter. Bake in a well-greased 8-inch skillet at 350°F until brown. Remove from the pan when cooled.

CORN CAKES

2 cups cornmeal

1 heaping tablespoon flour

1 teaspoon salt

2 teaspoons baking powder

1 tablespoon melted butter or lard

2 eggs, beaten

Buttermilk

Sift together dry ingredients. Add butter and beaten eggs. Mix in enough milk to make a thin batter, being careful not to let it get too thin. Pour out into a hot griddle and flip onto other side when brown. Amount of batter poured out depends on desired size of cakes. Good with butter and syrup.

CORN PONES

2 cups cornmeal
1 teaspoon baking powder
½ teaspoon salt
1 tablespoon lard
Milk

Mix together cornmeal, baking powder, and salt. Cut in lard and add enough milk to make a stiff batter. Form into pones with hands (or add some milk and drop from the end of a spoon), and place in a greased pan. Bake in a 425°F oven for 20 to 30 minutes.

CORNMEAL MUFFINS

1 egg, well beaten
1½ cups buttermilk
2 cups cornmeal, sifted
1 teaspoon salt
1 teaspoon soda
Melted lard

Mix together well-beaten egg and ¾ cup of the buttermilk. Add sifted cornmeal, salt, remaining ¾ cup buttermilk, and soda. Place pans (iron preferred) on top of range or stove; place in each division a teaspoonful of melted lard and let come to boiling point; when a blue smoke rises, fill each division half full of batter. Let rise while on top of the range, then place in a 400°F oven and bake until golden brown.

HUSH PUPPIES

1 cup self-rising flour
1 cup cornmeal
⅛ teaspoon salt
¼ teaspoon soda
1 egg
1½ cups buttermilk, or as needed
1 medium onion, chopped
Fat for deep frying

Sift together flour, cornmeal, salt, and soda. Add egg and buttermilk until it's the right consistency to hold its shape when rolled into a ball. Mix in onion, then roll into balls about 1 to 2 inches across and drop in deep hot fat. Fry until they're brown and crispy. Let them drain a bit on some paper and serve hot.

RYE BREAD WITH CORNMEAL

1 cup wheat flour
1 cup rye flour
½ cup cornmeal
1 teaspoon salt
1 teaspoon baking powder
3 tablespoons shortening
Buttermilk
½ teaspoon soda per cup of buttermilk

Sift together wheat flour and rye flour, cornmeal, salt, and baking powder. Cut in shortening. Add enough buttermilk to make a firm dough, adding ½ teaspoon of soda per cup of buttermilk. Mix thoroughly, then roll out to about ½-inch thick. Cut as you would biscuits, place on a greased sheet, and bake in a 450°F oven for 10 to 12 minutes.

Grits

Grits are a breakfast cereal very common in this part of the South. They are made from corn that is not harvested until autumn after frost, when the husks are dry and the kernels of corn are hard. Grits, a coarser grind than cornmeal, may be ground on the same millstones with the stones set a bit farther apart. Some millers told us that they have two sets of millstones, one for grits and one for cornmeal.

One of our contacts remembers that her mother would take out a portion of ground corn and sift it to separate the grits from the meal. The "meal" that went through the sifter would be set aside and used for bread. Everything that did not sift through—the grits and the hulls—was then poured into a bowl or pot to be washed. It was covered with water and the trash and hulls floated to the top and were discarded. The grits settled to the bottom. Some contacts recommend washing their grits, and some let the grits soak overnight before cooking them for breakfast. Others feel this isn't necessary.

To cook grits, add them to a pot of boiling water. The proportions are 1 cup grits to 4 cups water. Add salt to taste, usually ½ teaspoon per cup of grits. Cook at a moderate heat, low simmer, for about 30 minutes, or until grits have absorbed the water and are the consistency of applesauce or oatmeal. Stir often to prevent their sticking to the pan. Water may be added during cooking if you think they are too dry or haven't cooked long enough.

Grits are usually served on a plate for breakfast with butter or gravy, or for lunch or supper as a vegetable with butter, gravy, or cheese melted over them. They may be cooked the night before and heated the next morning, adding water if needed for the proper consistency.

Biscuits

Exie Dills talked about biscuits: "I was eighty-five the twenty-second of October, so it's been eighty years since I started making biscuits. At first I was so little I couldn't reach the table to work my dough. Mommy had a bread tray and I'd put that on the floor and make up my dough on the floor. I made up biscuits that way a many a time, and there never was one refused to be eat. And I don't say it to be bragging, but I've never been beat in making biscuits yet."

Through the years, biscuits have become almost a ritual for the morning meal in this area of the South. Stella Burrell told us her mother "always made homemade biscuits for breakfast." Even when loaf bread became common, she made biscuits, because "she didn't like toast."

Gladys Nichols still makes biscuits using her hands to roll them out: "Most of the time I stir them up with my hands and knead the dough until I get it kneaded real good. And then I squeeze my biscuits off and roll them out with my hands. [Squeeze off enough dough for one biscuit, roll dough between palms and flatten, then place on baking sheet.] I don't use a roller like most people do, 'cause I can make them faster than I can roll them out. I don't make little bitty ones either; I make great big ones."

Biscuits cooked with plain flour must have salt and soda added. When self-rising flour became available, cooks like Lucy York discovered it to be more convenient: "I use self-rising flour; don't have to bother too much about baking powder and so forth. It's a little more convenient."

Gladys Nichols shows us the bread tray she had made more than forty years ago. It is made out of basswood, which is very light and will not crack easily.

Fay Long takes her browned biscuits out of the oven of her wood stove.

However, others found it more difficult to switch to self-rising flour.

As Inez Taylor reminisced: "I never did cook too much when I was at home. Mama usually done most of the cooking, and Daddy done a lot of it. Daddy could make better biscuits than Mama could. He always got up to make biscuits every morning and every night for supper until they started buying self-rising flour. Then he never would make no biscuits, because he wanted to put all the stuff in it hisself [laughter]."

Self-rising flour soon became widely accepted by cooks, and eventually it was considered to be the number one staple on the kitchen shelf. Not many cooks today use plain flour for making biscuits. Inez Taylor told us: "I *cannot* make bread out of plain flour. I either get too much soda or too much salt."

The Frady gristmill.

The hopper is the V-shaped, funnel-like attachment on top.

Ground meal shoots into the trough to be bagged and weighed.

Ruby Frady waits for ground meal to come out of the hopper.

Addie Norton explained to us how she has made her biscuits throughout the years:

I just sift my flour, usually about two or three cups or however much I want to make. Then I put in about three big, good, deep tablespoons of lard and mix that all up till it's fine like, just in little balls. You know how it does when you mix it up. Then I put in milk, enough to dampen my dough. Work it pretty well and roll her out and cook her. I don't never time them. I just—when I think they've been in there long enough—go look at them and see if they're brown; then I take them out. It takes about fifteen or

twenty minutes if your stove's not too hot. About ten minutes will usually cook them if they're not too thick when you roll them out. Lots of people love thin biscuits and a lot of them love them up like that. When they're right thin it don't take long to cook them.

Now I use the self-rising flour. I didn't used to. Back then a lot of times it wasn't made up like it is now. You had to add your own soda and salt and stuff in it and your buttermilk. And I made them with my hands. They wasn't none of them little rolled-out ones; they were made out with my hands. I didn't roll them out then, I patted them in the pan. I don't ever put my hands in the dough any more because I make them littler and I can make them with a spoon. But now to make the biggest biscuits anywhere in the world, make them with your hands. You take your hands, you squeeze that lard, you get it all the same way, gets all through it good, and it ain't in wads and things like that. You get that all stirred up good, you know, all just alike, then put in your milk and mix it together right on for a long time. And then try and put it on your board before it gets too hard. I don't like those dry biscuits. I make mine just dry enough to hold them together so I can roll them out and cut them. And you have some good biscuits.

When Addie was asked how many biscuits she had to make to feed her four boys she exclaimed:

Fifty of a morning! If one or two of the young'uns was sick, they would leave one or two maybe. Hardly ever. Sometimes I'd have enough for the baby to have one or two before dinnertime, you know, and the rest were gone to school. But that's what it took to feed them of the morning—fifty biscuits. It took a great big half a dishpan full of flour nearly, quite a little bit of flour. And I had a great big dough board that Daddy made me. I've cut it in two one time and then cut off another piece off of it. It was great big, but now it's short. I'd pat out my biscuits on that board and put them in the pan. I had two great big pans. I could put twenty-five biscuits in one pan and twenty-five in the other. You know, when you get your biscuits cut out you got a little wad of dough left? Well, I'd just take and roll it out kinda thick and put it in there, you know, to cut it into biscuits. And my boys would quarrel over that little pone of bread. They thought it was better than the rest [laughter].

Like corn bread, biscuits recipes were shared with us by a majority of our contacts.

BAKING POWDER BISCUITS

2 cups flour
½ teaspoon salt
1 tablespoon baking powder
⅓ cup lard or shortening
½ to ¾ cup milk

Sift flour, salt, and baking powder together. Work in lard or shortening with fingers or fork. Gradually add the milk until mixture is well blended. Put out on a floured cloth, roll, and cut. Place on a baking sheet and bake in a 400°F oven for 10 minutes. Yield: *16 biscuits*.

QUICK BISCUITS

BESSIE UNDERWOOD

½ cup lard or other shortening
3 cups self-rising flour
1 cup milk

Work lard into flour, using a fork, until crumbly. Pour in milk and mix together into a good batter. Put out on floured surface, roll out, and cut. Bake in a 400°F oven for 10 to 12 minutes. "That makes fourteen biscuits and that does us all day."

SODA BISCUITS

NORA GARLAND

"I've had some awful good biscuits off a wood stove. Just as brown. I got the prize at the fair for my biscuits. Mix together four cups self-rising flour and a pinch of soda; add two tablespoons lard or other shortening and mix until meal-like. Add one cup milk and make into good dough. Put out on floured surface, roll and cut out. Bake at 425 degrees for eight to ten minutes." Yield: *32 biscuits*.

"RIZ" BISCUITS
ARIZONA DICKERSON

1 package dry yeast

1 cup warm buttermilk

½ teaspoon baking soda

2½ cups flour

1 teaspoon salt

2 tablespoons sugar or more, if desired

½ cup lard

Mix yeast with warm buttermilk. Add soda. Cut the lard into the dry ingredients. Slowly mix liquid mixture into dry ingredients. Roll out on a board and cut out biscuits. Let stand long enough to rise. Then bake about 12 minutes in 425°F oven. Yield: 24 biscuits.

CINNAMON BISCUITS
MARGIE HAWKINS

3 cups self-rising flour

1 cup Crisco

1/2 cup raisins (optional)

1 cup sweet milk, or whole milk

1 ground cinnamon stick

Mix dough. Add enough cinnamon to make dough a dark color. Add ½ cup raisins if desired. Roll out and cut as regular biscuits. Bake at 450°F for 10 to 15 minutes. Glaze: add milk (a few drops at a time) to 2 cups of powdered sugar until it becomes a creamy glaze. Spread over warm biscuits.

EASY PAN BREAD
OLENE GARLAND

"This is a good recipe to use if you don't want to make the mess or take the time to roll your biscuits out. Mix up desired biscuit recipe, adding more milk than usual to make a thinner batter. Pour into a greased pan and cook at 425 degrees until light golden brown."

PAN-FRIED BREAD
OLENE GARLAND

"Mix up desired biscuit recipe, and using a large spoon, drop batter into patties in a heated frying pan with ¼ inch of grease or oil and let cook and brown slowly one side, then turn and brown slowly on second side. Corn bread can be mixed and cooked the same way."

Dumplings

Cooks could create more interesting dishes using the biscuit dough for dumplings in stewed fruits, vegetables, and meats; crusts for vegetable, meat, and fruit pies; and a variety of desserts (see chapter 9).

DUMPLINGS
MARY ELLEN MEANS

4 cups flour*

⅓ cup lard or other shortening

1½ to 2 cups water

Mix together flour and lard. Add water and mix thoroughly. Toss dough on a floured surface until coated with flour. Divide into 4 balls and roll dough out, 1 ball at a time, to about ¼ inch or thinner. Cut in strips into 2-inch pieces. Add a few pieces at a time to boiling broth. Cook, uncovered, making sure that the whole dumpling is under the liquid part of the time. Cook about 5 to 10 minutes. Yield: 4 to 5 large servings.

*If using self-rising flour, heat water so dough will rise before you cook it.

After mixing up her recipe, Ruby Frady uses her hand to scoop the batter into a hot skillet.

After letting it cool for a few minutes, she inverts the skillet and easily empties the bread into her hand.

BUTTERED DUMPLINGS

FAY LONG

2 cups self-rising flour

2 teaspoons baking powder

½ cup shortening

½ cup instant nonfat dry milk (or 1 cup milk, more if softer dough is desired)

1 can clear chicken broth plus ½ can water (omit extra ½ can if milk is used)

Pepper to taste

Mix flour and baking powder; cut in shortening. Add milk to make a dough. Roll out and cut into desired shapes. Drop into boiling broth mixture, which has been seasoned with pepper. Reduce heat to medium and cook until dumplings are tender.

Cooking corn cakes takes longer than baking corn bread, but many people prefer them over baked corn bread.

Yeast Breads and Rolls

In earlier times, yeast used in bread making was not always easy to come by. Many women combined the yeast they had on hand with other ingredients to produce more yeast, which they dried into small cakes, thus ensuring a handy supply at all times.

Lettie Chastain told us about her mother making yeast and yeast bread, and about the hard work women had to do to keep the family going:

My mother used to make loaves of yeast bread, and she'd start with a little cake of yeast. You'd make yeast in cakes then. She'd have a pan about as big as a dishpan, and she'd let her dough rise about three inches. She'd shut it up in the safe [cabinet used for storing food], and we'd go to the field and work. When we'd come back to the house that night, it'd be all rose up. Then at dinnertime we'd have that great big old loaf of bread to eat on. That would save time, you see. We had homemade flour. It wasn't as pretty and white, but it was good. It would make big old thick pies and stuff, and it sure was good on those wood stoves. Mother made cobblers—chicken cobbler, potato or apple cobbler. In the summertime women had it hard. They had to go to the fields every day, do the canning, and then on Saturday do the washing and the ironing—all that besides cooking.

Three of our contacts told us how they used to make their own yeast but pointed out that, because homemade yeast often fails, it is more sensible and convenient to buy the packaged kind in the stores.

Dorothy Beck's version:

Boil three potatoes with the jacket on them, and you take fresh peach tree leaves and boil them until you boil all the strength out of them. Then you take the leaf part out and take your potatoes and mash them up in that peach leaf juice and then you add cornmeal to it to thicken it. Sometimes you can put a small cake of bought yeast in it. Then you roll it out in little patties the size that you want for a batch and lay them out in the sun to dry. I used to work at the Earl House and Mrs. Earl used to make all her yeast. She never bought any, and that's the way she made it.

Mary Pitts describes another method of making yeast at home:

Peel and boil three medium Irish potatoes with a handful of peach leaves or hops. Remove the potatoes and mash; strain water in which they were boiled back into potatoes. There should be approximately three cups of potatoes and water. Let become tepid. Dissolve two yeast cakes [packages] in one-third cup of water and add to mixture. Add one teaspoon sugar, one-quarter teaspoon salt, and set in warm place to rise overnight. Next morning stir into the yeast sufficient cornmeal to make a very stiff mixture. Let rise again from one and a half to two hours. Now add more cornmeal to make a stiff dough, roll out until one-third inch thick, cut into squares about two inches large, dry in shade, turning until dry and hard. Do not allow to sour, but turn daily until firm. Compressed yeast may be used as a starter. In recipe, use one yeast cake for one quart of flour. Two cakes or more may be used if a shorter [cooking] time is desired.

HOMEMADE LIQUID YEAST

BELLE LEDFORD

8 medium-size potatoes

1 quart lukewarm water or water in which
    potatoes are cooked

½ cup sugar

1 tablespoon salt

1 package dry yeast

Boil potatoes and mash fine. Add water. Add sugar, salt, and yeast, which has been dissolved in lukewarm water. Let stand in a warm place for several hours. Pour into ½-gallon glass fruit jars, filling about two-thirds full. Cover but do not seal. Put in cool place. Use 1 cup, or ½ cup if you have plenty of time, in place of yeast cake.

As with biscuits, the dough for yeast rolls may be pinched off and rolled between the hands or they can be rolled out on a floured surface using a rolling pin, the latter being the method that Rittie Webb uses. She then cuts them out and places them in her buttered iron skillet. In another iron skillet she melts butter and dots a small amount on top of each roll.

MARY'S ROLLS

MARY BROWN

1 package dry yeast

⅓ cup warm water

1 cup warm milk

⅓ cup melted butter or shortening,
    plus more for dipping rolls

¼ cup sugar

1 teaspoon salt

3½ to 4 cups flour

Dissolve yeast in warm water. Mix together warm milk, melted butter, sugar, and salt. Mix together the yeast and milk mixture. Gradually stir in flour. Mix for 5 minutes. Cover the dough and let rise until doubled in bulk. Roll out dough and cut with a biscuit cutter. Dip each round into melted butter and place in a pan. Cover with a cloth and let rise for 1½ hours. Bake in a 350°F oven for 30 minutes. Yield: 25 to 30 rolls.

EASY REFRIGERATOR ROLLS

MARY PITTS

2 packages dry yeast

1 cup warm water

1 cup hot milk

1 cup shortening

⅔ cup sugar

2 teaspoons salt

3 eggs, well beaten

7 to 8 cups flour

Dissolve yeast in warm water. Mix together hot milk, shortening, sugar, and salt in a large bowl and let it cool. Once cooled, add yeast mixture and the eggs. Mix in 4 cups flour, then stir in 3 to 4 more cups flour until the dough can be handled easily. Place dough in a greased bowl, cover, and refrigerate. The dough will keep 4 to 5 days. When ready to use, cut off amount needed and roll out ½-inch thick. Shape into desired pieces. Place on a baking sheet and let rise in a warm place for 2 hours. Bake in a 400°F oven for 15 to 20 minutes. Yield: Approximately 5 dozen rolls.

Rittie Webb.

POTATO REFRIGERATOR ROLLS

BELLE LEDFORD

1 cup milk
½ cup sugar
⅔ cup shortening
1 teaspoon salt
1 cup mashed potatoes
1 package dry yeast
½ to 1 cup lukewarm water
2 eggs, well beaten
5 ½ to 6 cups sifted flour
Melted butter

Scald milk in a larger boiler. Add sugar, shortening, salt, and mashed potatoes. Stir to mix and let cool. Dissolve yeast in lukewarm water and add to cooled milk mixture. Using a heavy spoon or potato masher, mix the yeast and eggs into

Rittie Webb at her stove.

this mixture and then begin adding the flour, a cup at a time. Mix well. Do not let rise.

Place dough in a greased bowl; turn it once to grease the surface. Cover and chill at least 2 hours or up to a week. About 2 hours before serving, take out the amount of dough needed and shape the dough as desired on a floured surface. Place in a buttered pan. Brush butter on top of each roll. Place in a warm place and let rise for about 1 hour, or until doubled. Bake in a 400°F oven for 15 to 20 minutes, or until light golden brown. Yield: *Approximately 5 dozen rolls.*

LIGHT ROLLS

ANNIE LONG

1½ cups milk

⅓ cup shortening

2 tablespoons sugar

2 teaspoons salt

1 egg, well beaten

2 packages dry yeast

½ cup lukewarm water

5 to 5½ cups sifted flour

Scald milk and mix with shortening, sugar, and salt. Let stand until warm, then add beaten egg and yeast, which has been dissolved in the ½ cup lukewarm water. Gradually add flour. Put on a floured surface and knead for a few minutes. Place in a greased mixing bowl and let rise until doubled. Roll out on a floured board, cut into rounds, and dip into melted butter before placing in a pan. Let rise until doubled. Baked in a 400°F oven for 15 minutes. Yield: *Approximately 5 dozen rolls.*

EASY HOT ROLLS

MARY PITTS

2 packages dry yeast

½ cup cold water

1 cup milk

2 tablespoons shortening

2½ teaspoons salt

2 tablespoons sugar

4½ to 5 cups flour

Melted butter

Dissolve yeast in cold water. Set aside. Put milk, shortening, salt, and sugar in a pan and heat only enough to melt shortening. Cool and then add yeast. Gradually stir in flour until you have a good stiff dough. Put on a well-floured board and knead for 3 to 5 minutes. Place in a greased bowl, cover, and let rise until doubled. When doubled, punch down and let rise again. Place on a floured board and roll out. Cut into desired shapes and dip in butter before placing in a pan. Let rise again until doubled. Bake in a 375°F oven for 15 to 20 minutes. Yield: *Approximately 4 dozen rolls.*

Pancakes, Muffins, and Sweet Breads

WHOLE-WHEAT PANCAKES

MARY PITTS

These pancakes will be "near 'bout big as a saucer."

2 cups whole-wheat flour

2 tablespoons brown sugar

1 teaspoon salt

1 package dry yeast

1 egg, beaten

2 cups milk

Mix together all dry ingredients, including the dry yeast. Add beaten egg to milk and slowly add the mixture to the dry ingredients. Stir well. Cover bowl with a towel and set in hot water for 1 hour. When ready, dip out the batter, using a ⅓-cup measure and fry in a greased pan. Yield: *Approximately fifteen 3-inch pancakes.*

BLUEBERRY MUFFINS

MARINDA BROWN

2 cups self-rising flour

1 cup sugar

½ cup melted butter or margarine

2 eggs

1 cup blueberries

Mix together flour, sugar, butter, and eggs only until flour is well moistened. Do not beat. Fold in blueberries. Pour into greased muffin cups and bake in a 350°F oven for 15 to 20 minutes.

Variation: Substitute 1 cup of grated apples for the blueberries, then mix together 1 cup chopped nuts, ½ cup brown sugar, and 1 teaspoon cinnamon and sprinkle on top of the muffins before you bake them.

MOLASSES SWEET BREAD

2 cups flour
½ teaspoon salt
1 to 2 teaspoons ginger
2 teaspoons baking powder
¼ teaspoon soda
1 teaspoon cinnamon
⅓ cup melted butter
1 cup molasses or ⅔ cup molasses and
  ½ cup sugar
¾ cup buttermilk
1 egg

Sift together dry ingredients and add melted butter and the molasses. Mix well, adding buttermilk and egg. Pour into a loaf pan and bake in a 350°F oven for 45 to 50 minutes.

QUICK AND EASY DOUGHNUTS

BESSIE UNDERWOOD
2 cups self-rising flour
¼ cup sugar
1 egg
¼ cup milk
Shortening for deep frying
Confectioners' sugar (optional)

Sift flour and sugar together. Add egg and milk to make a workable dough. Roll out and cut with a doughnut cutter. Drop in hot shortening. Turn when brown, and when the other side is brown take out and drain on paper towels or brown paper. May sweeten by sifting confectioners' sugar over them. Yield: *Approximately 16 doughnuts*.

CAKE DOUGHNUTS

ANNIE LONG
3 cups sifted flour
2 teaspoons baking powder
⅔ cup sugar
½ teaspoon nutmeg
1 tablespoon shortening
2 eggs
½ cup milk
Fat for deep frying
Confectioners' sugar
Cinnamon (optional)

Sift together flour, baking powder, sugar, and nutmeg. Add shortening by kneading in with fork or fingers. Stir in eggs and milk. Roll out; and drop in hot fat. Turn doughnuts when they rise to the top and turn brown. Watch carefully, and when brown on the second side take out with a slotted spoon. Drain on paper towels or brown paper. While still warm, drop into confectioners' sugar, plain or with cinnamon. Yield: *Approximately 20 to 25 doughnuts*.

OLD-FASHIONED GINGERBREAD

This recipe is at least a hundred years old, according to one of our contacts.

½ cup sugar
½ cup butter
1 cup molasses
2 cups flour
½ teaspoon soda
1½ teaspoon ginger
½ teaspoon cinnamon
½ cup sour milk [buttermilk]
½ cup raisins (optional)
½ cup chopped nuts (optional)

Cream together sugar, butter, and molasses. Sift together dry ingredients and beat into the sugar mixture alternately with sour milk. Mix well. Fold in raisins and nuts, if desired. Bake in a greased and lightly floured 13 × 9-inch pan in a 300°F oven for 1 hour.

ARIZONA'S GINGERBREAD

ARIZONA DICKERSON

2½ cups flour
2 teaspoons soda
½ teaspoon salt
1 teaspoon cinnamon
1 teaspoon ginger
½ teaspoon cloves
2 eggs, well beaten
½ cup sugar
1 cup molasses
½ cup vegetable oil
1 cup boiling water

Sift dry ingredients together twice. Set aside. Combine beaten eggs, sugar, molasses, and oil. Mix well. Add to dry ingredients and blend. Add boiling water and stir until smooth. Pour into an oiled shallow baking pan. Bake in a 350°F oven for 40 minutes.

NUT BREAD

3 tablespoons butter
1 cup sugar
2 eggs
2½ cups flour
3 teaspoons baking powder
1 teaspoon salt
1 cup milk
1 cup chopped nuts
1 teaspoon vanilla

Cream together butter and sugar. Add eggs and beat well. Sift together dry ingredients and add to butter mixture alternately with milk. Fold in the nuts and vanilla. Pour batter into a greased loaf pan and let rise for 30 minutes. Bake in a 350°F oven for 45 minutes.

CINNAMON ROLLS

2 teaspoons salt
2½ tablespoons sugar
1 cup milk
1 package dry yeast
5 tablespoons melted shortening
2 eggs, slightly beaten
2½ cups sifted flour
Soft butter
Sugar and cinnamon to sweeten
Confectioners' sugar
Water

Dissolve salt and sugar in ½ cup of the milk and mix yeast with the other half. Combine the 2 mixtures and leave in a warm place for 30 minutes. To this mixture add the melted shortening, slightly beaten eggs, and flour to make a stiff dough. Put in a covered bowl and leave in a warm place again for 30 minutes. Then beat the dough thoroughly in the bowl. Roll out dough on a floured surface about ⅓-inch thick. Spread with soft butter and sprinkle sugar and cinnamon on top. Then fold over in 3 folds, and cut in strips, about ¾-inch thick. Place close together in a greased shallow pan and let rise until doubled in bulk (about 30 minutes). Bake in a hot (400°F) oven for about 10 to 20 minutes. When lightly browned, remove from the oven, and while still warm in the pan, pour a sugar topping (confectioners' sugar thinned slightly with a small amount of water) over the rolls. Yield: *Approximately 20 rolls.*

9 The Syrup Shed

That's a special treat, now,
when you get a dried apple pie.
—Oma Ledford

In the days of near total self-sufficiency, the cook was limited, of course, to desserts made of ingredients that could be raised and processed on the farm. As one of our contacts said, "Mama always had a skillet full of peanuts or sweet potatoes ready for us when we came home from school." Olene Garland echoed the thoughts of many Appalachian cooks with regard to desserts, saying, "There was ten children in my family, so it was a pretty big chore for Momma to make a dessert for so many, but she was always wanting to treat us."

Sugar was not available as a sweetener in the Appalachian Mountains until the twentieth century. As a result, Appalachian families relied on natural sweeteners found in the region for desserts. Nearly all families raised sorghum cane and boiled down the cane juice into syrup, which made an effective substitute (see *Foxfire Book 3*, pp. 424–36). People also used honey by itself as a dessert and as a sweetener when it was available.

Lucy York told us: "If somebody found a honey tree, several families would go in together, cut the tree down, and divide the honey up between them all."

Her brother, Terry Dickerson, remembers: "One time somebody found a tree full of honey way up in the cove of Old Man John Garland's place, and I reckon they got permission to go up there and chop it down. I guess there was eight or ten of us went up there and cut that tree down, and when it fell, the hollow part where the honey was split plumb in two and that honey poured out all over the place. But we were still able to get a good bit of it and I remember carrying it home in buckets. That honey was just as white and pretty as what you see in the stores today." (For more information about honey, see *Foxfire Book 2*, pp. 28–46.)

With the expansion of transportation networks and innovations in manufacturing technology, commercial food products became more affordable and readily available in rural areas like the Appalachian Mountains. National self-service grocery stores, like Piggly Wiggly, supplied new ingredients, which opened up culinary possibilities for cooks in the mountain South. These ingredients, such as white cane sugar, coconut flakes, canned condensed milk, and gelatin products like Jell-O, combined with technological improvements to cooking implements, revolutionized cookery in Appalachia. No longer limited by the seasons or what could be grown locally, home cooks could explore new flavors and recipes. Desserts are a key marker of that change, because many of the ingredients included in the following recipes were purchased, not grown. Simple ingredients that are considered staples in many homes today were luxuries—white flour that did not have to be grown, milled, and bleached, butter that didn't have to be churned, spices from tropical climates, and, of course, white cane sugar that created light and fluffy baked goods.

These Appalachian recipes highlight the intersection of traditional foods and methods, like pulled sorghum candy, and the influence of new goods and techniques on foods such as cakes and cookies. This collection illustrates that regional foodways are part of a continuum and that authenticity is rooted in the people, not the past.

Candy

Sorghum and molasses were often used to make candies, through a laborious and involved process. Ruth Ledford instructed Foxfire students:

Get your molasses—real cane syrup, store bought don't work so well—and you put it on and cook it until when you hold it up it spins a thread. Then you take it off [the heat] and pour it out into a buttered bowl and cool it; then just roll it up [in a ball]. Then grease your hands with butter and then you just pull it. Now it takes two people to pull it. One can't pull it. You're supposed to pull it till it gets so hard it won't pull no more. [Pulling it] makes it get harder, and whenever you get it pulled you take it and twist it like that and just put it out on a [well-greased plate] or a piece of wax paper and cut it into little pieces.

The coupling nature of this process became important in social gatherings—boys and girls would often choose partners they were sweet on at community candy pullings. Ellene Gowder shared with us on candy pullings:

A candy pulling usually was after the season where they had the syrup making. When the cane would be cut and carried to the mill, and boiled down into syrup. But usually the last cooking, they would cook the syrup down much thicker, real thick, and it would become—oh—pretty hard. And when you would have those candy pullings, you would usually grease your hands so the candy or syrup wouldn't stick to your hands. And it was a lot of fun for the courting couples to pull the candy together. You would get a big handful of syrup, and start pulling it. When you first started, the syrup would be dark, but the longer you pulled it, the whiter it got. And eventually, you would pull it until it would be very white, you could

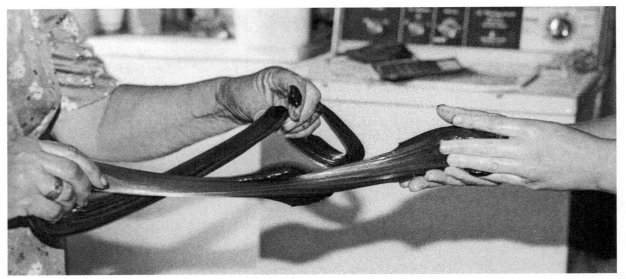

Pulling taffy.

pull it out into long strings, and let it get cold. And it would be so brittle that you could take a knife and chop it up into pieces.

The appearance of sugar, salt, and other such products also means that the repertoire of types of candies could be expanded. The following are several our contacts agreed to share with us.

MOLASSES CANDY

1 cup molasses
1 cup water
Dash of salt

Combine all ingredients and boil (do not stir) until it reaches the hard-ball stage. Remove from the fire and let stand until cool enough to hold in well-greased hands. Using a small amount at a time, pull the candy back and forth between the hands. After pulling for some time, it will change from a brown to a yellowish color, at which time it is done.

SALTWATER TAFFY

1 ¼ pounds sugar
1 ¼ pounds white corn syrup
2 cups water
1 tablespoon butter
2 teaspoons salt
½ teaspoon flavoring (peppermint, maple, almond, etc.)
Food coloring

Put sugar, syrup, and water in a saucepan and stir until boiling begins. Continue boiling (do not stir) until it spins a thread. Take from fire, add butter and salt, and pour into buttered platters. When cool enough, pull. Add flavoring and coloring while pulling. Cut into pieces and wrap each piece in waxed paper.

POTATO CANDY

MARGARET NORTON

1 large potato
Salt
1 box confectioners' sugar (about 3 ½ cups)
Peanut butter

Peel and boil potato. When done, mash up with a fork, add a little salt, and pour in a box of confectioners' sugar. This makes a stiff dough. Roll out on a dough board that has been well floured in a layer ¼-inch thick. Spread peanut butter all over top. Roll up like a jelly roll (make 2 rolls if you like). Put this in the refrigerator. Cut with a knife and serve. Good any time.

OLD-FASHIONED FUDGE

MARY PITTS

2 cups sugar
¼ teaspoon salt
6 tablespoons cocoa or 2 ounces melted chocolate
½ cup water or milk
¼ cup honey (or corn syrup)
2 tablespoons butter
1 teaspoon vanilla

Mix together in a saucepan sugar, salt, and cocoa. Add milk and syrup gradually. Boil gently, stirring often, until mixture reaches the soft-ball stage. Drop in butter and let cool before beating. Add vanilla. Beat until the mixture thickens and is hard to stir. Pour into a buttered dish. Cool before cutting into serving pieces. Yield: *Approximately 20 pieces of candy.*

COCOA FUDGE

ANNIE LONG

1 cup white sugar
1 tablespoon cocoa
½ cup milk
¼ cup butter

Mix sugar and cocoa together. Stir in milk and boil gently over medium heat for 30 minutes, or until mixture reaches the soft-ball stage. When the syrup forms a ball in cold water, remove from the heat and add butter. Cool, then beat until thick. Pour into a buttered dish and cut when cool.

PEANUT BRITTLE

3 cups sugar
1 teaspoon vinegar
1 cup peanuts

Melt sugar in a pan with vinegar, being careful not to let it burn. When melted, add peanuts, stirring as little as possible, and pour on a buttered platter; break up when cold.

DIVINITY

MARY PITTS

2 ⅓ cups sugar
¼ cup light corn syrup
½ cup water
½ teaspoon salt
2 egg whites, stiffly beaten

Mix together all ingredients except egg whites. Bring to a boil until it spins a thread when dropped from a spoon. Pour half the mixture over beaten egg whites. Let remaining mixture come to a boil again, add to previous mixture, and beat until stiff. Drop from a teaspoon onto wax paper or into a greased pan. Yield: *Approximately 24 pieces.*

POPCORN BALLS
LESSIE CONNER

On many farms, families also raised popcorn. Gathered dry in the fall, shelled off the cob, and popped over the fire in the living room fireplace, it could be used alone as a snack or combined with homegrown syrup to make popcorn balls. Lessie Conner taught us how:

In order to make the popcorn balls, she said, a large cast-iron skillet is needed, along with two large dishpans or bowls (one for the popped corn and one for the finished popcorn balls), one mixing bowl for the cooked syrup, and several kitchen spoons. A large skillet is needed because the syrup will boil up, and iron will heat more evenly and not burn the syrup as readily as another type of pan.

To make the syrup for the popcorn balls, pour a quart of sorghum in the large iron skillet to heat on the stove. Mrs. Conner said, "You can tell when the syrup is ready because it forms a 'hair' when dripped down from the spoon." It will take about five minutes to get to that stage. Pour the syrup into the mixing bowl to cook for several minutes. It should come right off the heat and preferably right out of the pan when it's completely cooked, or it will get brittle as it cools. Cover your hands with butter to keep the syrup from sticking to them while forming the balls. It is better to use cold rather than warm popcorn, because the syrup will stick better.

Mrs. Conner demonstrated two methods for forming the popcorn balls. The first method is to carefully place a small amount of popcorn into the palm of one hand and carefully (because the syrup could still burn) spoon about a tablespoon of syrup on top of it. Then pack the popcorn and syrup mixture together by hand. Use additional

Lessie Conner shows how to make popcorn balls.

butter on your hands after making a few balls or the syrup will start sticking to them. The second method is to add one or two teaspoons of baking soda to the syrup while it is boiling. The soda makes the syrup bubble and foam up, giving more candy to work with. Then pour the syrup into the mixing bowl and on top of that pour the popcorn. Stir that up with a wooden spoon and scoop it out with your hands to form the balls. After each popcorn ball is made, place it in a large dishpan or on waxed paper to cool.

Frozen Desserts

Before the development of ice boxes and freezers, home cooks had little access to methods of refrigeration, as discussed in chapter 3. However, during the winter, when snow was plentiful in the mountains, families could combine milk with sweeteners such as honey or syrup to make ice cream. Several contacts told us how to make snow cream: "Gather the snow carefully with a large spoon, keeping the snow fluffy. Place some of the snow in a large bowl; add milk—small amounts at a time—and stir into snow until it is at a nice, thick consistency. Add enough honey or syrup to sweeten, and add fruits or berries to flavor if desired."

Olene Garland explained another way her family made ice cream during the winter months:

We used two regular water buckets—which were lard buckets, a ten-pound and a five-pound bucket—and we would chip off the shoals from the falls—Sylvan Lake Falls—and chip it up fine enough to pack between the two buckets. We would pour the ice cream mixture into the smaller one; set it down inside the larger bucket; pack ice between the two and turn by the bail [bucket handle]. You had to put the lid on the bucket with the milk in it. We used to do that a lot. Sometimes we didn't have to go to the trouble to get ice from the falls—it was so cold we could often get ice by chipping it out of our water buckets.

With the year-round availability of ice and increasing access to ingredients like brown and white sugar, ice cream came into its own as a real dessert treat. Harriet Echols said, "We had ice cream parties, too—usually on Saturday night. See, most everybody had four or five cows, and we'd get about five ice cream freezers and invite the youngsters in, and we'd get in the parlor and get around the organ or piano and sing and play."

SYRUP ICE CREAM

MARY PITTS

3 cups dark corn syrup

6 tablespoons cornstarch

3 eggs, well beaten

2 cups whole milk

Cream or additional whole milk

1 teaspoon vanilla

Mix first 4 ingredients and cook in a double boiler until thick. Let cool, then add enough cream or whole milk to make 2 quarts. If you use cream, beat it well before adding it to the boiled mixture. Add the vanilla. Put in old-time ice cube trays (take sections out) and freeze. You may also use any shallow (1-inch) aluminum tray. Mary adds: "When it got icy—before it got hard—I'd take it out and beat it good and put it back in."

HAND-FREEZER ICE CREAM*

2 quarts milk

2 to 3 cups sugar

2 tablespoons vanilla

Crushed ice

Rock salt

Pour milk, sugar, and vanilla into the freezer container; cover, then pack the freezer with ice and salt. Turn the crank slowly at first, faster as the mixture thickens. Crank until it's almost too hard to turn. Eat right away, as it doesn't keep well.

*An electric ice cream churn may be substituted for a hand-crank churn, but alter the recipe to fit the size of the bucket if necessary. A 4-quart churn is recommended.

Variation 1: You may also add 2 beaten eggs to the milk mixture before putting it in the freezer. This will make the mixture more custard-like.

Variation 2: Add 1 cup of any mashed fresh fruit, such as strawberries, peaches, blueberries, and blackberries. For chocolate, you may add ½ cup cocoa to the sugar before adding it to the milk.

LIME SHERBET

MARY PITTS

1 package lime gelatin (such as Jell-O)
1½ cups sugar
1 cup boiling water
Rind of 1 lemon
Juice of 2 lemons (¼ cup)
1 quart milk

Dissolve sugar and gelatin in boiling water. Add rind and juice. Chill this mixture, then add milk. Put into a 13 × 9-inch pan with a cover and freeze. Stir frequently. It freezes in 2 to 3 hours.

Bread Puddings

White flour, which opened home cooks to a new and expansive repertoire of dessert recipes, was used in numerous baked goods present at nearly every meal. Resourcefulness, or simply wanting to avoid food waste, inspired the creation of bread puddings, a dessert common in many cultures. Bread pudding was one of the most convenient desserts and easily made from leftover biscuits. The use of biscuits instead of a stale yeasted bread gives this Appalachian version a unique texture and flavor.

BREAD PUDDING

RUTH HOLCOMB

2 cups fine crumbs from leftover biscuits
1 egg
1 cup sugar
2 tablespoons milk
1 tablespoon butter

Put the biscuit crumbs in a bowl. Add egg and sugar and mix thoroughly. Add milk and butter. Beat well. Pour into a greased pan and bake in a 350°F oven for 15 to 20 minutes. Yield: *4 servings.*

DAISY'S BREAD PUDDING WITH APPLES

DAISY JUSTUS

4 homemade biscuits, crumbled
1 egg
1 cup sliced and cooked apples*
¼ cup grated coconut
1 cup milk
1 cup brown sugar
¼ cup chopped nuts (pecans or walnuts)
1 teaspoon vanilla

Mix all ingredients and pour into a buttered small casserole dish. Bake in a 350°F oven for about 1 hour, or until a knife comes out clean, about 1 inch from the edge of the dish. Yield: *4 to 6 servings.*

*Raisins may be used instead of apples, or use both if you wish.

BLACKBERRY PUDDING

OLENE GARLAND

2 cups blackberries
½ to 1 cup sugar
2 cups water
4 to 5 homemade biscuits, crumbled
Butter

Bring blackberries, sugar as needed, and water to a near boil in a buttered baking dish. Add the crumbled biscuits and stir. Dot with butter and sprinkle with sugar, if desired. Bake in a 400°F oven until thick and glossy on top.

LEMON MERINGUE PUDDING

MARY PITTS

"This is a kind of bread pudding. Use leftover biscuits. You have to put that topping on it to get the kids to eat it. Had to fancy it up a little, but they always went back for seconds."

2 cups bread crumbs

4 cups milk

½ cup butter

1 cup sugar

4 eggs, separated

Juice and rind of 1 lemon

3 tablespoons confectioners' sugar

Soak bread crumbs in milk. Cream butter and sugar. Add beaten egg yolks, lemon rind, and all but 1 teaspoon of the lemon juice. Mix with bread crumbs. Pour into a baking dish and bake in a 350°F oven for 45 minutes, or until firm. Cover with a meringue made from the egg whites beaten with the confectioners' sugar and remaining lemon juice. Return to the oven and brown the meringue lightly.

ALEXANDER PUDDING

MONTENE WATTS

"Use sweetened fruit which has been spiced with cinnamon or ginger. Thin fruit with small amount of milk. Pour into bottom of dish. Slice leftover biscuits (cold) over fruit, being careful not to get it too thick. Then place another layer of fruit on top of biscuits. If the mixture seems too dry, make a small hole in the middle and pour small amount of milk in it. Set aside for a few hours (Mama would set that in the cupboard to sit awhile) and then eat anytime."

Pies

Pies in Appalachia took on many forms. A simple combination of flour, salt, lard, and water could produce a rich, flaky dough that served as the base for both sweet and savory treats and was filled with fresh ingredients like blackberries or cushaw. However, home cooks also took a more familiar route and used their favorite biscuit dough to use as a pie base. Some recipes, such as Cold Pie (page 175), simply call for leftover biscuits. These recipes illustrate the breadth of creativity, and sweet tooth, of Appalachian bakers.

LUCY YORK: *Pies are first put on the bottom rack of the oven and then moved up to a higher rack to brown.*

PIECRUST

ANNIE LONG

1½ cups flour

½ teaspoon salt

2 teaspoons baking powder

5 tablespoons lard

4 to 5 tablespoons ice water

Sift and then measure the flour. Sift flour, salt, and baking powder together. Work in lard with fingers or fork. Stir in ice water. Roll out on a floured board or cloth and make into piecrust. If crust needs baking before pouring in filling, bake in a 425°F oven for 5 to 7 minutes.

VINEGAR PASTRY

ARIZONA DICKERSON

"One teaspoon vinegar added to the pie dough makes a flaky pastry."

4 cups unsifted flour

1 tablespoon sugar

1½ cups shortening

1 egg

1 tablespoon vinegar

½ cup cold water

Blend dry ingredients. Cut in shortening. Blend egg, vinegar, and water together and sprinkle over the flour mixture 1 tablespoon at a time, tossing lightly with a fork until all is moistened. Gather into a ball with hands. Chill for several hours or overnight. Keep in a covered bowl. Yield: *2 crusts.*

BLACKBERRY PIE

MARY PITTS

To seed a quart of blackberries, put two cups of water in them and let them come to a boil on the stove. Let it cook for fifteen to twenty minutes, and then run it through a sieve and get all that juice and pulp out. And you can make a pie out of that just like you can with the berries. I've got tame blackberries right down here in the garden, and they grow in big bunches, each berry bigger than the end of my thumb. I juice them and make pies.

To start out [with blackberry pie], I put my berries in a saucepan. I put a cup or a cup and a half of sugar to a quart of blackberries and I put it on the stove till it comes to a boil. Then I use self-rising flour and make up my dough, just like I make my biscuit dough, and roll it out. I put them berries in a deep dish and cover them with dough—solid or in strips—and put it in the stove and brown it. Then I take it out

and put in the rest of my berries and put on the top crust. I dot the top crust with butter and sprinkle a little sugar on it and put it in the stove and brown it [at 400°F]. Yield: 10 to 15 servings.

TAME GOOSEBERRY PIE

2 cups gooseberries

¾ cup sugar

1 tablespoon butter

1 recipe biscuit dough

Mix berries with sugar and butter and cook, stirring to mash the berries, until thick. Pour the berries into a pie plate. Make up biscuit dough, roll it out, and cut ½-inch wide strips. Place the strips of dough crosswise on the berries and bake in a 450°F oven until the crust is brown. Yield: *6 to 8 servings.*

CUSHAW OR PUMPKIN PIE

SANDRA ROBINSON

1 cup brown sugar

¼ cup flour

¼ cup granulated sugar

1 teaspoon salt

1 teaspoon cinnamon

½ teaspoon ginger

½ teaspoon nutmeg

1 cup milk

3 eggs

3 tablespoons butter

2 cups cooked and mashed cushaw, candy roaster, or pumpkin

1 teaspoon vanilla

1 deep-dish unbaked pie shell

Nuts (optional)

Whipped cream (optional)

Sift together the dry ingredients. Add milk, eggs, and butter and beat well. Add cushaw and vanilla. Pour into deep unbaked pie shell. Bake for 15 minutes at 425°F. Reduce temperature to 350°F and bake for 25 to 30 minutes longer, or until a knife inserted 1 inch from edge comes out clean. If desired, garnish with nuts and whipped cream. Yield: *6 to 8 servings.*

Variation: For lemon cushaw pie, substitute white sugar for brown sugar, exclude spices, and add 1 teaspoon lemon extract or to taste.

SPICY PUMPKIN PIE
ANNIE LONG
¾ cup sugar
½ teaspoon salt
1 ¼ teaspoons cinnamon
½ teaspoon ginger
½ teaspoon nutmeg
½ teaspoon cloves
1 ½ cups cooked mashed pumpkin
3 eggs, well beaten
1 ¼ cups whole milk
⅔ cup evaporated milk
1 unbaked pie shell

Mix dry ingredients together. Blend in pumpkin and then the eggs. Gradually stir in the milk. Pour into unbaked pie shell and bake at 425°F for 15 minutes, then 30 minutes more at 325°F.

SWEET POTATO PIE
MARGARET NORTON
3 cups cooked mashed sweet potatoes
1 teaspoon cinnamon
¼ teaspoon nutmeg
1 cup sugar
1 tablespoon butter
¼ cup cream
1 prebaked pie shell

Add spices and sugar to sweet potatoes. Mix together the butter and cream and stir into sweet potato mixture. Pour into baked pie shell and bake the pie in a 325°F oven.

DRIED FRUIT STACK PIE WITH GINGERBREAD PASTRY
2 cups flour
1 teaspoon ginger
1 teaspoon cloves
2 teaspoons baking soda
½ teaspoon salt
¾ cup shortening
1 cup sugar
1 egg
½ cup dark molasses
Any canned fruit in thick sweetened syrup, such as cherries

Sift together dry ingredients. Cream together shortening and sugar until fluffy. Add egg and beat well. Mix in the molasses. Slowly mix the flour mixture into egg mixture. Divide dough into 3 or 4 balls; roll out to ¼-inch thick, and bake each circle about 10 minutes in a 350°F oven. Let pastry cool and then spread fruit between each layer of pastry and stack.

BEST-EVER LEMON PIE

BELLE LEDFORD

1 ¼ cups sugar

6 tablespoons cornstarch

2 cups water

3 eggs, separated

⅓ cup lemon juice

1 ½ teaspoons lemon extract

3 tablespoons butter

2 teaspoons vinegar

1 prebaked deep-dish 9-inch pie shell

Mix sugar and cornstarch together in top of a double boiler. Gradually add water. Beat egg yolks and lemon juice and then add to sugar mixture. Cook until very thick over boiling water 25 minutes. Add lemon extract, butter, and vinegar and stir very well before pouring into baked pie shell. Cover with meringue. (See Never-Fail Meringue below.)

KEY LIME PIE

JACK D. MARTIN

3 eggs beaten lightly with spoon

1 (14-ounce) can sweetened condensed milk

¼ cup sugar

⅓ cup Key Lime Juice

1 (6-ounce) ready-made graham cracker crust

Preheat oven to 350°F, combine all ingredients except the crust, and bake for 20 minutes. Remove pie from oven and allow to cool.

BUTTERSCOTCH PIE

ANNIE LONG

1 cup brown sugar

Pinch of salt

6 tablespoons flour

1 ½ cups milk

3 eggs, separated

1 teaspoon vanilla

¼ cup butter

1 baked pie shell

Mix sugar, salt, and flour together in a saucepan. Gradually add the milk and cook in saucepan stirring constantly until slightly thick. Beat egg yolks and gradually mix in a small amount of cooked mixture (approximately ¾ cup), then slowly stir this egg mixture into the remaining cooked mixture. Cook until very thick, about 4 minutes, stirring constantly. Take off the heat and add the vanilla and butter. Mix well and pour into baked pie shell. Make a meringue with the egg whites and spread on top of hot pie. (See the following recipe for meringue.) Bake in a 400°F oven for 10 minutes.

NEVER-FAIL MERINGUE

1 tablespoon cornstarch

2 tablespoons cold water

½ cup boiling water

3 egg whites

6 tablespoons sugar

Pinch of salt

1 teaspoon vanilla

Blend cornstarch and cold water in a saucepan. Add boiling water and cook until clear and thickened. Let cool completely. Beat egg whites with an electric beater at high speed until foamy. Gradually add sugar and beat until stiff but not dry. Add salt and vanilla, then gradually add cornstarch mixture and beat well until stiff peaks form. Spread over cooled pie filling. Bake in a 350°F oven for 10 minutes. This is a beautiful meringue which cuts smoothly and does not leak.

CUSTARD PIE
ANNIE LONG

2 eggs
2 tablespoons sugar
Pinch of salt
1 1/2 cups milk
1 teaspoon nutmeg or cinnamon
1 unbaked pie shell

Mix eggs with sugar and salt. Gradually add milk and nutmeg or cinnamon. Pour into an unbaked pie shell. Bake in a 400°F oven for 10 minutes. Reduce the heat to 325°F and bake an additional 20 to 30 minutes, until done. Pie is best served with a meringue. Yield: *6 to 8 servings.*

CHOCOLATE CUSTARD PIE
MARY PITTS

1/2 cup cocoa
2 cups sugar
1/4 cup cornstarch
2 1/2 cups milk
8 egg yolks, well beaten
1 cup butter
1 baked 9-inch pie shell

Mix together cocoa, sugar, cornstarch, and milk and cook over medium heat until thickened. Gradually add 3/4 cup of cooked mixture to beaten egg yolks, then slowly pour it back into remaining cooked mixture and cook an additional 5 minutes on medium heat. Take off the heat and add butter, mixing well. Pour into the pie shell. Let stand until set.

COLD PIE
DAISY JUSTUS

Use leftover cold homemade biscuits. Slice a layer of biscuits. Cover with applesauce, sprinkle with sugar. Repeat until you get as much as you want fixed. Cinnamon or nutmeg can be sprinkled on applesauce, if desired.

"HALF-MOON" PIES

"Half-moon" pies, a type of hand pie, is a popular dessert throughout Southern Appalachia. These are made by cooking and thickening sweetened berries or fruits such as strawberries, blueberries, blackberries, peaches, pumpkin, and possibly the favorite—dried apples. Blanche Harkins, an expert at making fried apple pies, demonstrated how to make these pies to Foxfire students:

To make 4 small pies, she uses 1 quart of dried apples. She places them in a saucepan, adds a small amount of water, cooks them until they are tender, and then mashes them up with a fork. She sweetens and add spices to suit her own taste.

She makes the piecrusts using the following measurements and instructions:

4 cups self-rising flour
1/2 cup lard or shortening
1 cup water

Make up crust like any other piecrust; divide the dough into balls about the size of a fist for each tart and roll the dough out into a very thin circle. Place the cooked apples on half the circle and fold the other half over the side with apples. Press the edges together with either your fingers or a fork, and make tiny holes or slits in the tarts, using a fork or knife, to let the air out as the tarts cook and to prevent the edges from turning up. Next, put enough shortening in a large iron

*"Half-moon" pies
being made by
Blanche Harkins.*

frying pan to almost cover the pies as they cook. After the shortening is heated, place the pies in the pan and fry until brown on both sides. Mrs. Harkins told us that if we preferred to bake them, to spread melted butter on the pies before placing them in the oven. The butter will give it a crispier crust as it bakes. For baking place in a 400°F oven.

Variation: These may also be filled with pineapple, as suggested by Connie Burrell, by evenly distributing one 16-ounce can of crushed pineapple between the pastries. To make a sauce, reserve the juice from the can and mix with ¾ cup sugar, 3 teaspoons butter, and 2 tablespoons all-purpose flour in a pan and bring to a boil. Pour over the pineapple pies.

Cobbler

As explained by Ruth Cabe, "A deep dish, or cobbler, is one that has no crust on the bottom. It has fruit on the bottom. Some people put fruit, a layer of pie dough, a layer of fruit, then their crust on top. They started it cooking on top of the stove because when they put it in the oven, the crust on top would get done before the layer of dough in the middle. By cooking it for a few minutes on top of the stove first, and then finishing it in the oven, it would cook evenly."

Cobblers are a favorite with families in this area. They are simple to make and can be served plain or with ice cream or whipped cream. During the summer, blackberries, blueberries, strawberries, huckleberries, cherries, rhubarb, sweet potatoes, and apples are gathered and preserved for winter use so they can be used for various dishes, preferably cobblers. Bertha Waldroop tells us how she makes a cobbler:

I make cobbler out of peaches or blackberries or cherries—I cut up the cherries and get the seeds out—use any fruit you want to. I use a square aluminum pan now, and make up a biscuit dough. I put the cherries, or whatever fruit I'm using, in the pan, usually a quart of fruit, and put some sugar on them—it takes a lot of sugar. And I use margarine now 'cause we don't have the butter like we used to have. For a quart of berries, I use about two tablespoons of butter, stir it around in the fruit, and cover the fruit with the dough. I do just like I was gonna bake biscuits—roll the dough out right thin, cut it in strips, and put it on top of the fruit. Then I put it in the oven and pour water about halfway up in the pan with the fruit. Bake it at 350 degrees about thirty minutes and when it browns on top, I take it out. If you wish to, it does make it awful good if you put some margarine on top of it. That makes it real good, and it's ready to eat.

APPLE COBBLER
DOROTHY BECK

"I take about five or six apples and cube them up and put them in a sheet cake pan and put a little water over them. I make a pastry using a cup of sugar and a cup of flour and about a half a cup of butter and just mix that up real good and sprinkle it over the top of your apples. Cook that at about 350 degrees for twenty or thirty minutes, or until done." Yield: *10 to 15 servings.*

SWEET POTATO COBBLER

2 cups cooked and diced sweet potatoes
⅔ cup molasses
¼ cup butter
½ cup milk
½ teaspoon ginger
Pinch of salt
1 recipe biscuit dough

Mix together all the ingredients except the dough and bring to a boil. Cut part of rolled dough into cubes and drop into boiling mixture. Cut remaining dough in thin slices and place on top. Put the pan in an oven and bake in 400°F oven until the crust is brown. Yield: *6 servings.*

RHUBARB COBBLER

IONE DICKERSON

"I cooked some rhubarb last week, and I told this woman up on Sylvan Lake, 'You could have heard me smacking my lips if you had been out on the porch [laughter].' That was the best stuff I ever put in my mouth! Oh, that was good!"

To make the cobbler, just cut the rhubarb up in inch pieces and put it in your pan. You have to put a little water and some sugar and butter in it. Slice your crust in lattice strips, put them over the top and bake. Or you can make a rhubarb crisp like apple crisp. Put your rhubarb in your pan, mix your oatmeal, flour, and sugar. You don't put spice in your rhubarb like your apple pie, though. Have it mixed up good, and sprinkle it over the fruit. Or you can make a thin sweet dough like a cake dough and pour it over that and cook it. It's good like that, too.

Fruit Desserts

Apples, a common local crop, retained their popularity as a food staple and became an easy ingredient to develop dessert recipes around. Other fruits, such as pineapple and coconut, became more common in dishes once non-local ingredients became more available in the mid-twentieth century.

BAKED APPLES SUPREME

6 large apples
½ cup brown sugar
½ cup raisins
1 teaspoon cinnamon
⅛ teaspoon salt
1 cup water
½ cup coconut

Wash and core apples but don't peel. Place in a baking dish. Fill apples with sugar, raisins, cinnamon, and salt. Add water to the baking dish. Bake 30 minutes in a 350°F oven, basting frequently. Sprinkle with coconut and bake 10 minutes more. Serve warm or cold. Yield: *6 servings.*

Variation: Replace brown sugar with honey, exclude raisins, cinnamon, and coconut, and add approximately ½ cup chopped nuts of choice, or more to taste. Prepare according to above directions.

APPLE FLUFF

IONE DICKERSON

"My mother used egg white in applesauce. Beat the egg white stiff [gradually adding sugar to it] and flavor it if you want to. Then mix your egg white with applesauce. Apple fluff, that's what we called it."

SPICY APPLE BROWN BETTY

1 cup sugar

¼ teaspoon cinnamon

¼ teaspoon nutmeg

¼ teaspoon salt

2 cups bread crumbs

3 cups pared, cored, and sliced apples

¼ cup water

3 tablespoons lemon juice

Grated rind of 1 lemon

2 tablespoons butter

Blend sugar, spices, and salt. Arrange a third of the crumbs in a greased baking dish. Add half the apples. Sprinkle with half the sugar mixture. Repeat the process, finishing with a layer of crumbs. Mix the water, lemon juice, and grated rind and pour over. Dot with butter. Bake for 45 minutes in a 350°F oven. Yield: *8 servings.*

PINEAPPLE CASSEROLE

½ cup margarine

¾ cup sugar

2 eggs, beaten

1 (8-ounce) can crushed pineapple

Crumbs from 4 slices of white bread

Beat margarine and sugar together; add beaten eggs and pineapple. Fold in bread crumbs. Put into a buttered dish and bake in a 350°F oven for 40 to 50 minutes. Yield: *4 to 6 servings.*

GRAPE JUICE SPONGE DESSERT

MARY PITTS

¼ cup cornstarch

6 tablespoons sugar

Dash of salt

⅛ teaspoon lemon juice

2 cups grape juice

1 tablespoon butter or margarine

2 egg whites

Combine cornstarch, sugar, and salt in a saucepan. Gradually add lemon and grape juice. Stir until well blended. Cook over medium heat until the mixture boils (stir constantly) and then boil 1 minute. Add butter and stir until melted and blended. Beat egg whites until stiff peaks form. Gradually pour hot grape mixture over beaten egg whites and beat until well blended. Pour into sherbet dishes and chill for 1 hour. Yield: 8 ½-cup servings.

LEMON MOUSSE

ARIZONA DICKERSON

1 (13-ounce) can evaporated milk

Juice of 2 lemons

1 tablespoon grated lemon peel

1 cup sugar

Graham cracker crumbs

Freeze milk in bowl long enough for ice to form. Whip. Add lemon juice and peel slowly while beating. As you continue to beat the mixture, add sugar slowly. Line a 9 × 9-inch pan with a thin layer of graham cracker crumbs. Pour lemon mixture into it. Sprinkle more crumbs on top, if desired. Cover with waxed paper and freeze. Yield: *20 servings.*

Custards

HARRIET ECHOLS: "We'd make boiled custards, you know, that's fixed with milk and eggs and sugar and flavoring, and it's delicious; but where you put a lot of eggs in it, it's so rich you can't eat much of it."

AUNT ARIE'S EGG CUSTARD (COOKED ON A WOOD STOVE)

1 recipe biscuit dough
1 egg, well beaten
1 cup milk
Handful of flour
1 teaspoon nutmeg
½ cup sugar

Line a small pie pan with plain biscuit dough rolled thin. In a separate bowl, mix together all remaining ingredients and pour it into the crust, using just a little wood so the fire won't be too hot. Bake it slowly until it "sets." It will "blubber up"—or bubble—and then the bubbles will settle.

EGG CUSTARD

BELLE LEDFORD
3 eggs, slightly beaten
2 cups milk
½ cup sugar
1 teaspoon vanilla
Dash of nutmeg (optional)
¼ teaspoon salt
1 unbaked pie shell

Combine first 6 ingredients in the order listed; pour into pie shell. Bake in a 400°F oven for 50 to 60 minutes.

Puddings

PUDDING AND CREAM PIES (TWO PIES)

STELLA BURRELL

"I just memorized this recipe, and I've always used it through the years for puddings and pies. I think it was something that I learned from my mother or grandmother when I was real young, and I still use it."

You would take 4 cups of milk, ½ cup flour, ½ cup sugar, 4 eggs, and your vanilla [1 teaspoon], and you would beat that all the time it was cooking. That will make 2 pies. If you're making pudding, you'd use the same recipe except you'd add about a tablespoon of milk for each cup to make it a little thinner. To vary the basic pudding recipe, for chocolate pie you just add cocoa [about 3 teaspoons] to it before you start your cooking process. And if you're making coconut pie, you would wait until it's almost finished to put your coconut in. If you were making lemon, you would add your lemon juice and the lemon rind; and you'd add bananas for banana pudding.

RICE PUDDING

DAISY JUSTUS
3 tablespoons butter
3 cups hot cooked rice (1 cup uncooked makes about 3 cups)
4 eggs
3 cups whole milk
¾ cup sugar (use more or less as desired)
1 tablespoon grated lemon rind
2 teaspoons vanilla
⅛ teaspoon salt

Lemon Sauce (recipe follows)

Stir butter into rice. Beat eggs, then add milk, sugar, lemon rind, vanilla, and salt. Stir together the 2 mixtures. Mix well and pour into a baking dish set in a pan of hot water. Bake in a 350°F oven for about 1 hour, or until a knife comes out clean. Serve warm with lemon sauce. Yield: *8 servings.*

LEMON SAUCE

½ cup sugar
1 tablespoon cornstarch or 5 tablespoons flour
⅛ teaspoon salt
1 cup boiling water
1 tablespoon butter
1 tablespoon grated lemon rind
3 tablespoons lemon juice

Combine the sugar, cornstarch, and salt. Stir in water gradually. Cook, stirring constantly, about 5 minutes. Blend in remaining ingredients. This sauce is also good on gingerbread.

CLASSIC SWEET POTATO PUDDING

MARY PITTS

4 large sweet potatoes, cooked and mashed
2 eggs
1 cup milk
1 cup sugar
½ teaspoon salt
½ cup butter
1 teaspoon nutmeg
1 cup seeded raisins
Never-Fail Meringue (pages 174–75), optional
Marshmallows (optional)

Mix well the ingredients except the optional ones and pour into a hot greased baking dish. Bake in a 350°F oven for 45 minutes, stirring pudding from the bottom occasionally to make sure that it is well cooked. When nearly done, smooth top over and let brown. When done, pudding may be topped with meringue, if desired, or dotted with marshmallows. Yield: *8 servings.*

BANANA PUDDING

ARIZONA DICKERSON

2 tablespoons flour
¾ cup sugar
¼ teaspoon salt
2 cups milk
3 eggs, separated
1 teaspoon vanilla
Bananas
Sweet crackers, such as vanilla wafers

Mix flour, sugar, and salt in top of a double boiler. Stir in milk. Cook over boiling water until thick. Beat egg yolks and gradually mix into hot mixture. Cook 5 minutes longer. Remove from heat and add vanilla. Let cool. Line a casserole dish with desired amounts of crackers and sliced bananas. Pour cooled sauce over them. Use egg whites for a meringue and put on top. (See Never-Fail Meringue on pages 174–75.) Brown the meringue in a 350°F oven for 5 minutes.

Gelatin Desserts

Gelatin desserts are often thought to have appeared in the mid-twentieth century, but when Foxfire students visited Arizona Dickerson, she shared a Jell-O recipe booklet copyrighted in 1930 that contained recipes from the early 1900s. Most were award-winning recipes presented at the Louisiana Purchase Exposition in St. Louis, Missouri, in 1904; the Lewis and Clark Exposition in Portland, Oregon, in 1905; and others of similar early dates.

RASPBERRY BAVARIAN CREAM

ARIZONA DICKERSON

1 package raspberry gelatin
1 cup boiling water
Raspberry juice plus cold water to equal
    1 cup liquid
¼ cup sugar
1 cup fresh raspberries, crushed and drained
    (save juice)*
½ cup whipped cream

Dissolve gelatin in boiling water. Add raspberry juice and cold water and sugar. Chill. When slightly thickened, beat with a rotary egg beater until the consistency of whipped cream. Fold in berries and cream. Turn into a mold. Chill until firm. Unmold to serve. May be garnished with whipped cream and whole berries.

*Strawberries or blackberries may be substituted for raspberries. Use the correct flavored gelatin for substitution used.

SNOW PUDDING

1 tablespoon plain gelatin
¼ cup cold water
1 cup boiling water
¼ cup lemon juice
¼ cup sugar
¼ teaspoon salt
3 egg whites

Soak gelatin in cold water; dissolve in boiling water. Add lemon juice and sugar. Chill mixture until set. Add salt to egg whites; beat to a stiff froth and combine with lemon mixture. Continue beating until mixture holds its shape. Chill and serve. Yield: *4 servings.*

FRUIT WHIP

1 lemon
1 cup sugar
1 tablespoon plain gelatin
¼ cup cold water
¼ cup boiling water
1 cup crushed fruit, such as berries, peaches,
    plums, or apricots
Pinch of salt
4 egg whites

Grate lemon rind into sugar. Set aside. Soak gelatin in cold water, dissolve in boiling water; add lemon mixture, and when sugar is dissolved, remove gelatin from the fire. Add the juice of the lemon and crushed fruit. Place the saucepan in ice water to cool, then whip until frothy. Add salt to the egg whites and beat until stiff. Fold them into gelatin mixture and whip the sponge until it holds its shape. Chill and serve with cream. Yield: *6 servings.*

Cookies

Of all the desserts, cookies probably rank number one with children. This is the one dessert children can help make unless they run into the problem Stella Burrell did with her mother: "Mama never let me cook many cookies. She said I always made too big a mess."

HONEY TEA CAKES

BELLE LEDFORD

"This was made during the war when we couldn't get sugar."

2 cups flour
½ teaspoon soda
1 teaspoon baking powder
½ teaspoon salt
2 eggs
1 cup honey
1 cup sour cream
1 teaspoon lemon juice

Mix and sift together dry ingredients. Beat eggs and honey together until smooth. Add egg mixture alternately with sour cream and lemon juice to the dry mixture until batter is smooth. Pour batter into greased muffin pans and bake in a 350°F oven for 15 to 20 minutes. Yield: *1½ dozen cakes.*

MOLASSES COOKIES

DOROTHY BECK

½ cup butter
½ cup sugar
1 egg
¼ cup molasses
2 cups sifted flour
½ teaspoon cinnamon
½ teaspoon ginger
¼ teaspoon allspice
¼ teaspoon cloves
¼ teaspoon salt
¼ teaspoon baking soda

Cream together butter and sugar; add eggs and molasses. Sift together dry ingredients and blend into the creamed mixture. Roll out and cut or put through a cookie press. Bake in a 375°F oven for 8 minutes, or until done. Yield: *4 dozen cookies.*

VANILLA WAFERS

1 cup sugar, plus more for topping
½ cup butter
1 egg, well beaten
1½ cups flour
2 teaspoons baking powder
½ teaspoon salt
½ cup milk
½ teaspoon vanilla

Cream together sugar and butter. Add egg and mix well. Sift together dry ingredients, resift, and stir into egg mixture alternately with milk. Add vanilla and let mixture chill. Turn out onto a floured surface and roll to a ¼-inch thickness; cut into 1½-inch circles and place on a lightly greased cookie sheet. Sprinkle tops with sugar. Bake in a 375°F oven for 7 to 15 minutes. Yield: *4 dozen wafers.*

CRISP SUGAR COOKIES

IONE DICKERSON

½ cup shortening

1 cup sugar

2 eggs, well beaten

2 cups flour

3 teaspoons baking powder

1 teaspoon vanilla

Cream shortening and sugar. Add eggs. Sift together dry ingredients; add to mixture. Add vanilla and beat well. Knead dough slightly and roll out thin. Cut out and place on a cookie sheet. Bake for 10 minutes in a 350°F oven. Yield: *4 dozen cookies*.

SUGAR COOKIES

ARIZONA DICKERSON

⅔ cup butter or shortening

1½ cups sugar

2 eggs

2 teaspoons vanilla

3⅔ cups sifted flour

2½ teaspoons baking powder

4 teaspoons milk

Cream the butter thoroughly. Slowly add sugar and beat well. Add eggs, one at a time, and beat. Add vanilla. Sift together dry ingredients and add to egg mixture alternately with the milk. Blend well. Chill the dough overnight. When ready to bake, roll out ⅛-inch thick. Cut out, using a floured cookie cutter. Put on greased baking sheets and sprinkle with granulated sugar. Bake in a 400°F oven for about 10 minutes. Yield: *5 dozen cookies*.

OLD-FASHIONED OATMEAL COOKIES

1 cup butter or shortening

1 cup brown sugar

½ cup water

2½ cups flour

1 teaspoon soda

1 teaspoon salt

2½ cups rolled oats

Cream butter and sugar. Slowly add water. Sift together flour, soda, and salt. Mix this with the first mixture. Stir in oats. Roll the dough out thin and cut with a cookie cutter. Bake in a 350°F oven for 10 to 12 minutes. Yield: *4 dozen cookies*.

Variation: Spread jelly between 2 cookies, seal up edges, and bake.

OATMEAL CRISP COOKIES

BELLE LEDFORD

1 cup shortening

1 cup dark brown sugar

1 cup granulated sugar

2 eggs

1 teaspoon vanilla

1½ cups sifted flour

1 teaspoon salt

1 teaspoon soda

3 cups uncooked quick-cooking oatmeal

½ cup chopped nuts (optional)

Cream together shortening and sugar. Add eggs and vanilla and beat well. Sift together flour, salt, and soda and add to creamed shortening and sugar. Add oatmeal and nuts, stirring well. Either shape into a roll and slice or drop from a teaspoon onto a greased cookie sheet. Bake in a 350°F oven for 8 to 10 minutes. Yield: *4 dozen cookies*.

SANDIES

BELLE LEDFORD

1 cup butter or margarine

⅓ cup sugar

2 teaspoons water

2 teaspoons vanilla

2 cups sifted flour

1 cup chopped pecans

Cream together butter and sugar. Add water and vanilla and beat well. Blend in flour and nuts. Beat well with a spoon. Drop from a teaspoon onto an ungreased cookie sheet. Bake in a 325°F oven for 15 minutes, or until lightly browned. Cool before removing from the pan. Yield: *40 cookies.*

Cakes

Although ingredients for cakes are often fairly simple, baking a cake in a wood stove could be tricky. Several contacts gave us helpful hints for baking cakes in this manner.

ADDIE NORTON: *I'd get my oven about 350 degrees. Then I'd put my cake in and put in one or two little sticks of wood every once in a while—just enough to keep it the same heat. It'll cook a cake just as pretty as you please. If it does get too hot when you've already got your cake or biscuits in there and you can't cool it off fast, you just have to take them out and let it cool down. You just don't put in too much wood.*

LETTIE CHASTAIN: *I put my cakes on the top rack in the oven unless it's a thick cake. Then I put it on the bottom rack. To keep it from burning on the bottom of the cake, I'm careful to not put much wood in the stove, just enough to get it hot.*

POUND CAKE

With the availability of new ingredients—especially with what our contacts called "cake flour"—through the years, cake recipes have become more sophisticated, but it seems that the pound cake, a cake usually cooked in a tube pan, remains the favorite in Southern Appalachia. Part of the reason pound cakes are so popular is the ready availability of the required ingredients, making it a convenient dessert to put together. The recipe calls for ingredients that are typically kept fully stocked in a kitchen: milk, eggs, flour, sugar, and shortening. Other cake recipes are often made in this area, but if the cook doesn't have the necessary ingredients for something different, she can always resort to making the pound cake.

Stella Burrell explained, "I have a plain cake that I've used if I wanted something real quick. It's something I keep the measurements for in my head. If I had a bunch that come in, that cake was something that I could just go ahead and be doing while I was doing other things. You could use most any easy sauce to go over a cake without having to think too much about it."

POUND CAKE

MARY PITTS

"Every time I make a pound cake, I pick up a salt shaker and just [makes a shaking motion with hand]. All sweets need a little salt. Not much—I just give a little shake."

1 cup shortening or lard

¼ stick margarine or butter

3 cups sugar

6 eggs

3 cups flour

¼ teaspoon salt

¼ teaspoon baking powder

1 cup milk

1 teaspoon vanilla or other flavoring such as almond

Cream shortening, margarine, and sugar. Add eggs, one at a time, and beat well. Sift together flour, salt, and baking powder twice and add with the milk and vanilla to creamed mixture. Beat well. Bake in a 325°F oven for 1½ hours.

OLD DOMINION POUND CAKE

MARY PITTS

2¼ cups flour

¼ teaspoon baking powder

1¼ cups sugar

1¼ cups butter

2¼ teaspoons vanilla

2 tablespoons lemon juice

6 large eggs, separated

⅛ teaspoon salt

1 cup sugar

1½ teaspoons cream of tartar

Sift together flour, baking powder, and 1¼ cups sugar. Cream butter and blend in vanilla and lemon juice. Add egg yolks, one at a time, beating well after each addition. Gradually blend in flour mixture. Beat egg whites until peaks form and add salt; then gradually add 1 cup sugar with cream of tartar, beating well after each addition. Beat until soft peaks form. Gently fold whites into batter. Turn into a greased and floured tube pan. Cut through batter one or two times, then bake 1 hour 20 minutes in a 325°F oven.

CHOCOLATE POUND CAKE

FAY LONG

3 cups sugar

1 cup butter

½ cup shortening

5 eggs

3 cups flour

½ teaspoon salt

½ teaspoon baking powder

4 heaping tablespoons cocoa

1 cup milk

2 teaspoons vanilla

Cream sugar, butter, and shortening until fluffy. Add eggs, one at a time, beating well after each addition. Sift flour before measuring and then sift with other dry ingredients. Add flour mixture alternately with milk. Add vanilla. Beat until well blended. Bake in a well-greased and floured tube pan in a 350°F oven for 1 hour 15 minutes.

PLAIN CAKES

Plain cakes differ from pound cakes in that they are baked in shallow, flat pans, as opposed to tube or Bundt pans, and are often iced or layered.

WHITE LAYER CAKE

½ cup butter

1 cup sugar

2 cups flour

½ teaspoon salt

3 teaspoons baking powder

1 cup milk

1 teaspoon vanilla

2 egg whites, beaten stiff

Cream butter and sugar. Mix dry ingredients and add alternately with milk to creamed mixture. Add vanilla. Fold in egg whites. Pour batter into three 8-inch layer pans. Bake in a 325°F oven for 25 minutes.

GOLD LOAF CAKE

MARY PITTS

"Mother always made this when she was making an angel food cake. She'd use her egg whites in the angel food and the yolks in this one."

½ cup butter

1¼ cups sugar

7 egg yolks

2½ cups flour, sifted

3 teaspoons baking powder

⅔ cup milk

1 teaspoon vanilla

Cream butter and sugar. Beat egg yolks until thick and lemon-colored. Add to butter and sugar. Sift flour and measure; then sift with baking powder three times. Add milk alternately with flour. Add flavoring and beat. Pour into a loaf pan. Bake 40 to 60 minutes in a hot (400°F) oven.

ANGEL FOOD CAKE

1 cup sifted cake flour

¼ teaspoon salt

11 egg whites

1 teaspoon cream of tartar

1¼ cups sifted sugar

1 teaspoon vanilla

½ teaspoon almond extract (optional)

Resift flour three times. Set aside. Add salt to egg whites and beat until foamy, then add cream of tartar and beat until stiff enough to hold a peak but not dry. Fold in sugar, 1 tablespoon at a time. Add flavoring. Fold in flour, 2 tablespoons at a time. Fold as little as possible to blend all ingredients. Pour batter into an ungreased tube pan and bake in a slow (325°F) oven for 45 to 60 minutes. When done, remove from the heat; invert the pan and cool the cake before removing from pan. Dust cake with powdered sugar or ice with a sugar icing.

DEVIL'S FOOD LAYER CAKE

NARCISSE DOTSON

⅔ cup shortening

1½ cups sugar

3 eggs

2½ cups flour

¼ teaspoon salt

3 teaspoons baking powder

1 cup milk

1 teaspoon vanilla

3 squares unsweetened chocolate, melted

Cream together shortening and sugar. Add eggs, one at a time, beating well after each addition. Sift together dry ingredients and add alternately with milk. Mix in vanilla and melted chocolate. Pour into two 9-inch layer pans and bake in a 350°F oven for 20 to 30 minutes.

COCONUT CAKES, SPICE CAKES, FRUIT CAKES, AND NUT CAKES

As dessert ingredients became more readily available, new products were incorporated into recipes, such as coconut, bananas, pineapple, and lemons, as well as an unlimited number of spices and flavorings.

Mary Pitts told us about having coconut as a child:

I've had coconut all of my life. You could get it at the store for a nickel or a dime apiece. I can just see my daddy taking a little hammer and going around that hard-shell hull, tapping it real good. You know, it's got a little monkey face—two eyes and a mouth—and you bore a hole in one of those soft spots and drain out all of that milk. They'd be a glass of coconut milk in there. That's good to put in your pies, and the kids love to drink it. It's good to drink. And he'd bust that open and the coconut would come out of that hull. It'd come out in great big chunks. You'd take a good sharp knife and peel the brown off the back of it and then you could grate it or grind it. Mother always grated hers and one coconut would always make a big bowl. I can just see them now. Us kids always did like to eat it. We got it at Christmas. Santa Claus always left some on the table.

SPICE LAYER CAKE

¾ cup butter
2 cups brown sugar
2 egg yolks
2¾ cups flour
1 teaspoon soda
1 teaspoon cinnamon
1 teaspoon cloves
1 teaspoon allspice
1 teaspoon nutmeg
1 cup buttermilk

Cream together butter and sugar. Add egg yolks, one at a time, beating well after each addition. Sift together dry ingredients and add alternately with buttermilk to the creamed mixture. Pour batter into three 8-inch round layer pans. Bake in a 350°F oven for 20 minutes. Frost this cake with Ivory Frosting (page 191).

SCOTCH CAKE

2 cups flour
2 cups sugar
½ cup butter
½ cup oil
¼ cup cocoa
1 cup water
½ cup buttermilk
2 eggs
1 teaspoon soda
1 teaspoon cinnamon
1 teaspoon vanilla
Scotch Cake Icing (page 192)

Combine flour and sugar. Mix butter, oil, cocoa, and water in a saucepan; bring to a rapid boil and pour into flour and sugar mixture. Mix well. Add buttermilk, eggs (one at a time), soda, cinnamon, and vanilla. Mix well. Pour batter into 2 greased and floured 9-inch layer pans or a greased and floured 13 × 9-inch sheet cake pan. Bake at 350°F for 30 minutes. When cool, frost.

DRIED APPLE CAKE

OLENE GARLAND

"Mrs. Garland [my mother-in-law] used a similar recipe for making what she called an apple torte, making four or five thin layers and spreading this mixture between and on top of layers."

1 white layer or pound cake
1 pint dried apples
1 pint water
½ to 1 cup sugar
1 tablespoon cinnamon

Bake the cake in four 8- or 9-inch round layer pans and adjust baking time stated in recipe so as not to overcook. Mix dried apples with water in a saucepan and cook until thick and the apples are mashed up. Sweeten to taste and add cinnamon. Let cool, then spread between the cake layers and on top of the cake, letting it drip down sides.

Variation: Spices—nutmeg, allspice, cloves—¼ teaspoon of each, can be added in addition to cinnamon.

PERSIMMON CAKE

NORA GARLAND

2 cups sugar
¾ cup butter or margarine
3 eggs
3 cups flour, plain or self-rising (if using
    plain flour, add 1 teaspoon soda and
    ½ teaspoon salt)
1 teaspoon vanilla
1 cup persimmons, scalded and mashed
    through a sieve or colander
Cream Cheese Icing (page 192)

"Cream your sugar and margarine. I use margarine now since I can't get the country butter. Add your eggs, one at a time. Mix the dry ingredients and add them to the blended ingredients. Add the flavoring. Stir in one cup persimmons. Make sure you cook them, mash them, and run them through a colander first to get all the seeds out. You can cook this in three layers or a Bundt pan, either one, at 350 degrees. You can tell when it gets done." (20 minutes for layers and 45 to 60 minutes for Bundt pan.)

CARROT CAKE

MARY PITTS

1 cup corn oil
2 cups finely grated carrots
3 cups self-rising flour
2 cups sugar
1 tablespoon cinnamon
1 teaspoon salt
1 teaspoon baking soda
1 teaspoon vanilla
4 eggs
1 cup chopped nuts

Mix together oil and carrots. Sift together dry ingredients and add to oil and carrot mixture. Mix in vanilla and beat in eggs, one at a time. Stir in nuts. Pour into a greased tube pan. Bake in a 325°F oven for 50 to 55 minutes. This cake is especially good after sitting for a couple of days, becoming moister.

JAM CAKE

NARCISSE DOTSON

1 ¼ cups butter

2 cups sugar

6 eggs

4 cups flour

2 teaspoons baking powder

*1 tablespoon each of cinnamon, cloves,
    allspice, and nutmeg*

1 teaspoon soda

1 cup buttermilk

2 cups jam, such as blackberry

Cream together butter and sugar. Add eggs, one at a time, beating well after each. Sift together flour, baking powder, and spice. Dissolve soda in buttermilk and add alternately with dry ingredients to the egg mixture. Mix in jam. Bake in four 8-inch or 9-inch layer pans in a 350°F oven.

FRUIT FILLING

1 cup raisins

1 cup chopped nuts

1 cup pear honey or fig preserves

Grated peel and juice of 1 orange

BUTTER FILLING

2 cups sugar

1 cup whole milk

½ cup butter or margarine

Mix together fruit filling and set aside. Mix and cook butter filling until slightly thickened. Spread the two alternately between cooled layers by spreading fruit filling on layer first and pouring butter filling over that.

NUT CAKE

MARY PITTS

½ cup butter

1 cup sugar

3 eggs

2 cups flour

2 teaspoons baking powder

1 teaspoon nutmeg

1 cup red wine

1 cup walnuts, or preferred nut

½ pound raisins

Cream together butter and sugar. Add eggs, one at a time, beating well. Sift together dry ingredients and add alternately with wine to creamed mixture. Fold in nuts and raisins. Pour into three 8-inch layer pans and bake in a 325°F oven for 1 hour. Frost with caramel filling.

Icings

In early days, honey and syrup were used as a topping for plain cake and spice cakes such as gingerbread. Several contacts told us how they made a glaze by boiling white sugar and water together until the sugar was dissolved, then pouring it over the cake while hot. With the addition of other products, more flavorful cake toppings were created.

To ice a cake, lay the bottom layer of the cake on a plate. Spoon the icing in the middle of the layer and spread it to the edge with a knife or spatula. Gently place the top layer on; spoon the icing in the middle of the layer and spread to edge and down the sides of the layers, while gradually turning cake around, until cake is completely iced. To spread coconut, sprinkle on top and gently stick to sides with hand.

PLAIN ICING

MARY PITTS

1 tablespoon butter
1 box confectioners' sugar
1 teaspoon extract (any kind)
¼ cup cream
Water (optional)

Soften the butter; add the sugar and extract, then add the cream. If the mixture is stiff, add a drop or two of water.

IVORY FROSTING

ARIZONA DICKERSON

2 egg whites
¼ cup brown sugar, firmly packed
1¼ cups granulated sugar
5 tablespoons water
1 teaspoon vanilla

Combine egg whites, sugar, and water in the top of a double boiler. Beat with a rotary egg beater until thoroughly mixed. Place over rapidly boiling water and beat constantly, cooking 7 minutes or until frosting will stand in peaks. Remove from the boiling water; beat in vanilla and spread on cake.

VINEGAR ICING

EXIE DILLS

"Take [one] cup of good apple vinegar, and you put two cups of sugar in that and boil it until it makes a syrup. It'll be as hard as it can be if you boil it *too* long. When it makes a thick syrup, you take it off the heat, and you put in a little lump of butter about that big [measuring about a tablespoon with her thumb] and melt it. It'll turn kind of white looking. You let the syrup cool till it's not runny, and you put that between [your cake layers] and then over the top."

Icing a cake.

SCOTCH CAKE ICING

½ cup margarine
¼ cup cocoa
6 tablespoons milk
1 teaspoon vanilla
1 box confectioners' sugar
1 cup chopped pecans
1 cup flaked coconut

Cream together margarine and cocoa. Add milk and vanilla. Stir in confectioners' sugar and mix thoroughly. Last add pecans and coconut.

CREAM CHEESE ICING

8 ounces cream cheese, softened
½ stick margarine, softened
1-pound box confectioners' sugar
1 cup persimmons, cooked and strained (see
    Persimmon Cake, page 189)

"Beat all this till it's smooth and add your persimmons last. Be careful about the persimmons. It wouldn't do to have any seeds in your icing."

BUTTERMILK ICING

BELLE LEDFORD

2 cups sugar
1 cup buttermilk
1 teaspoon soda
1 teaspoon vanilla

Mix all ingredients except the vanilla in a saucepan and cook until thick enough to spread. Add vanilla.

CARAMEL ICING

MARINDA BROWN

"My favorite cake was a white caramel cake I used to make and take out a lot. It always got a good reception. You can use any ordinary batter recipe that you know to make a white layer cake. I used a caramel filling, and it was just about the best cake I've ever made, I think."

1 box brown sugar, light or dark
½ cup milk
¼ cup butter
2 eggs, separated
1 teaspoon vanilla

In a saucepan, combine brown sugar and milk. Boil until mixture will spin a thread when dropped from a spoon. Remove from heat; stir in butter. Beat in egg yolks and vanilla. Beat egg whites stiff, then fold into filling. Spread mixture on white layer cake.

SOFT CHOCOLATE FROSTING

ARIZONA DICKERSON

4 squares unsweetened chocolate, cut in pieces
1 ¼ cups cold milk
¼ cup flour
1 cup sugar
2 tablespoons butter
1 teaspoon vanilla

Put chocolate and milk in the top of a double boiler and heat. When chocolate is melted, beat with a rotary beater until smooth and blended. Remove from the heat. Blend flour and sugar, then stir into the chocolate slowly until smooth. Return to the heat and cook until thickened. Add butter and vanilla and stir until well blended. Cool and spread on cake.

10 The Table

For Southern Appalachian communities, there may not be a more intimate space than the dining table. From holiday suppers to church grounds dinners, the rituals surrounding mealtime in this region are many, and tied to the institutions of family, faith, and community. The act of breaking bread with those closest to us—and, sometimes, with total strangers—is a time-honored tradition here and one often connected with our most precious memories.

There are many contexts in which food is the common ground where we meet. Many in this region hold dear memories of Wednesday night fellowship suppers at church, Sunday dinners at Grandma's house, Thanksgiving turkey, Christmas ham, and fund-raising barbecues. If there is any consistent signifier of regionality in this country, it is foodways. Southern Appalachia has carved out its respective piece of the culinary landscape with a strong collection of rich, long-standing food traditions.

For this, our final chapter, we present a collection of menus, libations, and other recipes that we view as indicative of this place and community culture. Some dishes have gone out of fashion, while others remain staples on the Southern Appalachian table. We bring these dishes together into classic mountain meals and explore stories and recipes for large gatherings. As Miranda Brown notes, cooking for family—and for friends and neighbors—truly makes up some of our happiest days.

Dinner on the grounds.

Menus

In most families today, menus are reserved for more formal occasions, with little to no planning for daily meals. However, our contacts provided us with suggestions for typical meals that they would prepare regularly. Menus varied seasonally, with fresh fruits and vegetables being more common in the summer while meats and preserved produce were more often found on the table during colder months. Though based on late twentieth-century traditions, these menus are rooted in traditional Southern Appalachian foodways. The following menus illustrate the creativity and ingenuity of Appalachian cooks. Even though they may not have had much, these cooks provided delicious and complex meals for their families and communities.

BREAKFAST

The first meal of the day often consisted of leftovers or simple ingredients like bread or fruit. Our contacts, though, shared other breakfast favorites that often became staples in the home. Before the convenience of electric, or even wood, stoves and automatic coffeepots, breakfast required considerable time for preparation. Gladys Nichols shared that "of course, the old-timers, they'd fly into that kitchen about four o'clock, and by five o'clock they'd have breakfast on the table. I don't like that early risin', but it usually required about an hour to cook breakfast for the family, you know, and get it on the table ready for them to eat. Of course, the old-timers, that's all they knew."

Typical breakfast foods:

Oatmeal
Meat, such as sausage or ham
Bread and butter

"That's all we had," said Jennie Arrowood.

Eggs
Chicken livers
Gravy
Biscuits

Other foods often served for breakfast include leftover corn bread, grits, mush, and fruits.

NOONDAY OR EVENING MEALS

Lunch and dinner menus often were much more involved, including a variety of dishes typically based on seasonal availability. Some families ate a larger midday meal, or dinner, while others preferred a larger supper, or evening meal. We collected a good sample of menus from our contacts:

Pork tenderloin
Rice, dressing, fried potatoes
Green beans, turnips, or greens
Sauerkraut
Blackberry pie

Pork chops, fried or baked
Fried green tomatoes
Potatoes
Biscuits and gravy
Peaches

Fried ham and brown gravy
Sliced onions and green beans
Candied sweet potatoes
Corn bread
Pumpkin pie

Cured ham and red-eye gravy
Baked sweet potatoes and butter
Chicken and broccoli casserole
Rice and gravy
Peas
Applesauce

Fried chicken
Stewed or fried apples
Green beans or peas or greens
Corn
Corn bread or biscuits and gravy

Baked chicken
Rice or creamed potatoes
Baked apples
Biscuits and gravy
Lemon pie or cobbler or Jell-O

SUNDAY DINNER AND HOLIDAYS

Sunday dinner has always been an important time for families in this part of the country. The cooks would have one or two menus that they would generally follow for the Sunday meal. Inez Taylor remembers these weekly feasts: "On Sundays sometimes my mother'd bake a ham or sometimes she'd just boil it. And she always had fried chicken with maybe rice or creamed potatoes. If we ever had company she'd always have big pans of corn, fried chicken, and fried ham. I usually don't have any choice but to cook for a big crowd, especially on Sundays. With us there was always a big family, and on Sunday I've seen Mama have three or four tablefuls."

Holidays were occasions that called for special meals and menus. Nora Garland recalled: "We killed a big, fat hen on Christmas, and we had plenty of meat—backbones and ribs—that we cooked. And we had sweet potato pie and apple tarts. And I soon learned to make doughnuts. I'd make about four or five dozen, and I bake them yet. I baked some last Christmas."

A TYPICAL SUNDAY MENU AT AUNT ARIE CARPENTER'S
Souse and/or sausage
Chicken and dumplings
Leather breeches
Hominy
Cabbage cooked in a frying pan in the broth from making souse
Potatoes cooked in a Dutch oven
Chowchow
Bread
Egg custards
Peach cobbler

Some special occasion menus consisted of:

Leather breeches with streak of lean
Ham hocks with Irish potatoes
Baked yams
Crowder peas cooked with pickled corn
Cracklin corn bread with sweet butter
Poke salad and pepper grass stewed together flavored with streak of lean
Pickled poke salad stalks
Spring onions, tomatoes, relishes
Buttermilk
Dried apple stack cake

Or:

Fried chicken and gravy, ham, or turkey
Stewed or mashed Irish potatoes or sweet potatoes if available
Boiled corn, on or off the cob
Green beans or lima beans or white half-runner beans
Other vegetables from the garden as available
Cooked apples or applesauce
Corn bread and/or biscuits
Pie, cobbler, or a special layer cake

Cooking for Crowds

Throughout our archives, many contacts recall cooking for large groups on a regular basis. Family members often numbered in the teens, either from the nucleus of parents and children or the consolidation of extended family members into one household. During the Depression, it was not unusual for families with more resources to share food with those who did not. Likewise, it was common custom to invite relatives, friends, and hometown or visiting revival preachers for Sunday dinner.

As it remains today, contacts interviewed for the first publication of this book (now, nearly forty years ago) noted how hard it was to get families together, as opposed to when they were younger. By the late twentieth century, and continuing into the present, larger gatherings are usually possible only around the holidays or on special occasions.

Nora Garland shared with us memories of her long years of preparing food for crowds:

Dinner spread.

When I was little we had the same thing all the time, nearly, for dinner and supper. We'd have beans, leather breeches beans, some kind of greens, and just things like that. We always had a big crowd. Mother never would throw anything away because she said somebody might come hungry. Daddy'd say, "Have you fed the dog?" She said, "No, I don't feed him till I see whether anybody's coming or not." A lot of people come by, and they was always hungry and ready to eat. And there was a good crowd of us—seven of us, nine with Mother and Daddy. But Mother never would throw nothing away because she said somebody might come hungry, and I'm just like her.

We'd take food to dinners at church. They call them covered-dish dinners now, but we didn't have no covered dishes. We just put it in anything we had. We'd cook chicken and make chicken pie and dumplings and we had plenty of meat, so we'd take fried ham and things like that.

Despite the gradual decline in the number of the large family meals, church suppers and reunions still afford opportunities for congregating—and for feasting on a great variety of dishes. Women often bring their specialties to church homecomings, all-day singings with "dinner on the grounds," and other community events. Covered-dish dinners in our area have quite a reputation for providing all one can possibly eat.

Our contacts shared their diverse experiences cooking for large groups, from school lunches to logging camps to commercial ventures. Despite the variation in venue, each story provides a snapshot of how Southern Appalachian cuisine and techniques were applied to community settings. School lunches are a common example of this. Most children brought home-cooked meals to school in lunch pails, but some institutions had in-house lunchrooms that served students hot meals. These lunchrooms provided a space for community meals and replicated many of the food traditions prevalent in the home. Rabun Gap–Nacoochee School (RGNS), a boarding school in Rabun County, Georgia, was one of the first locally to feature an on-site dining hall.

Mary Pitts shared some of her experiences as kitchen supervisor when she was a student at RGNS:

I've always liked to cook. Just give me the kitchen. I'd rather be in the kitchen than any other part of the house, especially on a rainy day and it cold outside. I think I took after my mother about that. She always loved to cook.

Well, the last year I was at Rabun Gap–Nacoochee School—my senior year, 1923 and '24—I had charge of the cooking. See, I went to school half a day and worked half a day. The morning cooks stayed there and cooked lunch, and there was girls to do the dishwashing. Then when I'd come at twelve-thirty to lunch, there was four other girls to do the supper cooking, and I helped do the planning and fixing of all of it. We had eight to ten tables, ten to a table.

We cooked on a wood stove bigger than this table is long. It had the firebox in the center, and we had two big ovens and biscuit pans that held sixty-four biscuits, eight biscuits each way. We made ten pans of biscuits for supper. We'd fry sausage and use that grease to make creamed gravy to pour over that. We'd pour it up in a big old dishpan on the edge of the stove so it'd stay hot. And we'd have homemade applesauce, and sorghum syrup made at the school, and butter stayed on the table all the time.

We even had possum dinners when I was in school. I cooked one year. We had possum and sweet potatoes. I don't remember the other vegetables; I just remember them greasy possums. But they were nice. Mr. Farmer, the one that brought the possums up from Toccoa, had put them up in cages and fed them for two weeks.

Other large groups, such as logging companies, required staff to provide meals throughout the week for workers who lived on site. Community meals provided a family dynamic and a sense of home to these men who spent long stretches of time away from their own homes. Connie Burrell describes cooking for one of these camps:

Back in the fifties, my husband and I cooked at three different sawmills. We cooked at Tacoma River, at Horse Creek down beside of Highlands, and at Rock Creek. The workers would just build their own camp. They'd build the kitchen and dining room off from the bedrooms.

But we cooked, that is, I cooked. Lawrence took care of the "lobby"—that's the bedrooms. I'd have to get up at about four o'clock in the morning, and I cooked three meals a day for as many as forty or fifty men by myself. There was plenty of them, and it took a lot of food. It'd take four or five pounds of bacon or sausage and about five dozen eggs for breakfast. You'd have to cook three or four big biscuit pans full, and the coffeepot'd hold about three gallons of coffee. We served milk, too.

You'd get through with one meal and have to start another one. You'd have to peel and cook about a half a bushel of potatoes. I'd fry them or stew them or mash them. I guess frying them'd be the easiest, but you still had to peel them. Lawrence would help me right smart when he wasn't working in the lobby. Mashing potatoes was a job because we just had a hand thing to mash them with. I didn't fry chicken too much, either. It was too hard to fry that much. I'd make chicken and dumplings sometimes, and chicken pie. We cooked bacon and beef and just different kinds of meat. We didn't have any wild game—didn't nobody have time to hunt. They'd just go out to the store and buy it by the truckload.

We had supper at about six o'clock, and I'd get through washing dishes and all at about eight o'clock. Lawrence helped some with the dishes. Between dinner and supper, I'd have a rest spell, but, Lord, I got tired. I never did get sick, though [laughter]. It was hard, but we didn't think nothing about it back then. The only thing was you just had to cook a lot of it.

While most restaurants today are a formal, business affair, Effie Lord had a uniquely casual and familiar business. At the time of the first *Foxfire Book of Appalachian Cookery*, Effie Lord's restaurant, Lord's Cafe, was approaching its silver anniversary (twenty-five years). Lord's was different from most restaurants. There was no wait staff, no formal menu, no one bussing dirty tables. Instead, patrons walked in, went to the kitchen, got a plate, and served themselves from the pots and pans of food on the big wood cookstoves. The patrons took their food back into the dining room, ate, then paid the two dollars and sixty cents on their way out the door. Though a business, Effie's setup created a family dynamic and transformed the restaurant into something more akin to a home kitchen. It's hard to imagine something like Lord's existing today, but it's important to talk about it—to see it—because of what it can tell us about this community and this culture. There is now a prevalent restaurant culture in Southern Appalachia, thanks to the growing interest around cultural foodways. We've seen an explosion of culturally based restaurants throughout the region, as well as restaurants following the same trends seen in urban markets. Yes, "farm to table" is a thing here, too. These businesses reflect the changing demographic of the region, due to immigration and a shift in local economic opportunities. Likewise, they provide a diversity of options that are redefining the culinary landscape and culture of the community. However, Effie's interview illuminates something meaningful: that amazing connection between food and community that isn't always visible in today's restaurant culture.

Now Mr. Lord's been dead going on twenty-four years, and I've run this café down here by myself for twenty-four years. Ever since I moved here I've been using a gas stove. It's just the same as cooking on a wood stove, but it takes a little bit longer on the wood stove. Slower cooking probably makes the food better then in an electric or gas stove, but I'd rather cook on gas 'cause I'd have a hard time getting in wood. There's nowhere to put wood in this place.

Here I serve meals every day except Sunday. I have to stay at home then. I'm not open to the tourists for breakfast, but I am to my regular local people who come in every day. I can't cook breakfast for a lot of people because I don't have time. Some want their eggs sunny-side up, and everybody wants their eggs different or different meats. So, I cook a few breakfasts for my locals, and while I'm cooking that I prepare dinner.

I have my customers come in the back and serve theirselves, and 99 percent of them carry their dishes back to the sink when they're through because I don't have any help. I have had help, but I had to wait on them. They just wanted to piddle. They were ashamed to wash dishes, sweep floors, mop or clean bathrooms, and I don't need nobody that can't help do, you know. So, I do all that myself.

Not having to pay help lets me keep the price down, anyway, and the people like eating this way. If a new one comes in, I have to tell them what to do, or if I'm back in the kitchen the customers will tell them. And it just tickles them to death to get to serve themselves, especially folks from out of town, and that all saves me a waitress. Besides, I have so many vegetables, two meats, the salad, tea, and dessert to fix, and it just takes all my time to cook. They all like it, especially these summer folks, because they really eat. I just charge two dollars and sixty cents—that's tax and all—and the tourists go back a second time. I don't have anything fancy with different names and all like most of them. It's all plain cooking. Mountain cooking. Home cooking. And they like that.

Most of the people I feed are regular mountain people, and they don't go for things like asparagus. They eat broccoli good now, but there's so many things that they don't like. So, I fix enough that if there's things that they don't like, there'll be other things they do. I have seven or eight vegetables a day, and I try to change every day and have a balanced meal—you know, something green, something

yellow. And today I had two kinds of potatoes—sweet potato patties and mashed potatoes. Then I had string beans and okra, tomatoes, corn, white turnips, kidney beans, some rutabaga turnips, and a slaw. So, you see, I have enough there.

I make a casserole out of squash, and the Florida people say I'm the only person they know that knows how to cook squash to eat. I take real small squash, scrape them, cut them up in thin pieces, put them in a pan, add onions, and then put crumbled-up Ritz crackers on top. Then I put butter, a tiny bit of water, and grated cheese on top of that, put foil over it and put it in the oven to cook. I just put green beans on and let them cook a long time. If I've got a ham bone I put that in them. I use bacon grease or whatever I have to season them with. I make a calico salad you don't ever see much nowhere, too. It's made out of onions, bell peppers, cucumbers, and tomatoes. You cut those up and weaken your vinegar a little bit and put a little sugar and salt in there. For bread, I serve mostly corn bread. I use self-rising meal and flour and always add extra eggs and soda and buttermilk. I bake it till the bottom gets brown, and then I take it out and put it under the grill. Then I take it up. To make apple cobbler, I just put sugar to canned or either fresh apples and then put a cake batter over the top of them.

My food don't stay there long. After I get it cooked, it stays about two hours, and then it's all gone. I just cook enough to last through the meal, and I put the leftover food in the garbage. Most cafés save it and make soup and just use it over and over, but I won't do it. The man I give it to feeds it to his hogs. I won't eat it, and I'm not going to serve it to my customers.

To prepare for your own crowd, try one of these high-volume recipes or prepare extra to share with friends and family throughout the week:

Lena Shope from the Wolffork Community will be gathering vegetables from her garden until fall.

Entrées for a Crowd

Soups and stews are delicious entrées that can easily be prepared for a large group or taken to a potluck dinner. Vegetable soup, a mixture of several vegetables cooked with tomatoes or tomato juice, is a common dish in this part of the South. People enjoy making it because the mixture is easily customized to suit their own taste. Two of our contacts told us how they make theirs:

EXIE DILLS: *Yeah, I made soup every fall, every summer. I just used corn and tomatoes and if I had them, shelled beans. And okra. That's all I put in mine. Some uses peas. I don't eat peas, so I don't put peas. You can put potatoes in if you want to, but I just never did. When you go to fix it for the table, you know, you can put cooked potatoes in with it then, if you want to.*

STELLA BURRELL: *When my boys were growing up, they got tired of just vegetable soup, and I would add beef to it. I would put usually about eight different kinds of vegetables in it— tomatoes with corn and green beans and lima beans, okra, and onions, and maybe a little pepper. I like vegetable soup with corn bread, but I eat it with crackers a lot now if I don't have the corn bread. That's another quick meal to serve if you've got somebody dropping in.*

OLD-FASHIONED VEGETABLE SOUP

3 pounds stew beef

4 cups water

1 cup cubed carrots

2 cups small cubes of Irish potatoes

1½ cups corn

¾ cup okra, sliced very thin

1 cup baby lima beans

½ cup chopped celery

1 medium onion, chopped fine

6 cups tomatoes or tomato juice

2 teaspoons salt

1 teaspoon pepper

½ teaspoon sugar

Cover beef with water and heat to boiling. Reduce heat; cover and simmer 1 to 2 hours until meat on shanks is fork tender. Let cool and pull meat from shanks into small cubes. Skim fat from cooled stock. Strain stock into large saucepan; add meat cubes and remaining ingredients. Heat to boiling, cover, and simmer for 1 hour, or until vegetables are tender. Additional water or tomato juice may be needed if mixture gets too thick. Yield: *Twenty to twenty-five 1-cup servings.*

As with vegetable soup, Brunswick stew recipes may also be easily modified. Many people make it without a recipe, mixing ingredients together to suit their particular tastes. Several contacts told us how they make Brunswick stew.

MARGIE LEDFORD: *I make Brunswick stew—that's some beef and some pork and some chicken and tomatoes and potatoes and some A-1 sauce. It's first one thing and then another. I don't have no recipe.*

LETTIE CHASTAIN: *We start cooking ours and put everything in it—corn, tomatoes, chicken, pork, beef, all your seasoning and butter and ketchup. Some people put sage in it, but I don't; and I put barbecue sauce. Put it on to cooking and we put our margarine and stuff in it, but I always just taste [some] of it. It's good if you put some broke-up soda crackers in it, but not too much, just some; then we put our seasoning in until we get it like we want it.*

BRUNSWICK STEW FOR A LARGE CROWD

BELLE LEDFORD

10 pounds ground beef

10 pounds chicken

3 pounds pork

4½ gallons tomatoes

4 gallons fresh, canned, or frozen corn

5 pounds onions, chopped fine and boiled or
   sautéed

½ gallon ketchup

1 pound butter

1½ cups Worcestershire sauce

5 ounces Tabasco sauce, or to taste

1 pound cheese (optional)

Salt and pepper to taste

Precook chicken, pork, and beef by boiling each until tender. Grind or cut chicken, beef, and pork into small pieces. Mix with remaining ingredients in a large pot and cook until good and done. Be careful with Tabasco sauce, using only the amount to suit taste. If canning this mixture place jars in a water bath and process them for 2 to 2½ hours. Yield: *12½ quarts.*

OLD-FASHIONED BEEF STEW

½ cup plus 2 to 4 tablespoons flour

1 teaspoon salt

¼ teaspoon pepper

2 pounds stew beef, cut into bite-sized pieces

2 tablespoons shortening

6 cups hot water

4 medium potatoes, cut into bite-sized cubes

4 carrots, cut into bite-sized cubes

½ cup sliced celery (optional)

1 medium onion, diced

1 tablespoon salt

1 cup cold water

Mix ½ cup flour, salt, and pepper and use to coat meat. In a large skillet, brown meat in the melted shortening. Add hot water and heat to boiling. Reduce heat; cover and simmer for 2 to 3 hours. Stir in the vegetables and salt and simmer 30 to 45 minutes longer, until the vegetables are tender. To thicken the stew, mix together the cold water and 2 to 4 tablespoons flour in a jar; shake until blended and stir into the stew. Heat to boiling, stirring constantly. Boil and stir 1 minute. Yield: *15 to 20 servings.*

HOG'S HEAD STEW

JOANNE CARVER

This recipe comes from the Carver family. Every harvest time, they plunge into a cooking-canning spree that goes for days and leaves them more than ready for the winter. The measurements given below yielded 63 quarts. To reduce the volume, cut proportionally by subtracting or adding other ingredients according to preference.

1 ½ hog's heads

2 shoulders or hams of venison

4 chickens

1 peck onions

1 gallon Irish potatoes

5 half-gallons each of tomatoes, corn, peas, and carrots

6 large cans tomato juice to thin (broth may be substituted for, or added to, the tomato juice)

1 package poultry seasoning

Bay leaves to taste

5 pounds salt (or to taste)

Worcestershire sauce to taste

Pepper to taste

Cook the meat until it comes easily off the bones. Cool, remove the meat from the bones, and grind it up (or run through a food chopper) together with the other ingredients. Place the mixture in quart jars, seal, and cook in a pressure cooker for 60 minutes at 10 pounds pressure. Then store away for the lean months.

Her mother's recipe for the same stew, provided to us by Brenda Carver, varies somewhat: 1 hog's head, 2 chickens, 4 pounds ground beef, 1 gallon potatoes, 1 gallon tomatoes, 4 number 2 cans each of peas, corn, and carrots. Chop and blend ingredients, can, cook in pressure cooker for 30 minutes.

Side Dishes for a Crowd

Side dishes allowed cooks the opportunity to pull in additional ingredients from the garden or root cellar to complement the entrée and round out the meal. Salads and covered dishes are a staple at potlucks, picnics, church suppers, and the family table. Early on, side dishes were simple— a variety of sliced vegetables arranged on a plate. However, over time, ingredients like mayonnaise were added to create some of the most beloved sides found at a potluck supper.

MARY PITTS: *My mother used olive oil to make mayonnaise. In a big, deep bowl, beat your egg yellow good with a rotary egg beater. We used the egg white for other stuff, and then we found out later you could use the whole egg and beat it. Then you put in one half teaspoon of oil at a time. It takes one standing putting that in and the other beating. Put a grain or two of salt in it, and you could tell when you got it thick enough. You could get it as thick as the mayonnaise you buy today. The more oil you put in it the thicker it got. It's real good, and my mother said she'd rather make it often and have it fresh made. You could put it in potato salads and things. We made mayonnaise way back in the thirties when my three oldest children was little. They loved just plain mayonnaise on loaf bread. It tastes different. To me it's better.*

Note: Belle Ledford says that plain cooking oil—she suggested Wesson—may be used instead of olive oil. You may season with salt and add a little lemon juice or a little vinegar.

MAYONNAISE DRESSING

1 egg yolk
2 tablespoons vinegar or lemon juice
    or 1 tablespoon of each
¼ teaspoon mustard
¾ teaspoon salt
⅛ teaspoon pepper
¾ cup salad oil

Beat egg yolk and add 1 tablespoon of the vinegar or lemon juice. Add mustard, salt, and pepper. Beat well. Drop oil, a teaspoon at a time, into the egg mixture, beating constantly, until ¼ cup has been added. Then add in larger quantities, beating thoroughly after each addition. As mixture thickens, add remaining vinegar or lemon juice a little at a time. Have all ingredients equally cold when mixing. Store in a cool place in clean jars. Yield: *1 cup.*

Potatoes were a common and prolific crop throughout the Southern Appalachians. They were served in a variety of dishes but were easily made into large potato salads for sharing with friends and families. There are almost as many variations for making potato salad as there are cooks, and it is still a favorite for taking along on outings.

OLD-FASHIONED POTATO SALAD
DAISY JUSTUS

Use leftover mashed potatoes, or cook as many potatoes as needed. Mash the potatoes and about 1 cup of chopped onions. Then use 3 or 4 tablespoons of vinegar, and salt and pepper; mix well. Serve on lettuce leaves.

POTATO SALAD

MARY PITTS

When I make potato salad, I usually peel about a gallon of potatoes and cube them before I cook them. They cook quicker that way. And then I drain all that water off of them and pour them on a tray and let them get cool. While they're cooling, I chop up a big onion and cucumber pickles and six or eight boiled eggs. By the time you get your eggs and all chipped up, your potatoes is nearly cold. And I just salt and pepper it, mix it all up with some mayonnaise, and set it back. When you get all that chipped up, you've got a bowl full.

Slaw can be made in as many different ways as potato salad, but the average slaw tends to "keep" longer. In fact, most names for slaw indicate how long they may be kept in the refrigerator. Cabbage is a hardy vegetable, and more recent recipes include instructions for freezing slaw.

DAISY JUSTUS: *Used to, when we made slaw, we'd take the thick cream of the milk and mix it and vinegar together and pour it over the cabbage. That was the way we made slaw. We still put tomatoes or onions in our slaw.*

SEVEN-DAY COLESLAW

MARINDA BROWN

Pack in layers in crock:

½ head cabbage, grated
1 carrot, grated
1 medium onion, chopped
½ sweet red pepper, chopped
½ green pepper, chopped
Thin layer of sugar on top

Mix together and bring to a boil:

¼ cup vegetable oil
½ cup vinegar
Sugar and salt (amount depends on how sweet or sour you want the slaw)

While still hot, pour the mixture over the vegetables in the crock. The peppers are optional, but they make it pretty and give it color. This recipe makes a quart and it will keep on and on, not just seven days.

FREEZER SLAW WITH CUCUMBERS, ONIONS, AND PEPPERS

BELLE LEDFORD

1 gallon chopped cabbage
1 tablespoon salt
4 small onions
4 cucumbers
2 carrots
2 small peppers
1 teaspoon celery seed
2 cups sugar
1 cup vinegar
½ cup water

Mix cabbage and salt. Let stand 30 minutes, then drain. Chop the onions, cucumbers, carrots, and peppers. Add to the cabbage, along with the celery seed. Set aside. Boil the sugar, vinegar, and water for 1 minute. When cold pour over the cabbage mixture, mixing well. Let stand 5 minutes before putting into containers to freeze.

Corn bread, a staple of the mountains, could be extended by adding it to a similar slaw or salad mixture:

CORN BREAD SALAD
NAWANA LAWRENCE

2 packages ranch dressing
2 cups sour cream
1 pan corn bread
2 cans pinto beans
3 tomatoes, diced
1 onion, diced
2 cups shredded cheese
10 to 15 pieces of bacon
2 cans whole corn, drained

Combine ranch dressing mix and sour cream. Set aside. Crumble ½ of corn bread into a large dish. Top with 1 can of pinto beans. Mix tomatoes and onions together and pour ½ onto the pinto beans. Layer ½ of ranch mixture on top of this. Repeat layers, topping with crumbled bacon. Refrigerate overnight.

As items such as pineapple and French-style green beans became available in local stores, cooks added them to their salad repertoires:

BEAN SALAD
BELLE LEDFORD

1 green pepper
1 stalk celery
1 large onion
1 can French green beans
1 can green peas
16 ounces white shoepeg (whole kernel) corn
1 small jar pimientos
¾ cup red wine vinegar
½ cup oil
1 cup sugar

Chop peppers, celery, and onions into fine pieces; add to other vegetables. Drain well before adding vinegar, oil, and sugar. Keeps in the refrigerator for weeks. Yield: *10 to 12 servings.*

FRUIT SALAD
BELLE LEDFORD

1 cup sour cream
1 cup mandarin orange slices, drained
1 cup crushed or chunk pineapple, drained
1 cup shredded or grated coconut
1 cup marshmallows

Mix together all the ingredients. Let stand 24 hours before serving. Yield: *8 servings.*

Before the popularity of gelatin, sweet salads consisted of fruit salad made from apples, raisins, nuts, and other fruits in season at the time. The fruits were generally tossed with mayonnaise. However, with the arrival of gelatin came a whole new series of congealed salads that incorporated both new and traditional ingredients.

RHUBARB AND STRAWBERRY SALAD
BELLE LEDFORD

1 large package strawberry gelatin
2 cups hot cooked rhubarb
2 cups sliced strawberries

Dissolve gelatin in cooked rhubarb. Let cool, then add sliced strawberries.

CUCUMBER AND PINEAPPLE ASPIC

3 lemons

4 cups cold water

1 can diced pineapple (about 2 cups),
    drained but juice reserved

1 cups peeled and diced tender cucumbers

1 package plain gelatin

2 cups hot water

Green food coloring

Lettuce

Mayonnaise

Juice lemons and add to cold water. Put pineapple and cucumbers into water. Use pineapple juice to sweeten to desired taste. Dissolve gelatin in hot water and add to mixture. Drop in enough green food coloring to make a delicate green. Turn into mold to jell. Serve on lettuce with mayonnaise.

Gravies and Sauces: "Mighty Good for Sopping Biscuits In"

It is simple to learn to make good sauces and gravies. Bland foods can be made more enjoyable when dripping with a good sauce, and in the mountains, it is a rare meal that does not include a thick gravy or sauce of some sort. These are typical:

CORNMEAL GRAVY

RUTH HOLCOMB

¼ to ½ cup grease from bacon or fatback, or lard

1 cup cornmeal

3 glasses water or milk or half of each

Have some grease or lard in a pan on the stove. Get it real hot and add the cornmeal. Stir it until the meal is brown. Stir in water or milk and stir constantly until it's as thick as you like it. That should serve about 4 people.

FLOUR GRAVY

ADDIE NORTON

"Meat that's been home cured; that's what makes good brown gravy. Meat that's kept in a freezer don't make a good brown gravy."

1 tablespoon grease

1 tablespoon flour

2 cups milk

Salt and pepper to taste

Heat grease in a skillet. Mix in flour and stir until the flour is smooth. Add the milk, stirring constantly until the gravy thickens. Add salt and pepper to taste. For white sauce, don't let flour brown; for brown gravy, let flour brown to desired color. Yield: 2 cups.

RED-EYE GRAVY

JAKE WALDROOP

"Fry slices of ham in a frying pan. After they are done, remove and add flour to the grease that's left in the pan. Let it brown. Add coffee and continue to stir. The coffee will make it a dark brown gravy. You may leave out the flour. Just add coffee to the grease left in the pan after you've finished cooking your ham. Stir it around. The gravy will be very thin, but have an excellent flavor and be mighty good for sopping biscuits in."

Giblet gravy.

CREAM SAUCE

STELLA BURRELL

I've got a cream sauce recipe that you do in a double boiler. It was something that you could do if you had somebody come in and you didn't have something fixed. I think I use about three tablespoons of butter and three of flour. You just add a little bit of flour at a time as the butter melts in the top of a double boiler. It takes about three or four cups of milk to thicken it. Salt and pepper it, too. You can add cheese, beef, chicken, or whatever to that sauce, or you can use it for scalloped potatoes, scalloped cabbage, mixed vegetables, or any way you want to fix it. It's something easy to fix.

Variations:

Cheese sauce—add grated cheese.

Egg sauce—add boiled or raw eggs.

Meat sauce—add dried beef, chicken, or turkey.

Vegetable sauce—add cream sauce to vegetables—scalloped potatoes, cabbage, etc.

Mushroom sauce—add ½ pound mushrooms, washed, peeled, and cut into quarters, or 1 (4½-ounce) can mushrooms.

GIBLET GRAVY

In 4 to 5 cups salted water cook the gizzard, heart, and neck of fowl until tender, approximately 1 to 2 hours. Add liver toward the last 30 minutes of cooking. Let cool and remove the meat from neck and chop giblets up into fine pieces. Follow the recipe and directions for making skillet gravy (Flour Gravy, page 207), except use broth from giblets for the liquid. Stir giblets into gravy and heat thoroughly.

Variation: Boiled eggs may be sliced and added.

BARBECUE SAUCE

1 ½ cups water

1 cup vinegar

½ cup tomato ketchup

½ cup chopped onion

2 tablespoons Worcestershire sauce or 1 teaspoon chili powder

1 teaspoon salt

½ teaspoon pepper

Bring all the ingredients to a boil, pour over your meat, and roast in a 350°F oven according to general rules, basting occasionally. Yield: *3 cups.*

TOMATO SAUCE (RELISH)

MARY PITTS

12 large tomatoes

1 green pepper

1 onion

2 cups vinegar

1 tablespoon sugar

1 tablespoon salt

2 teaspoons whole cloves

2 teaspoons whole cinnamon

1 teaspoon whole allspice

2 teaspoons whole nutmeg

Scald and skin tomatoes; chop green peppers and onions. Combine the 3 vegetables in a large pan with the vinegar and sugar. Mix spices and salt and tie in a square of cheesecloth. Drop into tomato mixture. Cook slowly 2½ to 3 hours. Yield: *4 cups.*

Desserts for a Crowd

No gathering is complete without a sweet treat to share. Whether for the holiday table, the annual cookie exchange, a special potluck, or even your freezer, these classic treats make plenty to share.

CRY-BABY COOKIES

MARY PITTS

"It makes a big batch [8 dozen]. We made 'em at Christmas time."

1 cup plus 2 tablespoons shortening

1 cup plus 2 tablespoons sugar

1 cup molasses

2 eggs, beaten

4¾ cups sifted flour

1 tablespoon baking powder

1 teaspoon salt

1½ teaspoons soda

2 cups grated coconut

2 cups chopped walnuts

1½ cups raisins

1 cup milk

Cream shortening, then add sugar, molasses, and eggs. Sift together dry ingredients, then combine with coconut, walnuts, and raisins. Add dry ingredients alternately with milk to creamed mixture. Drop by tablespoonful onto a greased baking sheet. Bake at 350°F for 10 minutes. Yield: *8 dozen cookies.*

CARAMEL COOKIES

JUDY MARCELLINO

(HER GRANDMOTHER'S RECIPE)

4 cups dark brown sugar

1 cup lard, margarine, or butter

4 large or 5 small eggs

6 to 7 cups flour

1 tablespoon soda

1 teaspoon cream of tartar

1 cup seedless raisins (optional)

1 teaspoon vanilla (optional) or 1 teaspoon
  or desired spice for varied flavoring

Cream together sugar and lard. Add eggs, one at a time, beating well. Sift together dry ingredients and pour into a large mixing bowl, making a pit in the center. Pour creamed mixture, vanilla, and raisins into the pit and work into the flour. Knead well. Form into 2 large loaves and let stand a few hours, then slice thin and place on a cookie sheet, being sure to leave plenty of room between each cookie for spreading as they cook. Place no more than 12 on a 17 × 13-inch ungreased pan. Bake in a 350°F oven for 10 to 15 minutes. Remove from the pan as soon as you take it from oven. The cookies will stick if left to cool on the pan. Yield: *8 dozen cookies.*

GINGER SNAPS

½ cup shortening or butter

1 cup brown sugar

1 cup molasses

6 cups sifted flour

1 teaspoon ginger

1 teaspoon soda

1 teaspoon salt

½ cup hot water

Cream together shortening and sugar. Beat in molasses. Resift flour with other dry ingredients and add to molasses mixture alternately with water. Turn out onto a floured surface and knead well; roll thin and cut into 2-inch circles. Bake on greased cookie sheets in a 350°F oven. Cool before removing from cookie sheets. Yield: *10 dozen cookies.*

OLD-FASHIONED TEA CAKES

MARY ELLEN MEANS

1 cup butter

2 cups sugar

4 eggs

2 teaspoons vanilla

2 teaspoons nutmeg (optional)

8 to 10 cups of self-rising flour

Cream together butter and sugar, then add eggs, one at a time, beating well. Add vanilla and nutmeg. Beat until fluffy. Gradually start stirring in flour until a fairly firm dough is formed. Place dough on a heavily floured surface and knead more flour into dough until it is firm enough to roll out. Working with only a small amount of dough at a time, roll out ½-inch thick, then cut out with a cookie cutter and place on an ungreased cookie sheet. Sprinkle sugar on each before baking. Bake in a 375°F oven for 5 to 8 minutes. Yield: *6 dozen cakes.*

YEAST POTATO DOUGHNUTS

1 cup sieved cooked potatoes (warm or cold)

1 cup liquid, reserved from cooking potatoes

¾ cup shortening

½ cup sugar

1 tablespoon salt

1 package dry yeast

¾ cup warm water

2 eggs, beaten

5 to 6 cups flour

Oil for deep frying

GLAZE

1 cup confectioners' sugar

1 tablespoon milk

½ teaspoon vanilla

Mix potatoes, potato liquid, shortening, sugar, and salt. Dissolve yeast in warm water; stir into potato mixture. Stir in eggs and enough flour to make dough easy to handle. Turn dough onto a lightly floured surface; knead until smooth and elastic, 5 to 8 minutes. Place in a greased bowl; turn greased side up. Cover. Let rise until doubled, 1 to 1½ hours. (Tip: Dough can be stored in the refrigerator 3 days before using. Refrigerate in the greased bowl immediately after kneading. If dough rises in the refrigerator, punch down and cover with a damp towel.) Pat the dough out on a lightly floured surface to ¾-inch thickness. Cut doughnuts with a floured 2½-inch cutter; let rise until doubled, about 1 hour. Heat oil (3 to 4 inches) to 375°F in a heavy pan. Fry doughnuts until golden, 2 to 3 minutes on each side. Drain on paper towels. Glaze doughnuts while warm. Store doughnuts at room temperature, covered with a towel. Yield: *Approximately 5 dozen doughnuts.*

PUMPKIN BREAD

MARY PITTS

4 cups cooked, mashed pumpkin

4 cups sugar

1 cup oil

1 teaspoon vanilla

4 eggs, beaten

5 cups flour

4 teaspoons baking soda

1 teaspoon salt

1 teaspoon cloves

2 teaspoons cinnamon

1 cup chopped nuts

1 cup raisins

In a large mixing bowl, using a wooden spoon to mix with, combine pumpkin, sugar, oil, vanilla, and beaten eggs. Mix well. Sift together dry ingredients and add to pumpkin mixture. Stir until well blended. Fold in the nuts and raisins. Pour into 3 or 4 greased loaf pans or, for a moister bread, use several coffee or bean cans, ungreased. If using cans, pour each can half full of batter. Bake in a 350°F oven for 1 hour.

Beverages

"Used to you couldn't make it too strong but what I could drink it."

Libations are always an important part of every meal, especially at large gatherings. Before the modern convenience of running water, people had to make, from scratch, beverages that were safe for consumption. These included coffee, milk, tea, cider (nonalcoholic), juice, beer, and wine.

COFFEE

Before the days of packaged, freeze-dried coffee, Gladys Nichols told us how she first prepared the real thing.

I've parched a many a pound of green coffee. That used to be my job when I was eight or ten years old. Mama would fly into that kitchen at about four o'clock and call me out to parch the coffee. I didn't have a stove to parch it on, either; I did it on the fireplace. I put my coffee beans in a pan and got me some coals out and put them on the hearth. I'd take a spoon and stir that coffee around and around until it turned brown. It's pretty easy done, but if you burned your coffee or scorched it a little it wasn't no good. Then I'd cool it down, put it in that old coffee grinder, and grind her up. Put it in the pot, and you've got some of the strongest coffee. If I had it today I'd like it better, but I wouldn't like that extra work. I didn't like that early rising, either, but it usually required about an hour to cook breakfast and get it on the table by five.

On a wood stove, the coffee-parching process was much the same. As Blanche Harkins said:

My mother had a large pan that covered the bottom of the wood stove. It fit down in there. She'd put her coffee beans on that pan and put it in the oven. You

Coffee beans were once ground in hand-turned mills like this one owned by Gladys Nichols.

CIDER AND JUICE

Apple cider was also a common beverage among mountain communities, since apples were an abundant crop that could easily be transformed into a delicious (and safe) drink. As part of the apple-pressing process, community members would gather together to make this drink. In the 1970s, Foxfire students visited Harry and Marinda Brown to help with their seasonal cider pressing. The process is documented in detail in *Foxfire Book 4* (pp. 449–51). To make cider, apples are gathered, washed, cored, and quartered (with peelings) before being fed into the hopper. The mill crank is turned as apples are added, and the mash, or pulp, is pushed into a container beneath the hopper. A disc with a separate crank is used to press the juice out of the pulp and is strained through cheesecloth. The resulting cider can be consumed immediately, chilled for later use, or preserved by canning or fermentation.

Aunt Arie Carpenter shared the process for making cider without a press. She said that a wooden trough with holes drilled in the bottom was filled with apples. A maul was then used to mash or crush the apples, and a plank was pressed down on top of the apples to squeeze the juice out. This cider was stored in wooden barrels or in the springhouse for drinking. After aging, some was used for vinegar or apple brandy.

Cider and other juices were popular drinks to serve to friends at gatherings. They were made more festive by the addition of spices and flavorings.

couldn't have your stove too hot. You wanted to parch the coffee slow. She'd open the stove and take the pan out and stir the coffee around. Then she'd put it back in. When the beans got brown like you've seen the coffee beans you buy in the store, they were ready to take out and grind. She had a grinder on the kitchen wall.

They didn't perk it back then. They boiled it in the grounds. Some people would break a raw egg in their coffee when it boiled. That'd make the grounds settle in the bottom of the pot or kettle, and they wouldn't pour out in your cup. Of course, the egg was cooked in the boiling coffee.

Tracy Speed places apples in the hopper as
Ernest Watts turns the mill crank.

A bucket of ground apples ready to be pressed into cider.

Ernest Watts transfers the apple pulp to a wooden tub.

The wooden disc is placed in the tub and the screw is wound down until it meets the disc.

Diagram of a cider mill.

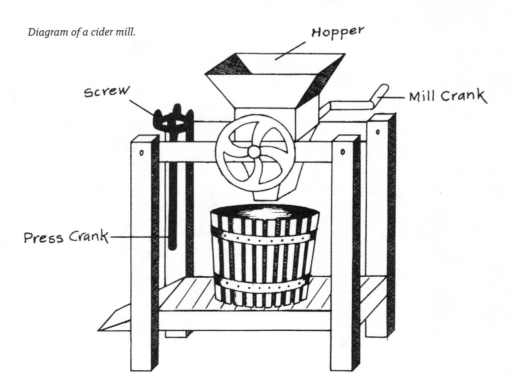

Juice is squeezed from the apple pulp as Ernest Watts uses a board for extra leverage.

The pan catches the unstrained cider.

Straining is the final step. Here, Marinda Brown and Suzy Angier do the honors.

MULLED CIDER

BELLE LEDFORD

1 quart apple cider

1 teaspoon whole allspice

1 teaspoon whole cloves

2 sticks cinnamon

6 thin lemon slices, if desired

Combine ingredients except lemon slices in a saucepan. Simmer, covered, for 20 minutes. Remove spices. Serve hot, with lemon slices, if desired. Yield: *6 servings (about ⅔ cup each).*

MERRY BREW

BELLE LEDFORD

½ cup firmly packed brown sugar

2 sticks cinnamon

1 tablespoon whole cloves

½ teaspoon whole allspice

1 cup water

2 quarts apple juice

1 lemon, thinly sliced

1 orange, thinly sliced

Combine sugar, spices, and water in a small saucepan; bring to a boil. Reduce the heat, cover, and simmer 10 minutes. Combine with apple juice and serve warm with the lemon and orange slices. Yield: *2 quarts.*

GRAPE JUICE

Mix 2 cups grapes and 1 cup sugar for each desired gallon of juice. Wash grapes and put in a hot sterilized gallon jar. Fill with boiling water. Seal and process by placing in water bath for 10 minutes.

BEER AND WINE

Homemade beers and wines could be found in most cellars throughout Southern Appalachia. We include a sampling of these alcoholic and nonalcoholic recipes here; the complete process for fermenting wine can be found in *The Foxfire Book of Wine Making*.

APPLE BEER

Peel apples and dry the peelings in the sun or by the stove. Put them in a crock, and add enough boiling water to cover. Cover the crock and let sit for about 2 days, until all the flavor comes out of the peelings. Strain and drink. You may add some sugar if desired.

PERSIMMON BEER

To make persimmon beer, gather persimmons and a good number of honey locust seedpods. Wash them both well and place them in a large crock or churn in layers until the crock is full. Pour enough boiling water in to cover them. Cover the crock with something and let it sit at least a week. Pour off or dip out the beer as desired. When drained, the crock may be filled with boiling water again to make a second batch.

Another variation is to gather and mash persimmons and place them in a crock. Pour enough boiling water in to cover them and let them work. Strain off foam, add sugar to taste, and let work

Lex Sanders's stock of canned goods includes grape juice (top shelf).

(ferment) some more. The beer is supposed to be very potent.

JAKE WALDROOP'S RECIPE FOR BLACKBERRY WINE

Jake keeps his in an earthenware jug with a corncob stopper. He makes grape wine the same way.

Gather 6 to 8 gallons of wild blackberries, wash them well, and put them in a big container. Mix in 5 pounds of sugar, then cover the top of the churn or container with a cloth, tied down so air can get in but insects can't. Let the mixture work for 8 to 10 days.

Strain the mixture through a clean cloth, squeezing the pulp so all the juice is removed. Measure how many gallons of juice you have. For every gallon of juice, add 1½ pounds of sugar. Let it work off. When it stops (when the foaming and bubbling is stopped on top), strain it again, measure the juice, and again add 1½ pounds of sugar to each gallon of juice. When it finishes working this time, it is done and can be bottled.

MUSCADINE WINE

Mash ½ bushel of muscadine grapes with your hands, put them in a large churn, and add 2½ pounds of sugar. Let it work for about a week, until it quits. Strain the mixture to get out the grape skins and impurities. Put back in the churn, add 10 pounds more sugar. Let it work about 8 to 10 days, until it quits and can be bottled. Yield: *4 gallons.*

MARY'S RHUBARB WINE

MARY PITTS

Put into churn:

1 gallon raw rhubarb stalks, sliced in
    ½-inch pieces
5 pounds sugar
1 teaspoon yeast
1 gallon warm water, poured over above mixture

Stir well each day for 7 days. Strain and add 1 pound sugar and work 7 days, until it quits and can be bottled. Yield: *2 gallons.*

Participants

THE STUDENTS

Eddie Bingham
Scott Bradley
Judy Brown
Laurie Brunson
Andrea Burrell
Harold Burrell
Vivian Burrell
Lynn Butler
Bit Carver
Brenda Carver
Rosanne Chastain
Vicki Chastain
Eddie Connor
Mandy Cox
Ken Cronic
Debbie Crowell
Kenny Crumley
Donna Dickerson
Bill Enloe
Ricky Foster
Shay Foster
Joey Fountain
Marty Franklin
George Freeman
John Garrard
Jeff Giles
Gary Gottchalk
Kim Hamilton
Phil Hamilton
Keith Head
Dana Holcomb
Debbie James
Mickey Justice
Georgeann Lanich
Tammy Ledford
Mike Lerson
Gayle Long

Don MacNeil
Pat Marcellino
Bridget McCurry
Michelle McDonald
Karen Moore
Paul Phillips
Allan Ramey
Sheryl Ramey
Aline Richards
Billy Robertson
Tracy Speed
Greg Strickland
Nancy Swenderman
Debbie Thomas
Don Thomas
Mary Thomas
Donna Turpin
Rhonda Turpin
Vance Wall
Chet Welch
Kim Welch
Frenda Wilburn
Lynette Williams
Rhonda Young
Wendy Youngblood

THE CONTACTS

Suzy Angier
Jennie Arrowood
Jerry Ayers
Lester Baker
Dorothy Beck
Bessie Bolt
Jessie S. Brady
Florence Brooks
Lawton Brooks
Pat Brooks
Harry Brown
Marinda Brown
Clyde Burrell
Connie Burrell
Stella Burrell
Mary Cabe
Ruth Cabe
Lola Cannon
Arie Carpenter
Evie Carpenter
Harley Carpenter
"Valley John" Carpenter
Billy Carpenter
Grover Carter
Roy Carter
Buck Carver
Mrs. Buster Carver
Connie Chappell
Lettie Chastain
Clifford Conner
Lassie Conner
Minyard Conner
Ethel Corn
Taylor Crochett
Edith Darnell
Arizona Dickerson
Ione Dickerson

Miriam Dickerson
Terry Dickerson
Exie Dills
Mrs. Carrie Dixon
Narcisse Dotson
Lon Dover
Thelma Earp
Harriet Echols
Ruby Frady
Nora Garland
Olene Garland
O. S. Garland
Carrie Dillard Garrison
Ruth Gibbs
Granny Gibson
Hillard Green
Albert Greenwood
Ethel Greenwood
Blanche Harkins
Ruth Holcomb
Mrs. John Hopper
Mary Hopper
Leonard Jones
Daisy Justus
Betty Keener
Gertrude Keener
Ada Kelly
Bessie Kelly
Lovey Kelso
Bill Lamb
Babe LeCount
Belle Ledford
James Ledford
Liz Ledford
Margie Ledford
Ruth Ledford
Virgil Ledford
Annie Long

Billy Long
Fay Long
Effie Lord
Garner Lovell
Lilly Lovell
Verge Lovell
Pearl Martin
Chuck Mashburn
Arie Meaders
Lanier Meaders
Bob Means
Mary Ellen Means
Marie Mellinger
Linsey Moore
Lizzie Moore
Gertrude Mull
Mrs. Gatha Nichols
Gladys Nichols
Addie Norton
Mrs. Algie Norton
Clark Norton
Mrs. Mann Norton
Mann Norton
Margaret Norton
Mrs. Edith Parker
Annie Perry
Beulah Perry
Esco Pitts
Mary Pitts
James Phillips
Fanny Powell
Monroe Reese
Lon Reid
Icie Rickman
Kenny Runion
Lex Sanders
Will Seagle
Nancy Sewell

Lena Shope
Maude Shope
Will Singleton
Lake Stiles
Myrtle Speed
Samantha Speed
Inez Taylor
Melvin Taylor
Nearola Taylor
Will Thomas
Mrs. Dillard Thompson
Bessie Underwood
Willie Underwood
Bertha Waldroop
Jake Waldroop
Hattie Watkins
Ernest Watts
Andy Webb
Mrs. Andy Webb
Rittie Webb
Wade Welch
Adaline Wheeler
Glenn Worley
Sara Worley
Lucy York

Index

Page numbers in italics refer to illustrations and captions; those in bold refer to recipes.

barbecue, barbecuing, 2, 11, 82, 127, 193

Barbecued Chicken, **92**

Barbecue Sauce, **208**

barrels, 9, 45, *46*, 212

bass, 136

basswood, *151*

baths, 27

bay leaf, 52, 53, 203

beans, 15, 34, 36; antique varieties of, 37–41, 43, 197; cooking of, 16, 17, 27, 33, 34, 38–39; dried, 37, 38, 39; gourd, 39, *40*, 41; green, 16, 33, 37, 38, **38**, 39; pickled, 37, 59, 65; soup, 37, **39**. *See also* leather breeches

Bean Salad, **206**

bear, *15*, 128

Beaty, Sallie, 114

Beck, Dorothy, 41, 157; recipes of, **95**, **123**, 177, **183**

beef and beef cattle, 77, 93; curing of, 114; gelatined, **94**; ground, 94, 95; raising of, 8, 9, 93; recipes for, **94**–**95**; slaughtering of, 93–94

Beef Stew, **95**, **203**

beer, 211; apple, **217**; persimmon, **217**; in Southern Appalachia, 217

beeswax, 9, 71, 76

Beet Pickles, **65**

beets, pickled, 41, **41**, 121

Bell, John, 113

bell peppers, 61, 62–63, 68, 200

Bennett, Margie, 3

berries, 9, 70, 71, 77, 118; in desserts, 169, 175, 177, 182. *See also names of individual types*

Best-Ever Lemon Pie, **174**

beverages, 211–181

biscuits, vii, 2, 75, 150–51, 170; baking of, 9, 12, 13, 32; with baking powder, **154**; for breakfast, 18, 195; cinnamon, **155**; dough for, 49, 171, 177, **180**; gravy and, 195, 199, 207–9; leftover, 170, 171, 175; quick, **154**; "Riz," **155**; soda, **154**

blackberry, blackberries, 9, 70, 71, 182; in pies and desserts, 16, **170**, **172**, 175, 177, 195

Blackberry Pie, 16, **172**, 195

Blackberry Pudding, **170**

Blackberry Wine, **217**

blenders, 53, 54, 67

blood, hog's, 79, 80

blossoms, fried, **50**

blueberry, blueberries, 9, 71; in desserts, 175, 177

Blueberry Muffins, **160**–**61**

Blue Book, 59

Boiled Creases, **121**

Boiled Onions, **47**

Boiled Poke, **120**

Bolt, Bessie, 17, 119–20

boneset, 126, *126*

Boneset Tea, **126**

borax, 116, 116n

boudin, 4

bouillon cube, 53

brains, hog's, 77, 80, **81**

bread, breads, 8, 47, 76, 79, 101, 144, 196; baked in cookstoves, 19, 29, 30, 32; baked in Dutch ovens, 13, 16–17; for breakfast, 194, 195; hearth cooking of, 8, 19; recipes for, **155**, **161**, **162**, **211**; rye, 8,

149; yeast, 157–60. *See also types of bread*

Bread and Butter Pickles, **64**

Bread Puddings, **170**–**71**

bread tray, *151*

breakfast, 18, 148, 150, 194–95, 199

bream, 136

brine, 59, 62, 64, 65, 67

brisket, 95

bristles, hog, 79

broccoli, **54**, 106, 195, 200

Broiled Chicken, **92**

Broiled Quail, **134**

Brooks, Florence, 37, 42, 50, 53, 64

Brooks, Lawton, 136, *137*

Brooks, Pat, 73–75

broth, 50, 71, 80, 81, 94, 123, 133, 148, 196, 203; chicken, 54, 92, 93, 155, 156, 208

Brown, Harry, 37, 51, 212

Brown, Marinda, 14, 33, 37–38, 84, 212, *216*; recipes of, **160**–**61**, **192**, **205**

Brown, Mary, recipe of, **158**

Brown, Miranda, 193

Brunswick Stew, **202**

burns, 32

Burrell, Clyde, recipe of, **62**

Burrell, Connie, 177, 198–99

Burrell, Stella, 33, 98–99, 146, 148, 150, 183, 185; recipes of, **71**, **133**, **180**, **201**, **208**

burying for food preservation, viii, 9–10

butchering, butchers, 4, 127. *See also* dressing

butter, 18, 55, 96–99, 145; churning of, 2, 3, 96–99; fruit, 73–75; molded, *98*; store-bought, 165

12–13, *13*, 15; popcorn and, 11, 14. *See also* hearths and hearth cooking

fish, 80, 135–42, **140**, 147; eggs of, *139*, 140; preparation of, 136, *138–39*

flank, beef, 95

flour: self-rising, 150–51, 153, 155; white, 165, 170

Flour Gravy, **207**

flowers, 37, 58; violets, 71

flues, 21

folklore, 2

food coloring, 72, 166

food mills, 53

food preservation, 9–10, 37, 58, 60, 82–83, 141, 194; smokehouses and, 107–17; springhouses and, 55. *See also methods of food preservation*

foodways and food culture, 1, 2; regional, 4, 165; Southern Appalachian, 5

4-H, 93

Foxfire (Broadway play), 7

Foxfire Book, The (1972), 36, 45, 107, 108, 127

Foxfire Book 2 (1973), 55, 119, 165

Foxfire Book 3, 19, 73, 119

Foxfire Book 4, 36, 45, 212

Foxfire Book of Appalachian Cookery, The, 144, 199; history of, 1–2, 3; revision of, 3–4

Foxfire Book of Wine Making, The, 217

Foxfire books, vii, 3, 8

Foxfire Magazine, The, 2, 3, 115

Foxfire Museum and Heritage Center, 11, 14

Foxfire program, 2, 3

Foxfire students, 17, 55, 58, 108, 113, 141, 175, 212

Frady, Ruby: corn bread of, **146**, *156*; gristmill of, 144–45, *152*, *153*

Franklin, North Carolina, 58

Free, Simmie, 115

Freezer Slaw with Cucumbers, Onions, and Peppers, **205**

freezing, freezers, 38, 39, 45, 55, 141, 169

fried apples, 195

Fried Cabbage, **41**

fried chicken, 84, 87–88, **92**, *92*, 195, 196, 199

Fried Creases, **121**

fried fish, **140**

Fried Green Onions, **47**

fried green tomatoes, **52**, 195

fried ham, 195, 197

Fried Okra, **47**

fried pigeon, 134

Fried Poke and Eggs, **120**

fried potatoes, 195

Fried Pumpkin or Squashblossoms, **50**

Fried Quail, **134**

Fried Ramps, **122**

fried sausage, 198

Fried Sweet Potatoes, **48**

fritter pan, *35*

frogs: dressing and cooking of, 127, *143*, **143**

frost, first, 44

fruit, fruits, 36, 194, 195; butters of, 73–75; canned, 55, 173; desserts with, **178**, 178–79, **179**, **182**, **190**, **206**; dried, 15, 50; pickled, 59, 69; preserving of, 3,

9, 58, 70–76; relishes of, 59, 69. *See also names of fruits*

fryers, 84

frying, 34, 43, 83, 92, 143; in fireplace cooking, 14, 16; of fish, 135, 140, 141; of game, 127, 128, 129, 131, 132, 133, 134; of gourd beans, 39, 41; of greens, 2, 44, 121, 122; of hominy, 45, 46; of meats, 9, 78, 80, 81, 94, 95; of potatoes, 48, 49; of pumpkins and squash, **50**, 51, 147; of sweet potatoes, 47, 48; of vegetables, 9, 41, 47, 52, 53; on wood cookstoves, 26, 33

frying pans, 13, 14, 16, 34, 41. *See also* skillets

fudge, **167**

Future Farmers of America, 93

game birds, 118, **133–34**

gardens, gardening, 8, 36–54, 201; organic, 36, 37

Garland, John, 164

Garland, Nolan, 84

Garland, Nora, 19–20, 70, 72, 99, 196–97; on cottage cheese, 103, 105; on fireplaces, 12, 15; recipes of, **122**, **154**, **189**

Garland, Olene, *88*, 164; recipes of, **41**, **93**, **155**, **170**, **189**

Garland, O. S., dresses chickens, *85–86*, 87

Garland, Ruth, 84

Garland, Seth, 84

garlic, 62, 79

gasoline, 23

gas stoves, 34, 199

gelatin desserts, 182, **182**